Patterns of Redemption in Virgil's Georgics

Current orthodoxy interprets the Georgics as a statement of profound ambivalence towards Octavian and his claim to be Rome's saviour after the
catastrophe of the civil wars. This book takes issue with the model of the
subtly subversive poet which has dominated scholarship for the last quarter
of a century. It argues that in the turbulent political circumstances which
obtained at the time of the poem's composition, Virgil's preoccupation with
violent conflict has a highly optimistic import. Octavian's brutal conduct in
the civil wars is subjected to a searching analysis, but is ultimately vindi-
cated, refigured as a paradoxically constructive violence analogous to blood
sacrifice or Romulus' fratricide of Remus, a prerequisite of the foundation
of Rome. The vindication of Octavian also has strictly literary implications
for Virgil. The close of the poem sees Virgil asserting his mastery of the
Homeric mode of poetry, the most sublime available, and the providential
world-view it was thought to embody.

LLEWELYN MORGAN is Teaching Fellow in Classical Languages and
Literature at Brasenose College, University of Oxford.

CAMBRIDGE CLASSICAL STUDIES

General Editors
P. E. EASTERLING, M. K. HOPKINS,
M. D. REEVE, A. M. SNODGRASS, G. STRIKER

PATTERNS OF REDEMPTION IN
VIRGIL'S *GEORGICS*

LLEWELYN MORGAN

PUBLISHED BY THE PRESS SYNDICATE OF THE UNIVERSITY OF CAMBRIDGE
The Pitt Building, Trumpington Street, Cambridge, United Kingdom

CAMBRIDGE UNIVERSITY PRESS
The Edinburgh Building, Cambridge CB2 2RU, UK http://www.cup.cam.ac.uk
40 West 20th Street, New York, NY 10011-4211, USA http://www.cup.org
10 Stamford Road, Oakleigh, Melbourne 3166, Australia

© Faculty of Classics, University of Cambridge 1999

This book is in copyright. Subject to statutory exception and to the provisions
of relevant collective licensing agreements, no reproduction of any part may
take place without the written permission of Cambridge University Press.

First published 1999

Printed in the United Kingdom at the University Press, Cambridge

Typeset in Times New Roman [AO]

A catalogue record for this book is available from the British Library

Library of Congress cataloguing in publication data
Morgan, Llewelyn.
Patterns of redemption in Virgil's Georgics / Llewelyn Morgan.
p. cm. – (Cambridge classical studies)
Revision of the author's thesis (Ph.D.) – Trinity College,
Cambridge.
Includes bibliographical references and indexes.
ISBN 0 521 65166 2 (hardback)
1. Virgil. Georgica. 2. Rome – History – Civil War, 43–31 BC –
Literature and the war. 3. Augustus, Emperor of Rome, 63 BC–14
AD – In literature. 4. Political poetry, Latin – History and
criticism. 5. Didactic poetry, Latin – History and criticism.
6. Virgil – Political and social views. 7. Politics and literature –
Rome. 8. Agriculture in literature. 9. Redemption in literature.
10. Rhetoric, Ancient. I. Title. II. Series.
PA6804.G4M67 1999
873'.01 – dc21 98-44171 CIP

ISBN 0 521 65166 2 hardback

CONTENTS

PREFACE

This book is a version of a doctoral thesis written at Trinity College, Cambridge, with the help of generous funding from the British Academy. It has benefited from the comments and contributions of many scholars, chief amongst them my supervisor Philip Hardie, my debt to whom will be evident from every page. Neil Hopkinson and Richard Hunter were kind enough to read sections of the thesis, and its examiners, Michael Reeve and Don Fowler, have consistently given me firm advice and firm encouragement. The thesis was completed during the first year of an Assistant Lectureship at University College Dublin, and the book during the first year of a Teaching Fellowship at Brasenose College, Oxford, and I owe a particular debt of thanks for the warmth of their welcome to the Department of Classics at UCD, especially Theresa Urbainczyk and Andrew Erskine, to the members of the Classics Department at Trinity College, Dublin, especially Kathleen Coleman, and the Fellows and students of BNC, the latter perhaps the most welcoming of all. Bill Lavelle, Jon Hesk and Peter Stewart have been rich and enthusiastic sources of ideas and information. The book is dedicated to Andrea Swinton, without whom it would never have been written at all, and to my father.

ὁ θάνατος οὐδὲν πρὸς ἡμᾶς

ABBREVIATIONS

CAH Cook, S. A., Adcock, F. E. and Charlesworth, M. P. (1923–39), edd. *The Cambridge Ancient History*[1]. Cambridge.

CHCL P. E. Easterling and B. M. W. Knox (1985), edd. *The Cambridge History of Classical Literature, Vol. I: Greek Literature*. Cambridge; E. J. Kenney and W. V. Clausen (1982), edd. *Vol. II: Latin Literature*. Cambridge.

De E Plutarch, *De E apud Delphos*.

De esu carn. Plutarch, *De esu carnium orationes II*.

FGrH Jacoby, F. (1923–58), ed. *Die Fragmente der griechischen Historiker* (16 vols.). Berlin and Leiden.

IG *Inscriptiones Graecae* (1873–).

Non posse Plutarch, *Non posse suaviter vivi secundum Epicurum*.

OLD *The Oxford Latin Dictionary* (Oxford, 1968–82).

RE A. Pauly, G. Wissowa and W. Kroll (1893–), edd. *Real-Encyclopädie der klassischen Altertumswissenschaft*. Stuttgart and Munich.

SH H. Lloyd-Jones and P. J. Parsons (1983), edd. *Supplementum Hellenisticum*. Berlin and New York.

SVF H. von Arnim (1903–5), ed. *Stoicorum Veterum Fragmenta, Vol. 1–3*; M. Adler (1924), ed. *Vol. 4*. Leipzig.

TGL C. B. Hase, W. Dindorf and L. Dindorf (1831–65), edd. *Thesaurus Graecae linguae ab Henrico Stephano constructus*[3]. Paris.

TLL *Thesaurus Linguae Latinae* (Leipzig, 1900–).

INTRODUCTION

I

In the introduction to his recent commentary on the *Georgics* – the most significant recent contribution to *Georgics* scholarship – Richard Thomas discusses Virgil's comparison of the mourning Orpheus to a nightingale who has lost her young to a predatory ploughman (4.511–15). As Thomas says, this ploughman must ultimately reflect Aristaeus, who was himself a farmer and was also responsible for the death of the wife Orpheus was mourning. And as Thomas also says, we have met this ploughman before, when the 'angry ploughman' extirpates the 'ancient homes of birds' in the process of creating 'shining' ploughland at 2.207–10. Thomas' pessimistic conclusion encapsulates his view of the whole poem: 'here, as throughout,' he writes, 'the complexity, ambivalence and ultimate darkness of the Virgilian world shine through'.[1]

This book will argue a diametrically opposite view of the *Georgics*.[2] What it will seek to establish is that the *Georgics*, far from being the bleakly pessimistic document envisioned by Thomas, can on the contrary be interpreted as a thoroughgoing exercise in Octavianic propaganda, a precise response to the requirements of the regime headed by Octavian which at the time of the poem's completion was emerging from the chaos of the Civil Wars; a text, in other words, capable of yielding a highly optimistic purport.

II

The year 29 BC was a momentous one for Octavian. By the defeat of Antony and Cleopatra at Actium in 31 and Alexandria

---

[1] Thomas (1988) 11.   [2] On these passages in particular see pp. 199, 210 below.

in 30 he had eliminated the final military challenge to his supremacy. His position thus corresponded to Caesar's on his final return to Rome after the Spanish campaign in October 45. Within six months Caesar was dead, assassinated by disaffected aristocrats, and this example seems to have weighed heavily with Octavian. It convinced him that military success alone was not sufficient to ensure the survival of his regime: the Roman elite must be brought along with him in any new dispensation. By as early as 36, in fact, Octavian was energetically appeasing upper-class sentiment.[3] In that year he gave an undertaking to restore senatorial government (App. *B Civ.* 5.13.132), words which he sought to substantiate by constructing a new senate house,[4] and by refusing to depose the former triumvir M. Lepidus from his position as *pontifex maximus*.[5] Horace's first book of *Satires* has been interpreted as part of this same campaign: one of the implications of Horace's choice of Lucilius as his literary model is that 'Horace and his friends cherish the true Republican ideal of *libertas*'.[6] However, Octavian's opponent Antony adopted an equally conservative rhetorical stance, repeatedly promising to restore senatorial control,[7] and there is evidence that in the competition to win the hearts and minds of the Roman elite Octavian was not as successful as he might have wished.[8] In 32, for example, both consuls and a large number of senators left Rome to join Antony's forces at Ephesus (Dio 50.2.6–7). In 30 M. Lepidus – son of Lepidus the triumvir and *pontifex maximus*, and nephew of M. Brutus the 'tyrannicide' – conceived a plan to assassinate Octavian on his return to the city.[9] In Octavian's absence in 30 Maecenas suppressed what

---

[3] Carter (1970) 170–3. It is from 36 that Servius and Donatus date Virgil's composition of the *Georgics: Vita Donati* 25; *Vita Servi* 25.
[4] Zanker (1987) 62. The old Curia had been obliterated by Caesar during his construction of the Forum Iulium: Zanker (1987) 34.
[5] *RG* 10; Dio 49.15.3; App. *B Civ.* 5.13.131.
[6] DuQuesnay (1984) 27–32, at 32.
[7] Dio 49.41.6, 50.7.1–2; cf. Suet, *Aug.* 28.1.
[8] Cf. Eder (1990) 96; Syme (1939) 279.
[9] Vell. Pat. 2.88; Livy, *Epit.* 133.

Velleius with some plausibility terms 'a prelude to renewed civil war'.[10]

With good reason, then, the period immediately subsequent to the defeat of Antony saw the continuation of Octavian's campaign of conciliation, and with increased vigour. As in 36, after the defeat of Sextus Pompey,[11] Octavian tried to take the credit for restoring peace: in January 29 the Senate – with Octavian still in winter quarters on Samos, but clearly co-ordinating events – decreed the closing of the temple of Janus, an event denoting the end of all wars throughout the world which, so it was believed, had taken place only twice before.[12] At the same time Octavian set about discharging his soldiers, spending the large sums he had obtained through the conquest of Egypt to buy land for them and thereby 'disassociating himself demonstratively from the detested practice of confiscation' which had caused him such unpopularity in the aftermath of Philippi.[13] Meanwhile a large number of religious and secular buildings were being built or renovated at his personal expense (*RG* 19–21): one building in particular was nearing completion, the magnificent Palatine temple of Apollo, with its rich interior decoration and carved scenes of Galatians and Niobids on its doors, 'images of the violence necessary for the preservation of the State and for the defeat of impiety', a significant reference point for my later argument.[14] In addition magnificent games were staged, and donatives and corn-distributions made to the people.[15]

But at the core of his programme remained the conciliation of the elite. Towards the end of 30, for example, Octavian took M. Cicero, son of the orator, as his consular colleague, a

---

[10] For a variant account see App. *B Civ.* 4.6.50.
[11] See App. *B Civ.* 5.13.130.
[12] Dio 51.20.4; Suet. *Aug.* 31.4; Varro, *Ling.* 5.165.
[13] Eder (1990) 102.
[14] Hardie (1986) 126; Prop. 2.31.12–14. The temple was dedicated in October 28. These and other details of the temple are apparently reflected in Virgil's poetic temple in the proem to *Georgic* 3: Corbaud (1899) 320–1. For the theme of 'necessary violence' in the *Georgics* see especially ch. 3 below.
[15] Dio 51.22.4–9; *CAH*[1] 10.119–20. Eder (1990) 102 estimates Octavian's total expenditure on such projects as 1,000 million sesterces.

gesture which neatly conflated 'Republicanism' and opposition to Antony (Plut. *Cic.* 49.6). Another undertaking in 29 was a preliminary purge of 'unworthy'[16] members of the Senate – apparently including some erstwhile supporters of his own – which again signalled his conciliatory intentions towards the traditional constitution in which the old elite had held sway.[17] This can be seen to be his most abiding concern in the period that followed. As Eder writes,

The interval between the triumphal reception prepared for the victor by the citizens of Rome (in mid-29 BC) and the official resignation of his all-encompassing power on 13 January 27 BC was utilized by Octavian to convince his fellow citizens not only that he deserved to be the first citizen, but that he was prepared to play this role in a *res publica* that was not a republic in name alone.[18]

In short, the evidence of Octavian's activity at this time points to a massive effort on his part to reconcile Rome, and in particular the Roman elite – in which respect the contrast with Julius Caesar is particularly great – to its new leading citizen.

In the summer of 29 Octavian returned to Italy. He landed at Brundisium, and in Rome on the 13th, 14th and 15th of August he celebrated a spectacular triple triumph for his campaigns in Illyricum, at Actium and in Egypt.[19] These triumphs and the closing of the temple of Janus became definitive emblems of the new regime.[20] Each is singled out at different points of the *Aeneid* to represent the entire Augustan achievement.[21]

It may also have been August when Virgil and Maecenas

---

[16] Suet. *Aug.* 35.1. On this *lectio* see Carter (1982) ad loc.

[17] See p. 126 below.

[18] Eder (1990) 101–2. Cf. Raaflaub and Samons (1990) 452 on the contrast with Caesar: 'in stark contrast to its (sc. the Senate's) situation under Caesar it was treated with respect and dignity ... In short the *res publica restituta* was much more than a mere façade; it contained enough republican substance to be credible and to encourage cooperation rather than resistance.'

[19] Suet. *Aug.* 22; Dio 51.21.5–9.

[20] The closing of the temple of Janus has prominence also at *RG* 13, Suet. *Aug.* 22, Dio 51.20.4, Livy 1.19.3. For the triple triumph see, similarly, Suet. *Aug.* 22, Livy, *Epit.* 133, Vell. Pat. 2.89.1.

[21] 1.293–4 (cf. 7.607–22); 8.714–19.

recited Virgil's new poem *Georgics* to Octavian.[22] The *Vita Donati* tells us, 'and there is no good reason to suspect the details',[23] that soon after his return to Italy (either before or shortly after his triumphs) Octavian visited Campania to recuperate from illness.[24] At the town of Atella Virgil and Maecenas took turns to recite the poem to him over a period of four days.

Amidst the torrent of self-promotion from Octavian at this juncture the *Georgics* is apt to seem a little anomalous. On the one hand it was the product of the patronage of Maecenas, Octavian's right-hand man,[25] and the circumstances might lead us to expect Virgil's poem also to contribute to the Octavianic propaganda offensive, which (as we have seen) had its origins much earlier.[26] On the whole, though, recent scholars have thought not. Wilkinson, for example, dismisses the notion that the *Georgics* were written to support Octavian's agricultural policy[27] on the grounds that the poets of Maecenas' circle 'were not a "propaganda bureau"'. 'We may surmise, then,' he goes on,

that the mainspring of the *Georgics* was not political; and this being so, that Virgil's own enthusiasms were more operative in generating the poem than any promptings from Maecenas.[28]

Up to a point Wilkinson's position on this issue is perfectly sound. It is hard to imagine the *Georgics* persuading anybody to take up farming; and the poem is certainly not propaganda

---

[22] Wilkinson (1969) 111 suggests it was 'on the eve of celebrating his Triple Triumph'; Thomas (1988) 11 has 'in August'.

[23] Thomas (1988) 11 n.1.

[24] *Vita Donati* 27.

[25] *G.* 1.2, 2.41, 3.41, 4.2.

[26] Cf. DuQuesnay (1984) 23 on Horace, *Satires* 1 in 36: 'it is hardly credible that amid all this activity, when Octavian clearly could and did expect his friends to support his cause in every way that they could, Maecenas, his closest friend and adviser, should publish and distribute a work which was irrelevant to the needs and the preoccupations of himself and his friends'.

[27] On this tenacious theory see White (1993) 107, who traces it back to the time of Dryden. Otis (1963) 145 still accepts it as an account of the poem at 'one level' of interpretation.

[28] Wilkinson (1969) 54–5.

in the sense of a commission imperiously handed down to the poet by Octavian or Maecenas. We now have in White's *Promised Verse* a much more nuanced account of the relationship between patron and poet in the Augustan period.[29] Nevertheless, the fact that the *Georgics* was a poem of Virgil's own inspiration does not preclude the possibility that it was politically directed: 'Augustan propaganda' *was* at times written by these poets, after all, and propaganda is propaganda whether the propagandist is under orders or merely possessed of 'a sense of shared direction'.[30] Wilkinson seems to assume that a privately motivated work of art cannot constitute propaganda: there is an implied antithesis in his remarks between political poetry and poetry which arises from Virgil's private 'enthusiasms'. This assumption is quite widespread. Galinsky, for example, moves from the very valid Whitean insight that the Augustan poets were not 'simply mouthpieces of the government' to the much more dubious conclusion that attributing an 'imperial "Augustan" purpose' to Virgil is simplistic because 'Augustan poetry transcends its own times' to make timeless observations about the human condition.[31] It is not hard to see that Galinsky's critical categories – the emphasis on the transcendental, eternal quality of Augustan poetry and the concomitant elevation of these poets out of their historical milieu – are fundamentally Romantic, and hence anachronistic. Post-Romantic criticism has a tendency to place the poet on a pedestal. A poet of value, a 'great' poet, is expected to have operated free of external influences, and thus not to have written propagandistic, public poetry but poetry from the heart, from his 'own enthusiasms'. West is typical of this approach when he claims that 'the *Aeneid* is still read and still resonates because it is a great poem'. It is a 'great poem' because it is, amongst other things, 'a contemplation of the general human predicament'. West then goes on to excuse the obviously political content of much of Virgil and Horace's poetry by reference to their private mental lives: 'in that day it was not foolish to hope and to

---

[29] White (1993).   [30] Galinsky (1996) 57.   [31] Galinsky (1996) 244–6.

6

believe'.[32] But are the poets' personal opinions in fact very relevant to an interpretation of Augustan poetry? When Stahl, for example, states that 'to a considerable degree ... Propertius wishes his poetry to be appreciated as autobiographical' and talks of 'reading the poet's heart' through criticism of his poetry, Wyke is clearly right, following Veyne, to wonder whether it really was the poet's wish or in fact merely 'that imposed upon him since by a modern post-Romantic *lecteur*';[33] and her objection has a wider application to Augustan poetry in general. There is still a widespread tendency to underestimate the *artfulness* of Augustan poetry and assume that personal input on the poet's part which has been so much a feature of post-Romantic literature. Thomas, in particular, has contributed more than anyone to our understanding of the highly artificial and impersonal nature of Augustan poetry in general and the *Georgics* in particular,[34] yet is still determined to believe that Virgil must have interposed his own personal experiences into his poetic scheme: 'the poem was begun, and much of it was written, in a time of the utmost political uncertainty', he writes, uncertainty which 'pervades the poem'.[35] We need to appreciate that assumptions of this kind are profoundly anachronistic.

Discernible also in Wilkinson's and Galinsky's objections to a politicized Virgil are certain closely related misconceptions as to the nature of propaganda. In popular imagination 'propaganda is intrinsically crude, strident, ugly and directed';[36] it is a word which 'has ugly connotations', as DuQuesnay says.[37] We imagine that a subtle, valuable poet such as Virgil or Horace could not, therefore, have written propaganda. Nevertheless propaganda (by any other name) is

---

[32] West (1990) x.
[33] Wyke (1989) 171, citing Stahl (1985) 248 and 372 n. 8, and Veyne (1988).
[34] See especially Thomas (1983a) on analogies between the structure of the Virgilian text and the text's contents, Thomas (1983b) on Virgil's imitation of Callimachus in the proem to *G.* 3, and Scodel and Thomas (1984) on parallelism between the *Georgics* and *Aeneid* and Callimachus' *Hymn to Apollo*.
[35] Thomas (1988) I 1.
[36] Wallace-Hadrill (1987) 222, citing Kennedy (1984).
[37] DuQuesnay (1984) 57.

what DuQuesnay convincingly argues that Horace's urbane, diverting *Satires* are, and the truth is that propaganda need not necessarily be the blunt weapon it is popularly supposed to be: far from being strident, in fact, 'the most potent propaganda is ... that which coalesces unnoticed with the existing values of a society'.[38] It may well be 'subtle, beautiful',[39] and it will not deal in blatant falsehoods.

An analogy from another area of artistic creativity – the visual arts – may serve to illustrate these preliminary remarks about subjectivity and propaganda. The *Surrender of Breda* is one of the most famous paintings by Velázquez (1599–1660). It is by general consent a masterpiece, and a masterpiece by a figure as eminent (respected, beloved) amongst painters as Virgil is among poets. It is also a work of propaganda, one of twelve paintings depicting Spanish military success which originally hung in the Hall of Realms, the focal point and symbolic heart of the Buen Retiro palace of Philip IV. The Hall of Realms was an opulently decorated statement of Philip's power, and the twelve victory paintings in the room were designed 'to create the impression of a triumphant reign'.[40] The *Surrender of Breda*, which commemorates a victory of Philip's general Spínola in 1625, is a very subtle but powerful article of propaganda. In it Velázquez completely revivified the traditional format of representations of surrender. Rather than depicting crushing victory on the part of the Spanish and the concomitant humiliation of the defeated Dutch – a standard approach – Velázquez manages to imply the invincible might of the Spanish, in particular by the famous motif of the raised lances, whilst laying most emphasis on the clemency and magnanimity of Spínola in victory. Contrary to convention Spínola is depicted dismounted, and he places a hand on his opponent's shoulder to restrain him

---

[38] Wallace-Hadrill (1987) 222.
[39] Wallace-Hadrill (1987) 222. To call it 'beautiful' is not to deny the possibility that its overall message may be politically or morally obnoxious; or to imply, for that matter, that it must have *worked* as propaganda.
[40] Brown and Elliot (1980) 168.

8

from making a standard gesture of submission.[41] 'By means of these subtle touches', Brown writes,[42]

Velázquez transformed the scene from a tableau of Spanish military power into a metaphor of Spanish moral superiority, which reflected the glory of the king in whose name Spinola commanded, and glorified the faith which he and his forebears had sworn to defend.

The *Surrender of Breda* is a masterpiece, of art and of propaganda. Some general points, relevant to Augustan poetry, can be made about it. On the one hand Velázquez's departure from the norms of victory painting signals that he, like Virgil, had creative autonomy: the direction his painting took was clearly not imposed from without.[43] But by the same token Velázquez's private ethical or political beliefs are of little or no relevance to the creative process. Is the less strident tone of this victory painting best explained by recourse to Velázquez's private convictions, his personal liberalism, say? No: it is the consequence of a superior intellectual appreciation on Velázquez's part of the nature of effective propaganda. The image, Velázquez appreciated, was actually made the more compelling for being less strident. If the *Georgics* can be shown to be propaganda I expect the same to apply: we will learn next to nothing about Virgil's soul. Furthermore – and perhaps this is the most important observation to be made – the recognition that the *Surrender of Breda* is propaganda in no way diminishes its value or interest as an aesthetic object, as (I hope) the foregoing paragraph has shown. Establishing that it or the *Georgics* is 'propaganda' only diminishes its value from a Romantic critical standpoint unhealthily preoccupied with the subjective experiences of the author.

More recent critics have in fact accepted, in contrast to Wilkinson, that the *Georgics* does offer itself as a commentary on recent events – though on the Civil Wars rather than

---

[41] Brown and Elliot (1980) 178–9.
[42] Brown (1986) 119.
[43] Significantly, the other scene of surrender among the twelve paintings, Leonardo's *Surrender of Jülich* (where the successful general is again Spínola), follows the conventions of the genre closely: Brown (1986) 116.

Caesarian agricultural policy – but typically these critics envisage in Virgil not an Octavianic apologist but a pessimistic, subversive poet who, though he does present the 'official line' in some sense, contributes in addition a personal dimension of his own which is at odds with and undermines the propaganda. Thus, seminally, Griffin feels himself unable to understand the rebirth of the bees at *G.* 4.528–58 as a happy ending. For him the rebirth does not outweigh the sufferings of Orpheus and Eurydice: 'an exquisite ambivalence surely prevails'.[44] The ambivalence Griffin attributes to Virgil is that between the personal values of the poet himself and the public values of the regime he (ostensibly, at any rate) serves. This distinction was inaugurated by Parry, with reference to the *Aeneid*,[45] and a similar distinction is presupposed by Thomas throughout his edition of the poem, who quotes this same context from Griffin's article in his introduction, with approval.[46]

This account of the poem has always sat uncomfortably with the external evidence of its composition and 'publication'. The image of Virgil and Maecenas reciting to Octavian at this of all junctures a work embodying 'the complexity, ambivalence and ultimate darkness of the Virgilian world' – so soon after Maecenas had crushed the conspiracy of Lepidus – must seem extremely implausible. Nevertheless support for the 'subversive' view of Virgil might be found in Quintilian's discussion of the rhetorical figure whereby *per quandam suspicionem quod non dicimus accipi uolumus*, 'by some hint we want something other than we say to be understood', cited by Ahl and Williams in connection with Lucan, *De Bello Ciuili* and Ovid, *Tristia* 2 respectively.[47] The various forms of

---

[44] Griffin (1979) 71.
[45] Parry (1963) 69 ('the continual opposition of a personal voice which comes to us as if it were Virgil's own to the public voice of Roman success'). Cf. especially Griffin (1979) 72–3.
[46] Thomas (1988) I 23.
[47] Quint. *Inst.* 9.2.65–99; Ahl (1976) 31–3; Williams (1994) 158–61. This defence of a subversive Virgil was made to me by Michael Reeve, *pers. comm.*

this figure are to be employed, Quintilian advises, *si dicere palam parum tutum est*, 'if it is unsafe to speak openly' (9.2.65–75). The technique is to couch criticism in ambiguous terms: the criticism must be susceptible to an innocent interpretation. Williams talks of 'subtle ambiguity':[48] and the watchword here is clearly subtlety. There is an innocuous superficial meaning, and then there is another offensive meaning, *latens et auditori quasi inueniendum*, 'hidden and, so to speak, for the hearer to discover'.[49] This schema in fact conforms very closely to the most careful analysis of Virgil's allegedly subversive techniques hitherto, that of Lyne. Discussing the Cacus episode in *Aeneid* 8, for example, Lyne enumerates the panegyrical elements of the story (Hercules, Aeneas and Augustus are 'ideal and exemplary instances of civilized heroes vanquishing ... powers which threaten civilization'), before pointing out the further details which in Lyne's view 'comment on, question, and occasionally subvert' the superficial panegyric. Lyne suggests that the panegyrical interpretation is 'the way in which the episode first appears to us'; it is the way 'I think Virgil wishes them (sc. Hercules, Aeneas and Augustus) initially to seem'.[50] As with Quintilian, then, subtlety is the key. There is panegyric, but if we are perceptive enough there are also disquieting, even subversive, 'further voices'.[51]

The main weakness of this model as applied to Virgil, it seems to me, is that – with all due respect to Lyne's critical acuity – there are many details in Virgil's poetry which qualify as disquieting but which could not by any stretch of the imagination be said to be subtle – unobvious, that is – or to require any particular perspicacity to spot. Is there, for example, any vacillation between panegyric and critique in the

---

[48] Williams (1994) 160.
[49] Cf. Demetr. *Eloc.* 291 on ἐπαμφοτερισμός, 'ambiguity'. On these passages in Demetrius and Quintilian see further Ahl (1984) 185–97.
[50] Lyne (1987) 28–9. On Lyne's analysis of this passage in general see Morgan (1998).
[51] On the alleged ambivalence of panegyric in the *Georgics* see especially Boyle (1979a) 78–80.

description of Aeneas on his return to the Trojan forces at *Aen.* 10.270–5?

> ardet apex capiti tristisque[52] a uertice flamma
> funditur et uastos umbo uomit aureus ignis:
> non secus ac liquida si quando nocte cometae
> sanguinei lugubre rubent, aut Sirius ardor
> ille sitim morbosque ferens mortalibus aegris
> nascitur et laeuo contristat lumine caelum.

The tongue of fire blazes on his head and the grim flame streams from his top and his golden boss vomits awesome fires – just as when in the clear night bloody comets glow gloomily, or the heat of Sirius, that bringer of drought and diseases to feeble mortals, rises and saddens the sky with sinister light.

Harrison may attempt to neutralize this imagery by recourse to 'focalization' (the simile, he thinks, is 'clearly seen from the subjective viewpoint of an enemy'),[53] but even so the comparison of Aeneas to the dogstar is a disquieting presence in the text: 'whoever it is to whom we ascribe these viewpoints, they are there, in the text, and the reader has the option of looking at the world that way'.[54] Furthermore there are similar examples of obvious 'disquieting' material where there are no alternative viewpoints available to defuse them: Aeneas' human sacrifice of the sons of Sulmo and Ufens at *Aen.* 10.517–20 and 11.81–2 stands out. Comparable, again, is the passage at the end of the *Georgics*, which I shall discuss at some length,[55] where the technique of *bugonia* is described. This is the method by which the hero Aristaeus achieves, in a way that must reflect recent actions of Octavian, the restoration of his Rome-like community of bees. The method, however, is unashamedly repulsive, a procedure by which 'putrid blood has produced bees' (4.285), 'a particularly brutal and repugnant sacrifice', a 'gruesome killing', a 'disgusting process':[56]

---

[52] For this emendation see Harrison (1991) ad loc.
[53] Harrison (1991) ad 272–5. On focalization see Fowler (1990).
[54] Fowler (1990) 57.
[55] See pp. 78, 134–41 below.
[56] Miles (1980) 254; Kromer (1979) 16; Mynors (1990) 300.

tum uitulus bima curuans iam cornua fronte
quaeritur; huic geminae nares et spiritus oris
multa reluctanti obstruitur, plagisque perempto
tunsa per integram soluuntur uiscera pellem.

Then a bullock just arching his horns from a two-year-old forehead is sought. Both his nostrils and mouth's breath are stopped up, though it struggles greatly, and it is beaten to death, and its flesh is pounded to a pulp through the undamaged hide.

This, I think, is unquestionably 'disquieting' material. But it does not seem in any way concealed, *latens*. It is in fact typical of much so-called 'negative' material in Virgil in that it is unequivocal. If such material makes the *Georgics* subversive of the Augustan dispensation, then it is uncompromisingly so: there is no equivocation.

In the interpretation of the *Georgics* which follows, then, I am not going to ignore or argue away the disquieting elements of the poem. This reading of the *Georgics* will prove the possibility of an interpretation of the poem which, without ever ignoring those details which have been used to argue Virgil's essential pessimism, can tease out of it an ultimately 'upbeat', propagandistic import. In my interpretation of details I shall often, in fact, be treading familiar ground. Ross's definitively pessimistic conclusion about the poem, 'conflict is the ultimate reality in that fire and water are the ultimate elements of all things',[57] is not, for example, a position I would want radically to differ from. What I shall suggest, though, is that in the cultural and historical context of the *Georgics* such a message has great *optimistic* potential.

When Griffin writes that 'anxiety and hope contend in the *Georgics*',[58] we could easily replace 'the *Georgics*' with 'Virgil's mind'; and this preoccupation with the author is widespread, as I have suggested, in *Georgics* scholarship. What I also hope to do in this reading of the poem is move criticism of the *Georgics* away from the current author-orientated emphasis to a fuller recognition of its status as a purposefully created artefact, a text designed for a readership. What we

[57] Ross (1987) 241.   [58] Griffin (1986) 12.

13

have in the *Georgics*, I shall suggest, is an artefact in many ways much richer in significance than the inert testament of personal ambivalence we find in most recent scholarly accounts. The *Georgics*, I shall argue, is a text quite as dynamic in its engagement with its readership as Lucretius' *De Rerum Natura*,[59] designed in a similar way to convert its audience to its point of view.

[59] Cf., for example, Schiesaro (1994) 83 on the *DRN*'s 'founding intention', 'to convert a sceptical, if not hostile, reader ... of the Roman upper classes, to the liberating truth of Epicureanism'.

PART ONE

PRIMA AB ORIGINE

Stop this day and night with me and you shall possess the origin of all poems
Walt Whitman, *Song of Myself* 25

CHAPTER I

THE OLD MAN OF THE SEA

I

It is my view – by no means an original one – that the key to an understanding of the *Georgics* lies in the myth of Aristaeus with which Virgil chose to conclude the poem. Thomas talks of 'the great question of the poem': 'What of Aristaeus, what of the song of Proteus depicting Orpheus' failure and loss?'[1] The passage will be the main focus of this book. A central tenet will be that any possible propagandistic agenda such as I have postulated in my introduction will necessarily carry implications of a distinctly literary nature. In the course of developing his political/propagandistic argument, in other words, Virgil at every stage considers its implications for himself, the poet, not in any Romantic, autobiographical way but in a highly literary way, according to the conventions of contemporary poetry. This depiction by the poet of his own implication in the events he describes is a motif very familiar from other poetry of the period.[2]

This first chapter, then, will be concerned with one aspect of the literary-generic dimension of the Aristaeus myth. At present, study of this dimension of the passage is dominated – and, I will suggest, somewhat vitiated – by the notion that the *Aristaeus* is an *epyllion*, that is, a short mythological epic of a type favoured in the Hellenistic period which contains, characteristically, a digression from the main narrative. More or less hand in hand with this notion has gone the idea that the main narrative and digression of this *epyllion* – roughly the myth of Aristaeus (315–452, 528–58) and the myth of Orpheus (453–527) – are in stylistic contrast to each other, the

---

[1] Thomas (1988) I 23.   [2] See pp. 56, 97–8, 101, 151 below; Lieberg (1982).

myth of Aristaeus being essentially 'Homeric' (or just 'epic') and the myth of Orpheus 'Neoteric' (or 'elegiac'), respectively. This, in outline, was the schema articulated nearly three decades ago by Otis,[3] and it remains in essentials the accepted view today. It is also, I think, in many respects sound, but unfortunately as commonly presented too confused to be particularly useful.

The confusion arises because these two views of the *Aristaeus* – the classification as an *epyllion*, and the distinction by style – are typically presented, as I have suggested, in tandem: the frame of the *epyllion* is Homeric, the inset Neoteric. The trouble is, however, that the two views are really not compatible. Either the *Aristaeus* is a representative of a characteristically Hellenistic (sub-)genre, the *epyllion*, or else, it would seem, the *Aristaeus* contains a section which may be termed 'Homeric', imitative of Homer: a section, that is, in ethos pointedly un-Hellenistic (according to the conventional use of the term).[4] How, by definition, could there be a partially 'Homeric' *epyllion*?[5] Not surprisingly, then, a degree of confusion on this point is evident. Two recent commentators on the *Georgics*, for example, use the term 'epyllion' to describe two quite distinct artefacts, the elliptical, pathetic *Orpheus*, and the *Aristaeus* in its entirety,[6] hamstrung between two definitions of the term *epyllion* which though at first apparently complementary are in fact – as applied to the *Aristaeus*

---

[3] Otis (1963) 190–214. Otis contrasts the epic 'objectivity' of the style of the frame with the Neoteric or elegiac 'subjectivity' of the inset.

[4] Gutzwiller (1981) 5.

[5] Compare Myers (1994) on embedded narratives in Ovid's *Met.*, which she argues 'seem to have in common a distinctively Alexandrian character' (94). We note that it is the *inset* which tends to be Alexandrian in style in the *Met.*, according to Myers' account, as compared with the more conventionally epic quality of the main narrative.

[6] Williams (1979) ad 4.315–424 ('The presentation of the myth, with its "digression" about Orpheus and Eurydice, is very much *in the style of the epyllion*') and ad 425–558 ('It is told *in the style of the epyllion*, with elliptical narrative, sensitive empathy, and concentration on the emotional reaction of its characters'); Thomas (1988) ad 4.315–558 ('As is often noted, the lines are *in the style of an epyllion* ... with frame and picture constituting the whole') and ad 453–527 ('It is a version which is not found before V. ... *in theme, style and emphasis absolutely typical of epyllion*, and is to be seen as [Virgil's] venture into that genre'). The italics are mine.

– mutually exclusive: as a type of poem consisting of frame and inset,[7] and as a form which is typically Hellenistic. Of the two, the latter usage is preferable. As has long been recognized, the *Orpheus* is stylistically closely akin to the short hexameter productions of the Neoterics such as Catullus' *Peleus and Thetis*, Cinna's *Smyrna*, Calvus' *Io*, and the pastiche of their work represented by the *Ciris*.[8] If we choose to employ the term *epyllion* (and it does have its uses) it is thus to the *Orpheus* that it should be applied. Traditionally, however, the term *epyllion* has been used of the entire *Aristaeus*, and has helped to foster the idea of a seamless (Homeric) frame enclosing a Neoteric inset.

This widespread view, then, of the *Aristaeus* as a frame-inset *epyllion*, part Homeric and part Neoteric is (as it stands) rather confused, and in fact fails to do justice to the complex literary ancestry of the *Aristaeus*. Otis drew the distinction between the 'Homeric' frame (the *Aristaeus*) and elegiac or Neoteric inset (the *Orpheus*) on the basis of an 'objectivity' and 'subjectivity' he perceived in their respective narrative styles. This approach is of some use as an analysis of the Orpheus inset, but does not get us very far with the Aristaeus frame: Aristaeus' piteous cry to his mother, *mater, Cyrene mater* (321), for example, is not especially 'objective'. The truth is that the Aristaeus frame as a whole does contain a great deal of 'Homeric' material, strikingly so,[9] but equally there is considerable intertextuality evident with Callimachean and Neoteric contexts: for example the *Aristaeus* is an *aetion* in which a leading character is Cyrene, eponymous patron of Callimachus' home-town, and I suggest later extensive reference in the passage to Hesiod. What we appear to have, in

---

[7] The notion that a Hellenistic genre of *epyllia* existed, identifiable by certain characteristic features, and in particular a structure consisting of a subordinate story embedded in the primary narrative, is advanced by Crump (1931). Allen (1940) and Gutzwiller (1981) 1–2 have succeeded in debunking Crump's assertion that the *epyllion* constituted a precisely delimited genre, as much as anything by proving that the digressive inset was far from being a ubiquitous feature of Hellenistic or Neoteric short ἔπη. Nevertheless the frame-inset model has continued to exert influence on scholarship of the *Aristaeus*.

[8] See pp. 162–7 below.

[9] Cf. Thomas (1988) ad 4.315.

fact, in the body of the *Aristaeus*, is a blend of the two traditions, Callimachean and Grand Epic.

II

Otis' scheme over-simplifies the dynamics of the *Aristaeus*, then, but nevertheless contains a lot of truth. In other words I do consider that the Orpheus inset is Neoteric-elegiac in colouring, and I do think that the passage in the *Aristaeus* which surrounds the *Orpheus* might usefully be termed 'Homeric'. In my analysis, though, this 'Homeric' passage is rather more limited in extent than Otis suggests. It consists not in the whole of Aristaeus' adventures, but in the climactic one, his capture of Proteus at 4.387–529. In this context I believe we can usefully talk of a 'Homeric' episode, and on what seem to me considerably firmer grounds than Otis', namely that the passage involves direct, intensive and sustained imitation of a *locus* in the Homeric poems, of an order we encounter nowhere else in the Virgilian corpus.

Virgil's Proteus episode is an ambitious imitation of *Odyssey* 4.383–570. Sustained verbal imitation of the Homeric passage gets under way at around line 396 (see my concordance in Appendix I). It is divided into two sections (an anticipation of the capture of Proteus, followed by the real thing, as in the Homeric original) by a passage (418–25) describing Proteus' cave partly derived from *Od.* 4 and partly from another Homeric context (*Il.* 13.32),[10] and is apparently carefully structured around two references to *Od.* 4.400 early in the first half (at 401) and at the beginning of the second (426–7). In this Proteus episode, as Thomas notes,[11] Virgil 'adapts a poetic model as closely as anywhere in his corpus'. It is in fact probably the most sustained close imitation of a poetic model that Virgil ever undertakes. It follows that it is a closer imitation of Homer than anything in the *Aeneid*, Virgil's full-scale

---

[10] See Thomas (1988) ad locc. On the reference to *Il.* 13 and the contamination of the depiction of Proteus with another sea god, Poseidon, see also Thomas (1988) ad 430–1.

[11] Thomas (1988) ad 4.387–414.

'Homeric' undertaking, and it does not require a trawl through Knauer's index to see it.[12] We need only ask ourselves where in the *Aeneid* we find an entire Homeric event – complete with main character – transferred to the Virgilian text to appreciate how exceptional and unparalleled a case of *imitatio* Virgil's version of Proteus is. The presence of Homer here should give us pause: at the close of a poem which elsewhere advertises its indebtedness to the Hellenistic poets, Callimachus especially, and *their* favoured models – in Callimachus' case, Hesiod[13] – Virgil apparently does a most un-Callimachean thing: he copies a Homeric episode and figure – Proteus – far more comprehensively than he ever does in the *Aeneid*. How we can set about explaining so intensive a piece of Homeric imitation at *this* point in *this* poem is the main question addressed by this chapter.

III

Russell, in his investigation of the ancient concept of imitation,[14] establishes the inalienability of *imitatio* and *aemulatio* ('rivalry'). His 'fifth principle' of literary imitation is that *imitatio* always has a competitive element.[15] The author who copies a model in the manner considered proper by the ancients must harbour the ambition to *equal* that model, typically by elegant alterations to the original. Imitation without this emulative element is liable to the charge of plagiarism: it is a *furtum*. The *locus classicus* for this aspect of ancient literary theory is Ps.-Longinus, *Subl.* 13.2–14.3, which advises the μίμησις τε καὶ ζήλωσις of models as the best means to the creation of a 'sublime' style, μίμησις and ζήλωσις being terms closely corresponding to the Latin *imitatio* and *aemulatio*. Imitation and emulation are thus two sides of the same coin,[16] and examples of this ambivalent attitude to one's models – the deference of imitation and the aggressiveness of

---

[12] Knauer (1964) 361–527.   [13] Cf. 2.176 and Thomas (1988) ad loc.
[14] Russell (1979).   [15] Russell (1979) 16. See also Fiske (1920) esp. 43–6.
[16] Russell (1979) 10.

rivalry – are readily to be found in Latin authors. Pliny the Elder (*HN praef.* 22–3) contrasts the practice of other writers on natural history who copy their authorities word for word without acknowledgement with the practice of Virgil and Cicero (in his philosophical works). Both Virgil and Cicero, Pliny implies, indulge at times in verbatim imitation of their models, but in them the practice is justifiable: in Cicero's case because the imitation is candidly acknowledged, and in Virgil's case because it is a mark of courage, since it is a means of *rivalling* the model (*ut certarent*). The author of the *Rhetorica ad Herennium* gives a similar definition of *imitatio* in rhetoric: *Imitatio est qua impellimur ... ut aliquorum similes in dicendo ualeamus esse*, 'Imitation is the means by which we attain to ... an ability in speaking equal to certain models' (1.2.3).

A fine example of the application of this terminology is provided by Aulus Gellius at *Attic Nights* 13.27. Discussing the use made by Virgil (at *G.* 1.437) of a line of the late Hellenistic poet Parthenius, Gellius describes the exercise in terms of *rivalry*:

Partheni poetae versus est:
Γλαύκῳ καὶ Νηρεῖ καὶ εἰναλίῳ Μελικέρτῃ.
eum uersum Vergilius aemulatus est, itaque fecit duobus uocabulis uenuste inmutatis parem:
Glauco et Panopeae et Inoo Melicertae.

There is a line of the poet Parthenius,
To Glaucus and Nereus and marine Melicertes.
This line was emulated by Virgil, and by the graceful change of two words he rendered his line equal to the original:
To Glaucus and Panopea and Melicertes son of Ino.

Virgil's task – in which in this case he achieves success – is by creative imitation of the line to *rival* it, create a line to be its equal. This is a usefully succinct illustration of the ancient notion of imitation: imitation (or good imitation) *entails* emulation. Immediately afterwards Gellius cites an occasion when Virgil *failed* to equal a line of Homer: *non ... parem neque similem fecit*. Here the arena for competition is a single line. In the case of Virgil's *imitatio* of *Odyssey* 4, where the imitation of the model is so very much more sustained and eye-catching than usual – and, as I will suggest, seeks by structural means to make the arena for competition Virgil's whole poem – this element of emulation is that much more obviously in evidence.

IV

Further consideration of the passage will, I think, confirm the validity of this interpretation. We have so far noted a stylistic and verbal resemblance between the two Proteus passages of Homer and Virgil. I now wish to suggest that there is also what we might call a 'structural' resemblance.

Contemporary criticism of the *Georgics* – as will be clear even from my argument so far – is particularly associated with the name of Richard Thomas. His excellent edition of the poem (my occasional criticisms of which only confirm its enormous prominence in the critical literature), along with numerous articles, has served to illuminate many aspects of the *Georgics* – especially in the area of Hellenistic models – previously neglected by scholarship. One area of research to which Thomas' contribution has been especially great is the issue of structural parallelism between ancient works of literature. In two articles, 'Callimachus, the *Victoria Berenices* and Roman poetry' and 'Virgil and the Euphrates' (co-authored by Ruth Scodel), Thomas established the existence of precise structural parallels between the *Georgics* and two works of Callimachus, the *Aetia* and the *Hymn to Apollo*.[17] In the first article Thomas argued for the pervasive influence on Latin poetry of the fragments of poetry found in the Lille papyri (the *Victoria Berenices*) and specifically for a pattern of correspondences between the opening of Book 3 of the *Aetia* (where Parsons placed the *Victoria*)[18] and the equivalent points of Propertius' elegies, Statius' *Silvae* and the *Georgics*: in each case the opening of the third book. In the second

---

[17] Thomas (1983b); Scodel and Thomas (1984).
[18] In the first publication of the papyri: Parsons (1977) 46–8.

article Scodel and Thomas pointed out how the name *Euphrates*, which occurs only three times in Virgil's corpus, occurs each time precisely six lines from the end of a book, *Georgics* 1 and 4 and *Aeneid* 8 respectively. Their convincing explanation was that the position was intended to mirror the Ἀσσύριος ποταμός of Callimachus' Second Hymn,[19] also lying six lines from the end of the poem, and identified by a scholiast (rightly or wrongly)[20] as the Euphrates.

This kind of thing should not surprise us any more, let alone provoke scepticism, and generally speaking it no longer does. As Jenkyns says, 'it is very hard to believe that [Virgil] could not have been conscious of what he was doing when he planted the name Euphrates where he did',[21] though *why* he did so may be a more vexed issue.[22] A considerably more fastidious piece of parallelism to be found in the *Georgics* is that noted by Edwin Brown at 1.429–33: the acrostic featuring the initial letters of Virgil's *cognomen, nomen* and *praenomen* (in that order) in an equivalent location to Aratus' famous λεπτός acrostic.[23] Similar, again, though as yet unexplained, is the careful placement of the name *Maecenas* in the proemia of each book of the *Georgics*, at line 2 in the first and fourth books, and line 41 in the second and third.[24] Not for the first time we are obliged to accept the quite phenomenal meticulousness both of much Hellenistic poetry and of the Roman verse it influenced.

At various points in the *Georgics*, then, Virgil equates his poem with the *Phaenomena* of Aratus and Callimachus'

---

[19] In *Georgics* 4 and *Aen.* 8, perhaps indirectly: see Jenkyns (1993) although I find it hard to agree with Jenkyns' assertion that (at the time of the *Aeneid*) 'the *Georgics* was much better known both to Virgil and his likely readers than Callimachus' Second Hymn', and with his suggestion that the two later instances might not evoke the Callimachean passage at all, but only the earlier Virgilian example(s) (116). Jenkyns seems to me to underestimate the enormous programmatic importance Callimachus had for the Augustan poets.

[20] See Williams (1978) 91.

[21] Jenkyns (1993) 115.

[22] See n. 19 above.

[23] Brown (1963) 102–5; cf. Fowler (1983).

[24] See Thomas (1988) ad locc.

Hymn to Apollo and *Aetia*. In the case of Callimachus the resemblance is structural: Virgil's whole text, as it were, is rendered similar to the model. In his edition Thomas also notes
(*en passant*) another parallel with an earlier work of Greek
literature, this time in Book 4. This correspondence, needless
to say, is between the two episodes involving the character
Proteus, both of which occupy the fourth book, and begin at
closely equivalent lines in their respective works of poetry, the
Georgics and the *Odyssey*. Yet given Thomas' enthusiasm for
parallelism of this kind he is perhaps surprisingly diffident
about this one. He writes (at 4.387–414),

In this section ... V. adapts a poetic model as closely as anywhere in his
corpus. Cyrene's instructions, and Aristaeus' execution of them, are based
closely on the famous incident from Hom. *Od.* 4.351–570 ... It is presumably coincidental that Eidothea's speech begins at *Od.* 4.383, Cyrene's at *G.*
4.387, though V., like many others, may well have felt *Od.* 1–4 (the *Telemachy*) to be in part a separable section of the epic – in which case the
structural parallelism is perhaps intended.

Part of the reason for Thomas' caution is his sense that the
Georgics is in essence a Callimachean poem.[25] Another reason, perhaps, is the distance of this correspondence from
either end of the book. The issue arises of visibility. Both
Thomas' parallels stand close to permanent textual features,
the beginning of Book 3 and the conclusion of Book 4, and
are consequently easily picked up by a reader. The Proteus
parallel, by contrast, is stranded in the middle. *Georgics* 4.387
may be reasonably close to the end of a book (180 lines or so);
but *Odyssey* 4.383 is not even halfway. How could such a
parallel be recognized?

The answer, I would argue, lies in the format of contemporary texts. I have already suggested how unusually intensive is
the *aemulatio* of Homer constituted by Virgil's Proteus. But it
is noticeable that the imitation of the *Odyssey* episode does
not begin until a while after the first mention of Proteus at line
387. The material at 387–400 is gleaned from a number of

---

[25] Thomas (1988) I 3.

sources, including Callimachus' passing reference to Proteus in the *Victoria Berenices*[26] and passages of Homer from outside *Odyssey* 4.[27] Some details, undeniably, originate in *Odyssey* 4: *caeruleus* (388) picks up ἅλιος (384), and *G.* 396–7 are indebted to *Od.* 388–9. But the real proximity of the two passages only becomes clear at the emphatic moment when Cyrene begins to explain to Aristaeus by what means she will help her son entrap the sea god. The temporal expression of 401, *medios cum sol accenderit aestus*, 'when the sun has kindled the midday heat', is an adaptation of *Od.* 400, ἦμος δ᾽ ἠέλιος μέσον οὐρανὸν ἀμφιβεβήκῃ, 'when the sun has bestridden mid-heaven', as also is line 426, the opening line of the second half of Virgil's description (the actual capture, as opposed to Cyrene's anticipation of it). But the line numbered 401 in modern texts of the *Georgics* can easily be shown to have been originally line 400, since *G.* 4.338 is generally accepted as a later interpolation from the *Aeneid* (5.826).[28] Our *G.* 4.401 is thus not only a close imitation of *Od.* 4.400: as *G.* 4.400 it is also the precise stichometrical equivalent – by line and book – of its model in the *Odyssey*.

This perhaps makes the situation seem rather more simple than it is. An original text of the *Georgics* may be fairly easy to reconstruct, but deciding what a text of the *Odyssey* might have looked like in Italy in 30 BC is another matter altogether, and I relegate most of my rather complicated discussion of this parallel to Appendix II. What can be established slightly more easily (though again I leave the details to the Appendix) is the visibility of such a parallel. The correspondence at *Od.* and *G.* 4.400 is so striking not only because of the parallelism of both book and line, but also for the precise line at which the two poems happen to coincide: a round hundred. We have

---

[26] *SH* fr. 254.5–6, εἰς Παλληνέα μά[ντιν, | ποιμένα [φωκάων], apparently supplies to Virgil Proteus' homeland, Pallene (391); whilst *uates* (387, 392) picks up μάντις, and ποιμένα (with Lloyd-Jones' φωκάων) is perhaps reflected by *pascit . . . phocas* (395). See Thomas (1988) ad locc.

[27] *G.* 4.388–9 bear a resemblance to *Od.* 3.179, and 392–3 translate *Il.* 1.70: see Thomas (1988) ad loc. Crabbe (1977) 349–51 would also like to see reference here to Catullus' *Peleus and Thetis*.

[28] Thomas (1988) Mynors (1990) ad loc.

noted how Thomas' parallels played on features of the text which remained invariable from individual copy to copy: book divisions. It is significant that the only other permanent structural feature in contemporary texts, the progressive line-numbering (or 'running stichometry') to be found in the left margin of a text, occurred at every hundredth line.[29] A four-hundredth line of a poetic text was more than likely – as I argue in the Appendix – to have had such a stichometrical mark in its left margin.

We may or may not, ultimately, be able to establish a precise, line-to-line parallel between the *Georgics* and the *Odyssey*: in view of the difficulty of postulating a single particular fixed Homeric text at any given historical juncture (or geographical locale) probably, on balance, not. But a general parallel (after the fashion of the *Aetia* parallel in Book 3) in the close vicinity of line 400 of the fourth book seems unquestionable. Now, if we are to consider the Euphrates and *Aetia* parallels significant we are obliged to do the same with this one. As to its significance, we have already considered the necessarily 'emulative' dimension of Virgil's verbal imitation of *Odyssey* 4. A similar rationale seems to lie behind this structural parallel. What can be the effect of such a parallel but to make the copying text *resemble* the original? Surely the stichometrical correspondence is an (arch)[30] expression on a structural plane of the emulation of Homer – the attempt to equal his achievement – represented by Virgil's verbal imitation of the *Proteus*. The imitation of Homer's Proteus episode at the precisely equivalent point of Virgil's poem has the effect of styling the *Georgics* in a sense 'equivalent' to the first four books of the *Odyssey*: a Latin *Telemachy*, written, of course, by a Latin Homer.[31]

---

[29] For a good illustration see Hunt (1911) 82 and pl. 4 no. 44, an ε marking *Il.* 1.500.

[30] For the 'meta-allusive' quality of this example of imitation, cf. Smith (1990) 460.

[31] It is not, I think, coincidental that after this intensive imitation of *Od.* 4 at the end of the *Georgics* the *Aeneid* begins with close imitation of *Od.* 5. Interesting in this context are the statistics in Davison (1956) on the relative popularity of individual books of the Homeric poems. Judging by papyrus finds the favourite book of the *Odyssey* in Egypt was, by some distance, Book 4. Cf. Haslam (1997) 59.

V

I have so far considered two aspects of Virgil's Proteus passage: that it is an imitation of Homer of unparalleled ambitiousness, and that it occupies a position in the *Georgics* equivalent to the position of its model in the *Odyssey*. My explanation has been that Virgil by these means intended to depict his *emulation* of Homer, his striving to *equal* the Greek poet.

A similar motive can be attributed to Virgil in the *Eclogues* and in the prologue to Book 3 of the *Georgics*. The frequent close imitations of Theocritus in his pastoral poems are clearly designed to style Virgil Theocritus' equal in the Latin language. The same is presumably true of the parallel with *Aetia* 3 at the start of *Georgics* 3: Virgil is asserting his poem's equivalence to the four-book *Aetia*, and by implication his own equality with Callimachus. Each of these claims is the act of a highly confident poet. Theocritus was one of the very leading figures of Hellenistic literature. Callimachus was *the* leading figure. For a poet of a culture which traditionally felt such inferiority regarding the artistic achievements of the Hellenistic world these are very significant statements.

But outshadowing both these earlier claims is the implication of comparability with Homer that we seem to find in *G.* 4. Throughout Greek history Homer was the object of enormous hyperbole. The view of Homer inherited by Augustan Rome from the Hellenistic age considered it axiomatic that Homer was altogether unique: *beyond* emulation, in other words. This was the cornerstone of Callimachean poetics, which was itself merely the literary dimension of an almost universal idolatry of the poet in Hellenistic culture. Brink describes the hugely exaggerated evaluation of Homer's achievement current at this period,[32] according to which he was not only the poet *par excellence*, often ὁ ποιητής without qualification,[33] but also became considered the original source of all other literature as well and even – amongst the

---

[32] Brink (1972).   [33] Harmon (1923); see also Skiadas (1965) esp. 95–103.

allegorist scholars of Pergamum especially – the source of all knowledge whatsoever. Later writers such as Ps.-Heraclitus in his *Quaestiones Homericae* and Ps.-Plutarch in the *De Vita et Poesi Homeri* sought to establish that all subsequent philosophical or scientific doctrines were anticipated in the Homeric poems.[34] In saying this they are generally supposed to be following the lead of the second-century critic Crates of Mallos, first head of the library at Pergamum, the most important Hellenistic scholarly establishment after the library of Alexandria.[35]

A relief in the British Museum by the sculptor Archelaus of Priene – the so-called *Apotheosis of Homer* – illustrates the enormously high esteem in which the Hellenistic world held Homer.[36] It appears to commemorate the success of the (contemporary) poet depicted standing on the middle right. In the relief Homer sits receiving sacrifice, holding a scroll and sceptre and in general closely resembling a figure of Zeus in the same relief: Homer, it implies, is Zeus's parallel in the realm of poetry.[37] Near Homer there are figures representing the *Iliad*, the *Odyssey* and the *Batrachomyomachia* and also, crowning him, Time and *Oikoumene*, the Inhabited World, all identified by inscriptions. As Pollitt writes, the crowning of Homer by these two indicates that 'Homer's epics will last for all time and are universal'; and they are the fountainhead of all subsequent literary genres.[38] The relief may perhaps reflect the iconography of the Homereion (incorporating a *temple* of Homer) established by Ptolemy IV Philopator at the end of the third century at Alexandria, the same context as the poetry of Callimachus and only about twenty years after his death.[39] Whether the link is direct or not (Brink thinks probably not),[40] Archelaus' relief and Philopator's Homereion

---

[34] See, for example, *Quaest. Hom.* 4.4; and Buffière (1962) ad loc.
[35] On Crates and scholarship at Pergamum see Mette (1936); Pfeiffer (1968) 234–51; Hardie (1986) 27–9; and with some timely criticisms of Pfeiffer, Porter (1992).
[36] There is a clear reproduction of the relief in Smith (1892–1904) III 245.
[37] Brink (1972) 551 n. 20.
[38] Pollitt (1986) 16.
[39] Webster (1964) 144–7; Pollitt (1986) 16.
[40] Brink (1972) 551.

clearly partake of the same complex of Hellenistic notions regarding the absolute pre-eminence of Homer and his poetry. Homer is the godlike source of all literature (specifically, here, the poetry of the Hellenistic poet who apparently had the relief made), and the relevant definition of literature – if we look at the attributes of the Muses, Homer's patrons, depicted towards the top of the relief – is catholic. One of the Muses points to a globe, identifying herself as Urania, Muse of Astronomy and of natural philosophy in general.[41] The widespread interpretation, by Crates and others, of the Homeric and Hesiodic poems as texts of natural philosophy – the study of the fundamental processes of the universe and conventionally the highest possible poetic theme,[42] and thus the appropriate theme for the highest poetic genius – will exercise us in the next chapter. But suffice to say that Antipater of Sidon is not expressing an unorthodox view in the second century when he calls Homer nothing less than the ἀγήραντον στόμα κόσμου παντός, 'ageless mouthpiece of the entire universe' (*AP* 7.6.3–4).

It is against this conceptual background that we must understand Virgil is suggesting his commensurability with Homer: not merely with a great Greek poet, nor even merely with the greatest, but with a figure commonly considered nothing less than the origin of all literature and even the source of all Greek intellectual culture whatsoever. Virgil's only real precedent in making such a claim was Ennius, who at the start of the *Annals* described a dream in which Homer appeared to him and explained how he was reincarnated in Ennius.[43] As such, Ennius suggested, he was capable of following in Homer's footsteps and composing heroic epic. Hardie rightly judges Ennius' claim astonishingly bold: the dream is 'an extraordinarily confident version of epic succes-

---

[41] Hardie (1986) 23; see *RE*, s.v., for the iconography and functions of Urania.

[42] For the conventionally elevated status of natural-philosophical themes, and in particular the myths of Gigantomachy, which were understood as allegorical expressions of the fundamental conflict between order and chaos, see Innes (1979); Hardie (1986) 85–90.

[43] Skutsch (1985) 147–67.

sion'.[44] Ennius' assertion of his equality with Homer is apparently reflected by Horace when he records the description of Ennius as *alter Homerus*, 'a second Homer' (*Epist.* 2.1.50), though he attributes the evaluation to *critici* rather than to Ennius himself.[45] Horace himself appears to be sceptical about the description,[46] and from a Hellenistic standpoint, at any rate, it was almost a contradiction in terms: Homer was irreplicable. Euphorion famously termed him ἀπροτίμαστος, 'unapproachable'.[47] Half a century after the *Georgics* Velleius provides evidence that such notions had been fully assimilated in Rome (1.5.1–2):

clarissimum deinde Homeri inluxit ingenium, sine exemplo maximum, qui magnitudine operis et fulgore carminum solus appellari poeta meruit; in quo hoc maximum est, quod neque ante illum, quem ipse imitaretur, neque post illum, qui eum imitari posset, inuentus est.

It was at this moment that the brilliant genius of Homer shone forth, the greatest without parallel, who by virtue of the greatness of his work and the brilliance of his poems has alone deserved the name of poet. The main basis for his reputation is that before his time no one was found for him to imitate, and after his time no one capable of imitating him.

Some time later Quintilian briskly dismisses the notion of *aemulatio* of Homer, *quod fieri non potest* (*Inst.* 10.1.50), and Virgil himself is credited with having responded to those who accused him of plagiarizing Homer with the apophthegm that it was easier to steal Hercules' club from him than a line from Homer (*Vita Donati* 46): even to plagiarize Homer in the Latin language – as we have seen, plagiarism was considered an inferior form of *imitatio* – was a major achievement, let alone to emulate him. But in Virgil, and in the *Georgics* particularly, the audacity of seeking to emulate Homer is all the more striking because he has hitherto – and in the course of this very poem – advertised his allegiance to Callimachean

---

[44] Hardie (1993) 103. Cf. A. S. Gratwick in *CHCL* II 60 ('this stupendous claim').
[45] According to Jerome the expression was used of Ennius by Lucilius, perhaps as a 'satirical reference to Ennius' dream': Rudd (1989) ad Hor. *Epist.* 2.1.51–2.
[46] Brink (1982) 92–3; Rudd (1989) ad 2.1.51.
[47] Euph. fr. 118 Powell; *TGL*, s.v., glosses the term 'pro οὗ δυσχερὲς ἐφάψασθαι τῆς δυνάμεως'.

poetics and the extravagant appraisal of Homer's achievement which that entailed.

VI

The classic expression of Homer's status as the cultural wellspring of Greece is, as Brink writes,[48] the ancient equation of the poet with Ocean, the divine source of all waters, according to a celebrated passage in the *Iliad*. At *Il.* 21.193–7 Achilles explains to the corpse of Asteropaeus,

> ἀλλ' οὐκ ἔστι Διὶ Κρονίωνι μάχεσθαι,
> τῷ οὐδὲ κρείων Ἀχελώϊος ἰσοφαρίζει,
> οὐδὲ βαθυρρείταο μέγα σθένος Ὠκεανοῖο,
> ἐξ οὗ περ πάντες ποταμοὶ καὶ πᾶσα θάλασσα
> καὶ πᾶσαι κρῆναι καὶ φρείατα μακρὰ νάουσιν.

But it is not possible to fight with Zeus the son of Cronos: with him not even king Achelous vies, nor the great strength of deep-flowing Ocean, from whom all rivers flow and every sea, and all springs and deep wells.

In Augustan Rome Dionysius of Halicarnassus re-employs Homer's description of Ocean to describe Homer himself (*Comp.* 24):

> κορυφὴ μὲν οὖν ἁπάντων καὶ σκοπός,
>   ἐξ οὗ περ πάντες ποταμοὶ καὶ πᾶσα θάλασσα
>   καὶ πᾶσαι κρῆναι,
> δικαίως ἂν Ὅμηρος λέγοιτο.

The summit and target of all authors,
  'from whom all rivers and every sea
  and all springs . . .'
may rightly be said to be Homer.

As Ocean is the source of all waters, so Homer is the origin of all literature. The conceit is evidently fairly routine. Dionysius makes no attempt to identify the quotation, and he omits any mention of the name Ὠκεανός. And indeed the likening of Homer to Ocean is a very common motif in the Augustan

---

[48] Brink (1972) 553–6.

period and later, as Brink and Williams have established.[49] But it can be dated back rather further. Philopator's Homereion in Alexandria seems to have contained a painting of Homer in the aspect of Ocean by the artist Galaton. This, at any rate, would explain Aelian's bizarre description of the painting at *VH* 13.22:

Πτολεμαῖος ὁ Φιλοπάτωρ κατασκευάσας Ὁμήρῳ νεών, αὐτὸν μὲν καλῶς ἐκάθισε, κύκλῳ δὲ τὰς πόλεις περιέστησε τῷ ἀγάλματι, ὅσαι ἀντιποιοῦνται τοῦ Ὁμήρου. Γαλάτων δὲ ὁ ζωγράφος ἔγραψε τὸν μὲν Ὅμηρον αὐτὸν ἐμοῦντα, τοὺς δὲ ἄλλους ποιητὰς τὰ ἐμημεσμένα ἀρυομένους.

Ptolemy Philopator built a temple to Homer, and established it in fine style. He placed in a circle around the statue all the cities who laid claim to Homer. The artist Galaton painted Homer himself vomiting, and all the other poets collecting what he vomited.

As Webster suggests,[50] Aelian must unknowingly have been using a satirical epigram which wilfully misunderstood the image of Homer as Ocean, source of all poetry. Williams convincingly argues that its ancestry stretches back even before Callimachus, whose imagery of sea, muddy river and pure spring in the *Hymn to Apollo* presupposes the Ocean / Homer equation.[51]

Given the prevalence of this particular conceit it is hard not to see it operating also in the scene in *Georgic* 4 which immediately precedes the episode involving Proteus. At 4.380–3 Cyrene pours a libation – to Ocean:

> et mater 'cape Maeonii carchesia Bacchi:
> Oceano libemus' ait. simul ipsa precatur
> Oceanumque patrem rerum Nymphasque sorores,
> centum quae siluas, centum quae flumina seruant.

His mother said: 'take up goblets of Lydian Bacchus; let us pour an offering to Ocean'. Then she at once prays to Ocean, father of all things, and the sister Nymphs, who protect a hundred forests and a hundred rivers.

---

[49] Brink (1972); Williams (1978) 98–9. See, in addition to Dionysius, Ov. *Am.* 3.9.25–6; Manilius 2.8–11; Ps.-Longinus, *Subl.* 9.13, 13.2–3; Quint. *Inst.* 10.1.46; *AP* 9.184.3–4.

[50] Webster (1964) 144–5.

[51] Williams (1978) 88: 'there are firm indications that it was already a commonplace in the Hellenistic period'.

The passage which I have argued constitutes emulation of Homer follows after this libation scene; and it is clearly tempting to read *Oceanus* as a signpost to the presence of Homer. The epithet *Maeonii* in line 380 surely ensures that we do. To specify the wine Cyrene employs in her drink-offering as *Lydian* wine serves perhaps two functions in the primary narrative: it indicates its quality (though there were better, and better-known, wines than the Lydian), and it alludes to Bacchus' reputed origins in Asia Minor. But as Thomas (again, somewhat tentatively) suggests, it could also fulfil an additional function as an allusion to *the Maeonian*, a favourite Augustan soubriquet for Homer.[52] As early as the fifth century there was a tradition to the effect that Homer's father was called Maeon;[53] it may or may not predate the debate waged *ad nauseam* in the Anthologies on the question of Homer's ethnic origins. One answer to that question had Homer as a native of Smyrna.[54] Smyrna was in Lydia, and an earlier name for Lydia was Maeonia.[55] Μαιονίδης – alternatively 'the Lydian', or 'the son of Maeon' – is regularly encountered as a variant appellation for Homer in the Hellenistic epigram: our earliest instance is in a poem of Antipater of Sidon.[56] *Maeonides*, or more commonly the Latin adjective *Maeonius*, became a commonplace alternative to *Homerus* in Roman verse as well.[57] The fact that it is to *wine* that the term is applied may help to confirm the reference. Bacchus was for both Hellenistic and Augustan poets a symbol of artistic inspira-

---

[52] Thomas (1988) ad loc.: '*Maeonii* could suggest Homer, given the Homeric surroundings'. Claudian, at the beginning of his epic *De Raptu Proserpinae*, depicts his poetic inspiration in terms of the mystic experiences of the initiate at Eleusis. The last vision he sees is the drunken Iacchus, leaning on a thyrsus. The way it is described, *Maeonius ... thyrsus*, perhaps captures the same double reference as *Maeonius ... Bacchus* in the *Georgics* – Lydian Bacchus/Homeric inspiration – as would be appropriate at the outset of an epic.

[53] See *FGrH* 4 F 5, a fragment of Hellanicus.

[54] See, for example, *Anth. Plan.* 299; Ps.-Plut. *de Vita et Poesi Homeri* B2, citing Pindar.

[55] Serv. *auct.* ad *G.* 4.379; Pliny, *HN* 5.110.

[56] *AP* 7.2.2. See also 5.30.2; 7.15.2, 138.3, 213.8, 674.2; 9.28.6, 97.5, 192.2, 575.5, etc. Antipater died around 125 BC: Gow and Page (1965) II 32.

[57] Maeonius: Hor. *Carm.* 1.6.2, 4.9.5–6; Prop. 2.28.29; Ov. *Ars. Am.* 2.4; *Rem. Am.* 373; *Ciris* 62; *Laus Pisonis* 232; Stat. *Achil.* 1.4; *Anth. Lat.* 1111.13. Maeonides: Ov. *Am.* 1.15.9, 3.9.25; *Tr.* 4.10.22; Persius 6.11.

tion,[58] mainly as a consequence of the common association of poetic inspiration with religious ecstasy or drunkenness. Horace, *Epistles* 1.19.1–5 reflects this motif:

> Prisco si credis, Maecenas docte, Cratino,
> nulla placere diu nec uiuere carmina possunt
> quae scribuntur aquae potoribus. ut male sanos
> adscripsit Liber Satyris Faunisque poetas,
> uina fere dulces oluerunt mane Camenae.

If you believe old Cratinus, my learned Maecenas, no poems can please or survive for long which are written by water-drinkers. Ever since Liber enlisted crazy poets among his Satyrs and Fauns, the sweet Muses have usually smelt of wine in the morning.

But Macleod convincingly argued that Horace here lends Cratinus' maxim an additional, contemporary programmatic sense. In the lines that follow these (6–8) the comedian is ranked with Ennius and Homer, apparently as exemplifying 'old-fashioned' (the implication of *prisco*, line 1) approaches to poetry:

> laudibus arguitur uini uinosus Homerus;
> Ennius ipse pater numquam nisi potus ad arma
> prosiluit dicenda

By his praises of wine Homer is proven bibulous. Father Ennius himself never leapt forth to tell of arms unless drunk.

Horace at first seems to align himself with the wine-drinkers, but Maecenas' epithet, *docte*, is strongly redolent of the sober poetic ideals of Alexandria, and *si credis* implies that Cratinus' dismissal of the water-drinkers is not necessarily to be accepted without question.[59] Macleod's view is that Horace's poem uses a pre-existing programmatic image (itself a development of a non-programmatic body of epigrams censuring teetotalism), which set in opposition water-drinkers, who represented Callimacheans, and wine-drinkers, representing adherents of conventional heroic epic.[60] A similar image is

---

[58] See Callim. *Epigr.* 8; Hor. *Carm.* 2.19, and Nisbet and Hubbard (1978) 316–17; Prop. 3.2.9.
[59] Macleod (1977) 364.
[60] On this complex of imagery see also Crowther (1979) and Knox (1985b).

employed in a poem composed by the Augustan poet Antipater of Thessalonica (*AP* 11.20), where a contrast is clearly drawn between Callimachean ὑδροπόται, identifiable by the reference to the *Hymn to Apollo*, and poets such as Archilochus and Homer who are associated with wine:

> φεύγεθ᾽ ὅσοι λόκκας ἢ λοφνίδας ἢ καμασῆνας
> ᾄδετε, ποιητῶν φῦλον ἀκανθολόγων,
> οἵ τ᾽ ἐπέων κόσμον λελυγισμένον ἀσκήσαντες
> κρήνης ἐξ ἱερῆς πίνετε λιτὸν ὕδωρ.
> σήμερον Ἀρχιλόχοιο καὶ ἄρσενος ἦμαρ Ὁμήρου
> σπένδομεν· ὁ κρητὴρ οὐ δέχεθ᾽ ὑδροπότας.

Away with you, all who sing of *loccae* and *lophnides* and *camasenes*, tribe of thorn-gathering poets, and you who drink frugal water from the holy spring, practising contortions as your verses' ornament. Today we pour wine for the birthday of Archilochus and manly Homer; our bowl is not at home to water-drinkers.

Wine and Homer were thus apparently strongly linked in Hellenistic and Augustan programmatic symbolism. When Virgil has Cyrene exhort her son to take up 'Maeonian Bacchus' in order to pour a libation to Ocean, after which the poet undertakes his most ambitious ever imitation of Homer, he is surely tapping the rich body of imagery with which Greek literature had surrounded the figure of Homer. The libation-scene would seem to be alerting us to the imitation of Homer to come. The image may be partially paralleled in Archelaus of Priene's relief, in which sacrifice is made to Homer as, we must presume, the source of inspiration for the contemporary poet pictured on the middle right in whose name the scene was apparently carved. In the poem by Antipater just cited, as well, libation functions as a gesture of respect and deference to the two Archaic poets, with the implication also that Homer and Archilochus are in some sense Antipater's literary models.

VII

Yet even if there is this further function as a metatextual reference to Homer to explain it, the introduction of Ocean to the story at 381 may nevertheless strike us as rather per-emptory. This would, I think, be mistaken. Ocean is not pre-viously *named* in the *Aristaeus*, but he plays nonetheless, I want now to suggest, a much more prominent role in the epi-sode than has hitherto been appreciated. He does so by virtue of an unjustly neglected reference in the *Aristaeus* to Hesiod's *Theogony*. By virtue of this allusion to Hesiod we can appre-ciate that Cyrene's watery cave is not just any underground river-source. Virgil strongly encourages us to identify it with the home of Ocean and the children of Ocean who are listed at *Theog.* 337–70.[61]

At *G.* 4.360–2 Aristaeus enters the *sacrum caput*, 'sacred source', of the river Peneus. He finds himself in a marvellous watery environment inhabited by nymphs (334–47) and rivers (366–73), both sets of whom are listed by name. Thomas sur-mises that the scene of Cyrene and her fellow nymphs has for its main model a Homeric context, *Il.* 18.35–64, the scene when Thetis responds to Achilles' lament for Patroclus which contains a catalogue of Nereids. But since in its *details* Virgil's list of nymphs is not Homeric (only Clymene at 345 corre-sponds to any of the Homeric nymphs), Thomas suggests that both they and the list of rivers which balances them derive from two Callimachean prose treatises, the Περὶ Νυμφῶν and the Περὶ Τῶν Ἐν Τῇ Οἰκουμένῃ Ποταμῶν.[62] This is a very plausible suggestion. The evocation of *Iliad* 18 at the begin-ning of the episode, also, is unquestionable. But another pas-sage in earlier literature that Virgil's parallel catalogues of nymphs and rivers cannot fail to recall – besides any Homeric or Callimachean context – is that of the complementary lists of *rivers* and *nymphs* at *Theogony* 337–70, representing the sons and daughters, respectively, of Ocean. Only one of the Virgilian nymphs actually corresponds to the Hesiodic, but this is a prominent one, Clymene again, who in a neat *mise en abîme* is depicted singing a kind of eroticized *Theogony* (347, *aque Chao densos diuum numerabat amores*, 'and she

---

[61] Cf. Quint (1983) 34: 'This is the cave of Ocean.'
[62] Thomas (1986) 190–3.

enumerated the many liaisons of the gods from Chaos on') which may also constitute a reference to the original prologue of Callimachus' *Aetia*, 'which alludes to the Hesiodic account of the genesis of the universe and the gods from Χάος, the original αἴτιον'.[63] Furthermore, two of the nymphs are pointedly specified as being daughters of Ocean, Clio and Beroe, *Oceanitides ambae* (341).[64] The rivers correspond more closely. Three of them, the Phasis, Caicus and Eridanus, appear in both Virgil and Hesiod (and the presence of the Peneus, *Theog.* 343, may be taken for granted), strongly suggesting that Virgil means the reader to bear the Hesiodic passage in mind. These rivers have their sources in the cave (*caput*, 368): Aristaeus, we recall, gained entrance to it via the source (*caput*, 319) of the Peneus. There is only one possible mythological contender for the original source of all these rivers, and that is Ocean, ἐξ οὗ περ πάντες ποταμοὶ ... νάουσιν.[65]

The location of Ocean directly *beneath* the earth, rather than, as more often, around its perimeter, also perhaps requires some explanation. Clearly, first of all, the idea of ocean as source of all waters entails a central location. But as I shall argue at some length in the next chapter, Homer's Ocean had broader significance for the Greeks than just as a metaphor for the poet himself. Descriptions of the god elsewhere in the *Iliad* than Book 21 (in particular in Book 14) were one of the means by which it was argued that Homer's poetry was a

---

[63] Hardie (1985) 90; Call. fr. 2 Pf.

[64] Many later authors follow Hesiod in making all nymphs the daughters of Ocean: see Callim. *Hymn* 3.42–5, Ap. Rhod. *Argon.* 4.1414 (νύμφαι, ἱερὸν γένος 'Ωκεανοῖο); Catull. 88.6 (*genitor Nympharum ... Oceanus*).

[65] Those critics, such as Zenodotus, who preferred *Il.* 21.193–7 *without* 195, the reference to Ocean, clearly thought that the river Ἀχελώϊος (194) – on which the relative clause ἐξ οὗ περ πάντες ποταμοὶ ... νάουσιν then became dependent – could fit the bill of universal source. As such the Achelous was considered equivalent to Ocean; see Σ *Il.* 21.194, and Erbse (1977) ad loc.; Grenfell and Hunt (1899) 78–9 (scholia on *Il.* 21); Powell (1925) 248; see also Serv. ad *G.* 1.9. It is thus perhaps of interest that the cave of Achelous at Ov. *Met.* 8.562–73 much resembles Cyrene's cave, as Hollis (1970) notes ad 562 ff. On the pointedly epic associations of the figure Achelous in Ovid's treatment, see Hinds (1988) 19; Barchiesi (1989) 57–64.

References spanning the Classical period depict Ocean's domicile as a cave (Aesch. *PV* 133, 303; Claud. *Fesc.* 12.34–5), where his daughters dwell (*PV* 133). Quint. Smyrn. 3.748 and 12.160 speak of the home of Tethys, Ocean's wife, as ἄντρα.

vehicle for information about the fundamental physical processes of the universe. On this interpretation the Homeric poems were texts of natural philosophy which anticipated the cosmological doctrines of later philosophers. Statements of Homer to the effect that Ocean was the father of all things were interpreted as anticipating Thales' doctrine that water was the fundamental constitutive element of the cosmos, the element from which all others derived. This (as Servius here notes) is the view of Ocean which underlies the *second* mention of Ocean in Cyrene's libation, *Oceanum ... patrem rerum* (382). Thales presented a physical model of the cosmos corresponding to his theory of creation: the earth, according to Thales,[66] sat on top of the watery substrate of the universe which was supposedly indicated by Homer by means of the figure of Ocean. It is not, then, in contradiction of ancient concepts of Ocean to depict his domicile as lying underground, accessible via a river-source in Thessaly. In general, as I shall suggest in my next chapter, the conceptions of Ocean as the margin of the world and the source or origin of the world dovetail in a rather vague sense of his metaphysical liminality, be it in geographical space or historical time.[67]

VIII

To recap, then: I have suggested that Virgil's Proteus episode demands to be read, amongst other things, as a bold emulation of nothing short of the archetype of *all* poets, Homer. Furthermore, I have argued, this undertaking is advertised by the poet in the scene of libation to Ocean which just precedes it. In addition, it appears, the figure of Ocean – who, it can be established, was intimately associated with Homer at this time – has been present in a covert fashion for a much longer

---

[66] See, for example, Sen. *Q Nat.* 3.14.1.
[67] Servius seems to display knowledge of some such interpretation of the Virgilian passage. At *G.* 4.364, glossing part of Virgil's description of Cyrene's watery home, Servius for some reason cites for comparison Egyptian rites the upshot of which is a revelation that everything originally derives from a great water-source underground (*ex qua cuncta procreantur*). 'Hence', he continues, referring to 382, 'the expression in accordance with Thales *Oceanumque patrem rerum*'.

period: the cave to which Aristaeus gains access through the fount of the river Peneus, Virgil implies, is the cave of Ocean.

It is tempting at this point to bring in the end of Callimachus' *Hymn to Apollo* again. Williams interprets Callimachus' meaning in the finale to the *Hymn* to be that only his own poetry, taken from the spring, retains the purity of the ultimate source of the spring, the Homeric πόντος, which Williams equates with Ὠκεανός.[68] If we can broadly accept Williams' interpretation, certain parallels with the scheme of *G*. 4 present themselves. Led by Cyrene, patron of Callimachus' home town,[69] Aristaeus enters a spring and finds beneath, beyond or behind it – in a context at first sight Homeric but thereafter with strong Hesiodic and Callimachean colouring –[70] Ocean, and his Homeric encounter with Proteus. Might Aristaeus' entry of the spring figure Virgil's retracing of Callimachean inspiration to its source, Homer, of whom Virgil subsequently advertises his emulation?

IX

But there was more to the practice of *imitatio* than merely imitation. An integral part of the game of ancient *imitatio* was the meaningful *variation* of the model: an imitating poet proved his mastery of the model by his ability to introduce significant divergences from it: in this way *imitatio* became *aemulatio*.[71] Virgil's imitation of Parthenius of which Gellius so approved, as we saw,[72] was made comparable to the original by Virgil's felicitous alterations: *fecit duobus uocabulis uenuste inmutatis parem*. Too close imitation, by contrast, was open to the charge of plagiarism. A large part of the achievement was successfully to integrate foreign material into a new

[68] Williams (1978) 85–9.
[69] *Hymn* 2.65–96.
[70] Hesiod, of course, was claimed by Callimachus as his poetic model. He was also however a figure treated, like Homer, as a cosmological poet: see, e.g., Hardie (1986) 140. His is an appropriate poetry, then, to mediate between the two traditions.
[71] Lee (1981) 20.
[72] See p. 22 above.

context. What I wish to do now is investigate some of the alterations Virgil makes to his Homeric model. This will provide some preliminary indication of what Virgil intended to convey in the Proteus passage over and above the literary-generic dimension of his undertaking that I have been discussing in this chapter. But also, paradoxically, by the very nature of *imitatio* some of the best indications of how indebted this passage is to Homer involve Virgil's departures from his Homeric model: as we shall see, great significance seems to be conveyed by the slightest deviation from the Homeric original, and this is testimony of the extent to which the Virgilian episode is designed to be understood in the light of the Homeric. The divergences derive the effect they have from the otherwise near total congruity of the two passages.

A good illustration of this is provided by Virgil's rendering of Proteus' transformations. Virgil copies the dual Homeric structure (his choice of a passage displaying such a typically Homeric piece of repetition is not, presumably, accidental),[73] a speech of instruction by a sympathetic superhuman followed by its execution in the narrative. But true to the principle of *uariatio* details are transferred from one passage to the other, as my table in Appendix I indicates. Thus, for example, though in the Homeric original the description of Proteus' transformations *before* the event (by Eidothea, 417–18) is the less detailed, and that in Menelaus' narrative (455–8) the more so, in Virgil's version the longer treatment comes first, in Cyrene's speech (406–10), whilst the shorter is transformed into a kind of recapitulation in the authorial narrative (440–2): Virgil's *uariatio* has the effect of *tidying up* the model, a typically versatile piece of creative imitation.[74] The transformations themselves are also varied.[75] Those of Homer's longer list – lion, δράκων, panther, boar, water, tree – are

---

[73] Such repetition is, as Hardie (1993) 15 puts it, 'a mark of the [epic] genre'.

[74] On this process as it is displayed in Virgil's imitation of Homer in the *Aeneid*, see Schlunk (1974) 8–35. Another point at which Virgil may be seen to display concern for the 'propriety' of his Homeric imitation is in his restrained treatment of the unpleasant smell given off by Proteus' seals, a detail to which Homer gives far greater emphasis: see Thomas (1988) ad 395, 415, 431.

[75] Cf. Thomas (1988) ad 407–10.

replaced by Virgil with a boar, tigress, *draco*, lioness, fire and water. In three cases there is a correspondence of metamorphoses – *draco*, boar, water – and in two also of terminology. Homer's term for 'pig', σῦς, was identical with a standard Latin term; and *draco* is a loan-word. So much for the similarities. But what of the divergences? Why does Virgil substitute a tiger for Homer's panther, for example, and a lioness for Homer's male lion? One possible answer might be that these alterations – striking, as I have suggested, given the otherwise general congruity of model and version – point us back to an earlier context in the poem. At 3.242–83 the effects are described of *amor*, one of the violent natural forces to which Virgil repeatedly describes the *Georgics* world as being subject. The effects of *amor* are illustrated by the behaviour, when under its influence, of various members of the animal kingdom (245–6, 248):

> tempore non alio catulorum oblita leaena
> saeuior errauit campis ...
> ... tum saeuus aper, tum pessima tigris;

At that time the lioness, oblivious of her cubs, roams more savage on the plains ... then savage is the boar, then the tigress is at her worst.

We may recognize at least two of Proteus' manifestations: the lioness and the tigress. There is also a boar; and a *Sabellicus sus* also appears later (255).

As the natural force of *amor* inflicted itself, then, upon the lioness, tigress and boar in Book 3, so Aristaeus imposes himself upon Proteus when the latter is in the form of (amongst other things) a lioness, tigress and boar. What could be the significance of this? The innovations seem to relate Aristaeus' activity to that of a violent natural impulse. Aristaeus in fact appears to *usurp* the violent power of that impulse: he seems, like Aeneas, to be what Hardie terms a 'synecdochic hero' who subsumes into his person the elemental forces of the universe.[76] Thus, for example, in the *Aeneid*

---

[76] Hardie (1993) 4.

the developing imagery of *storm* is an important means by which Aeneas' movement from being the victim of events to being controller of events is depicted. In stark contrast to Aeneas' condition at the mercy of the storm as the poem begins is his *identification* with the violent power of storm as he defeats Turnus (*Aen.* 12.923).[77] Aeneas' control and employment of the storm at the end of the poem figures both his total control of the world (he is identical with the powers of the universe) and also the constructive power of destructive forces such as storm within the providential cosmic scheme which the god-like Aeneas at the end of the poem embodies. Further investigation of the figure of Proteus, in particular the exegesis of the figure by the allegorists of Homer, will help to show, I hope, that Virgil's intentions here in the *Georgics* are comparable. I argue in the next chapter that Virgil's treatment of the Homeric Proteus is mediated by a Hellenistic interpretation of the capture of Proteus as an allegory for the Stoic model of cosmic Creation. The capturer of Proteus, according to this interpretation, was a figure for the simultaneously destructive and creative demiurgic force of Stoic cosmology. The assimilation of Aristaeus to cosmic powers of destruction, I shall suggest, is bound up with Virgil's negotiation of the constructive potential of destruction such as that visited on Italy by the Civil Wars.

For now, however, the relevant issue is how Virgil's development of the imagery of his poem in the Proteus episode reflects his stylistic indebtedness to the *Odyssey*. The first point to be made here is how careful Virgil is not to puncture the carefully constructed Homeric atmosphere of his own passage. *All* the animals in the Virgilian metamorphosis, even his own imports, *could* be Greek. The *tigris* and *leaena* – Greek words – seem deliberately to have been chosen so as to blend in with their Homeric context. But more importantly, Virgil's subtle adaptations of his model – especially with regard to the lioness – demand, and presuppose, that the reader of the

[77] Hardie (1986) 176.

43

Georgics simultaneously follow closely the corresponding passage in Homer's *Odyssey*.

Another divergence made by Virgil from his Homeric model which is very rarely, if ever, noted is his introduction of *chains* to the story of Proteus' capture. In the *Odyssey* Proteus is subdued by brute strength alone (κάρτος τε βίη τε, 415). Menelaus and his companions threw their arms around him (ἀμφὶ δὲ χεῖρας | βάλλομεν, 454–5). But in the *Georgics*, while the necessity to apply force is equally emphasized, that force has a physical instantiation, *uincula*. Both the departure from Homer and an etymological connection between *uincula* and *uis* are signposted by Virgil. The chains are mentioned no less than six times in the course of the encounter. In two cases (396–8, 399–400) their effect is equated with *uis*:

> hic tibi, nate, prius *uinclis capiendus*, ut omnem
> expediat morbi causam euentusque secundet.
> nam *sine ui* non ulla dabit praecepta, neque illum
> orando flectes; *uim duram et uincula* capto
> tende

Him, son, you must capture with chains, so that he may unfold the whole cause of the sickness and prosper the outcome. For without force he will give no instructions, and you will not prevail upon him by pleading. Bring hard force and chains to bear on the captive.

It seems clear that this etymology was not Virgil's own invention. Isidore of Seville notes the fairly obvious derivation of *uinculum* from *uincio*, 'bind' (*Etym.* 5.27.6), but he also adds an alternative, *uel quia ui ligant*, 'or because they bind by force'. Augustine (*Dialect.* 6.11) also seems to favour the latter derivation, connecting *uinculum* with *uiolentus*;[78] but then both he and Virgil's contemporary Varro (whom Augustine is often following) habitually confuse words derived from *uis* with words to do with 'binding'. Thus Augustine in the same context (6.12) derives *uincio* itself from *uis*; and Varro went so far as to explain the name of the goddess Victoria by the fact not that conquered people were *defeated*, but that they were *chained* (*Ling.* 5.62). Ancient etymology, in fact, per-

---

[78] Cf. Isid. *Etym.* 10.279 (*uiolentus, quia uim infert*).

ceived all of these terms as being part of a single semantic group.[79]

In the *Georgics* violent power is something associated particularly with those natural forces with which the farmer is obliged to contend; and it is probably no coincidence that a number of these forces – *Venus, uentus* and perhaps also *morbus*[80] – were thought to be connected etymologically with *uis*. Again, I have more to say about Aristaeus' chains in my discussion of Homeric allegory in the next chapter, but this may suffice as a provisional explanation of their presence in the Proteus episode: they are a concrete symbol of the (paradoxically constructive) violent force, *uis*, which Aristaeus brings to bear on Proteus, and also, again, serve to assimilate his action to the processes of the natural world.[81] Once more, however, this quite major departure from the Homeric scene is signposted with great sophistication. I have already quoted Homer's brief account of Menelaus' initial assault on Proteus at 454–5, ἀμφὶ δὲ χεῖρας | βάλλομεν. As my table shows (Appendix I), Virgil reuses it twice, at 405 and 439–40. In the first

---

[79] See, for example, Isid. *Diff.* 1.523 – in Maltby (1991) s.v. – on competing explanations of the word *uictima*. For the prevalence of *uis*-etymologies in Virgil's didactic predecessor Lucretius, see Friedlander (1941) 26–7.

[80] For the derivation of *Venus* from *uis*, or those words considered related to it, see Varro, *Ling.* 5.61–3; Isid, *Etym.* 8.11.76; August. *De civ. D.* 6.9, p. 264. *Ventus* is etymologized by Isidore (*Etym.* 13.11.1), *dictus … uentus quod sit … uiolentus*, and he also (*Etym.* 4.5.2) gives an intriguing derivation of the word *morbus*, along with *Venus* perhaps major instantiation of the destructive potential of the natural world in the *Georgics: inde ueteres morbum nominaverunt, ut ipsa appellatione mortis uim, quae ex eo nascitur, demonstrarent*. It appears to me that both *mors* and *uis* are part of Isidore's etymology of *morbus*, that is that the *-bus of morbus* is a derivation of *uis*. This is more plausible in the light of contemporary pronunciation of the two letters *u*-consonant and *b*, which were much closer in sound than the English *w* and *b*. There seems to have been a significant fricative element to the pronunciation of *b*, and in the first century AD there actually starts to be found inscriptional confusion of *u*-consonant and *b*: see Allen (1965) 41. With these examples compare Ross (1987) 144–5 on *G.* 2.454–7, into which he reads Varro's etymology (*Ling.* 5.37) *uitis a uino, id a ui*.

[81] The same seems to be true of another Virgilian embellishment of the Homeric original. At 425–8, as Thomas (1988) ad loc. notes, there is an un-Homeric emphasis on the extreme heat of the setting for Aristaeus' struggle with Proteus (see p. 88 below). As Thomas writes ad 1.84–93, 'When things go wrong in the *Georgics* … the disaster is accompanied or motivated by an imbalance of the elements.' Here once again Aristaeus' actions seem to be equated with destructive processes earlier in the poem. Cf., e.g., Ross (1987) 157–67 on the 'fire of love' and 177–83 on the *sacer ignis* (*G.* 3.566) of disease.

instance Menelaus' only weapons, his hands, are juxtaposed with Virgil's innovation, chains: *manibus uinclisque tenebis*. In the second the two are exquisitely combined into one synonym of *uincula*: *manicisque iacentem occupat*. Virgil, in other words, is playing a game with his own departures from Homer. The 'hands' of 405 direct us to the Homeric model and thus emphasize the non-Homeric innovation of *uincula*. 439–40 go a step further, substituting a synonym for *uincula* which does the same, but in a single word: *manicae*, 'handcuffs'. Once again the conceit implies exceptional familiarity on the part of the reader with the Homeric text, and a recognition on the part of that reader of Virgil's intimate engagement with Homer at this juncture.[82]

X

We might try to go even further. I shall conclude this intensive reading of the Proteus episode with what might perhaps be an even more explicit acknowledgement on Virgil's part of his debt to the Homeric text. At 528–30 Proteus completes his song and returns to the sea:

> haec Proteus, et se iactu dedit aequor in altum,
> quaque dedit, spumantem undam sub uertice torsit.
> at non Cyrene;

Proteus concluded and leaped into the deep sea; and where he leaped he churned up the foaming water deep down in the eddies. But not Cyrene;

What Cyrene did or did not do at this point has been a cause of debate. Mynors' suggestion of *discessit* as the suppressed

---

[82] Whilst there is no mention of chains in the *Odyssey*, it is possible that chains entered the Proteus tradition *before* Virgil's time. Horace's second book of *Satires* (published about 30 BC) may or may not predate the *Georgics*. At 3.71 Horace writes, *effugiet tamen haec sceleratus uincula Proteus*. But what really matters is less when, precisely, chains entered the myth of Proteus than Virgil's emphatic indication of the divergence between his own text and Homer's. More strange altogether is Ps.-Heraclitus' summary of the *Odyssey* capture-scene (64.3): δεσμοὶ μετὰ τοῦτο καὶ Μενέλαος ἐνεδρεύων. Ps.-Heraclitus is talking specifically about Homer's text, yet still commits the anachronism of introducing chains. Did the chains enter the story with Ps.-Heraclitus' allegorist sources?

verb is surely right:[83] Cyrene does not do precisely what Proteus has just been stated to have done, that is, depart into the sea. But the question then becomes quite why Virgil needs to deny that Cyrene might do the same as Proteus. What should lead us to suppose that Cyrene might go the same way as he does?

It has been an unspoken assumption of my whole reading of Virgil's *Proteus* that this is a style of poetry of a highly intellectual and artificial nature, one that demands an exceptional degree of attention from its readership. It is no exaggeration to say that almost every word is significant. The exceptional proximity of the *Georgics* to the Homeric text at this point – along with the significant tiny deviations – can only admit of this interpretation; and recent discoveries such as Scodel and Thomas' Euphrates parallel have only confirmed that this is the way Virgilian poetry demands to be read. My suggested answer to this question about *at non Cyrene*, if correct, bespeaks an even greater degree of sophistication in Virgil's methods of reference and imitation. Here is the suggestion, then: we might only be led to expect Cyrene to disappear in the same manner as Proteus by our familiarity (as exemplary readers of the *Georgics*) with the Homeric line (570) which Virgil imitates at 528–9, ὡς εἰπὼν ὑπὸ πόντον ἐδύσετο κυμαίνοντα, 'with these words he dived under the foaming sea'. This line is employed twice in Homer's passage, once (here) of Proteus, and once, with the requisite change of gender, of Eidothea, Cyrene's Homeric analogue (425), ὡς εἰποῦσ' ὑπὸ πόντον ἐδύσετο κυμαίνοντα. A reader with an eye very firmly on *Odyssey* 4 *would* therefore have reason to expect Cyrene to depart in a similar fashion to Proteus, since that is what she does in the *Odyssey* model.

This most explicit deviation from the Homeric model also serves to mark Virgil's final departure from the *Odyssey* (see Appendix I): *at non Cyrene* may serve also to inform us that the emulation of Homer stops here. Is it a coincidence that the

---

[83] Mynors (1990) 321, following Serv. *auct.* ad loc.

end of the *aemulatio* of Homer coincides with Proteus' return to the *sea* (πόντος in the Homeric line) – commonly synonymous with 'Ocean' even in ancient times?[84] Is it, for that matter, a coincidence that Virgil chose to represent the Homeric mode in his text by means of an episode framed by a Homeric character's emergence from and return to the sea?[85]

XI

These last readings may help to corroborate my wider argument, and they may be interesting in their own right. They may also, I accept, be too tenuous to convince. But the core argument of this chapter stands without them. For some reason Virgil chooses to place the most ambitious *imitatio* of Homer (and probably of any poet) he ever undertakes in Book 4 of the *Georgics*. Its position, as it happens, parallels the position of its model in the *Odyssey*. And in addition, it seems, the *imitatio* is signposted. In a text as demonstrably intellectual and artificial as the *Georgics* imitation of Homer cannot but be extremely significant, and it demands an explanation. Homer was at this juncture in literary history a far too momentous figure for a piece of imitation of this order to be inert. This, then, according to my explanation of the passage, is one aspect of Aristaeus' descent to Cyrene's cave and subsequent capture of Proteus: it dramatizes Virgil's mastery of Homeric poetry, the highest possible form of literary inspira-

---

[84] See Williams (1978) 88 on Callimachus' assimilation of πόντος, 'sea', and 'Ὠκεανός, which was apparently anticipated by Xenophanes. See also the anapaests praising Homer preserved on a first-century papyrus, Page (1942) no. 93a, where the imagery is either the same or at any rate very similar to that of Ocean, but Homer is likened to πόντος τις. In mythical terms 'Ὠκεανός, properly, ran around the outermost edge of the world; according to the later, more scientific, conception it was, strictly, ἡ ἔξω θάλασσα, our Atlantic and Indian Oceans. But see West (1966) 201: Ocean is strictly 'quite distinct from the sea, though later equated with it'; at this time, as, e.g., Hor. *Carm.* 1.3.21–3, and Ov. *Met.* 9.594 show, the distinction between Ocean and ordinary sea was frequently and easily confounded.

[85] On the sea as an image of the epic genre see *G.* 2.41–5 and Thomas (1988) ad loc.; Prop. 3.9.3–4, 3.3.22–4; Hor. *Carm.* 4.15.3–4; Wimmel (1960) 227–33; Coleman (1988) ad Stat. *Silv.* 4.7.1.

tion, the source of all other poetic inspiration, a necessary prerequisite (incidentally) of his composition of the *Aeneid*: a return to the *beginnings* of poetry.[86]

[86] Emulation of the *Odyssey*, specifically, might also be seen to constitute a new beginning, more narrowly, in Latin literature alone: according to Charisius (1.84.8–9 K) Livius Andronicus' rendering of the *Odyssey* was the oldest Latin poem (*antiquissimum carmen*).

CHAPTER 2

ARISTEIA

I

At the beginning of the Third *Georgic* the poet pictures himself flushed with success. Dismissing as hackneyed a representative selection of Callimachean and Neoteric themes, he expresses the wish to attempt a new direction in poetry, one that will allow him, it is implied, to match the achievements of Ennius,[1] Lucretius[2] – and even Octavian himself: at 10 the imagery depicting Virgil's future accomplishment becomes dominantly[3] that of a military triumph – the procession of captives, the victor's palms, the votive temple, the celebratory *ludi* and dramatic performances.[4]

This prologue has been a source of particular controversy even in a poem as fiercely contested as the *Georgics*. In one respect, however, it is not nearly as controversial as it used to be: these days, at any rate, by far the prevailing opinion has it that Virgil's prediction refers not to his current poem, the *Georgics*, but to the great epic to come, the *Aeneid*.[5] If the anticipated poem seems so very *unlike* what the *Aeneid* was to become, the argument goes, this is only because its details were still vague in Virgil's mind.[6]

The main piece of evidence habitually cited in favour of the view that it is the *Aeneid* which is the subject of the proem is

---

[1] 3.9 echoes Ennius' epigram *Varia* 17–18 V., *uolito uiuos per ora uirum*, and 10–11 Lucretius' praise of Ennius, 1.117–19.

[2] Compare line 3 and *DRN* 1.50, and see Mynors (1990) ad loc.

[3] Thomas (1983b) details the epinician element of the passage (apparently derived from its structural model in Callimachus' *Victoria Berenices*).

[4] Buchheit (1972) 99–103 explains the triumphal resonance of *deducam, rediens, refert* and *palmas*; see also Mynors (1990) ad 10–11.

[5] The consensus that the prologue refers to the *Aeneid* seems to date from Wilkinson (1969) 323–4, which is also a useful summary of earlier literature on the subject.

[6] Thomas (1988) ad 1–48.

the content of the poetry envisaged, which though hardly (in details) a very faithful representation of the *Aeneid* is considered to bear absolutely no relation to the content of the *Georgics*. The work prefigured is an *epic*, with everything – martial and panegyrical content – that categorization at this juncture entails. As such it is akin in aspiration to the compositions of Ennius, as line 9 implies, and Lucretius (who assimilates his own project to Homeric and Ennian epic at *DRN* 1.117–26). The work, furthermore, is contrasted with examples of subject-matter typical of Callimachean and neoteric production (4–8).[7] The *Georgics*, on the other hand, cannot be described as an epic, therefore is not the object of the prediction.[8]

But does the *Georgics* have *no* affiliation with epic? There is, in fact, a common, and long-standing, view of the *Georgics* as a *transitional* poem,[9] a poem which exploits the flexibility of the category of didactic to negotiate the stylistic territory between the neoteric affiliations of the *Eclogues* and the Grand Epic pretensions of the *Aeneid*. Farrell, in particular, has recently proposed the existence in the poem of a progressive 'strategy of allusion', in the course of which the literary-generic aspirations of the poem climb from the explicitly Hesiodic/Callimachean affiliations of the earlier part of the poem[10] to the Homeric quality of the *Aristaeus*: 'the allusive structure of the entire *Georgics*' is 'arranged in such a way as to build ... deliberately through the earlier books to this great Homeric conclusion'.[11]

The question is, what might constitute the epic anticipated at 3.8–39 and 46–8? When might it be true to say that Virgil is wearing the hat of epic poet? Only when he is engaged upon a large-scale work such as the *Aeneid*, or also perhaps at that

---

[7] Thomas (1988) ad 3–8.

[8] Thomas (1988) ad 1–48 ('The temple clearly represents an epic, and ... the lines look to the *Aeneid* ... The view that the temple represents the *Georgics* will not stand').

[9] See, for example, Hardie (1971); and also Thomas (1988) I 1–3.

[10] Perhaps most notably 2.176, *Ascraeumque cano Romana per oppida carmen*, and the Euphrates parallel at 1.509.

[11] Farrell (1991) 256, and *passim*.

point at the end of Book 4 of the *Georgics* where, I have suggested, by stylistic and structural parallelism he contrives to make his poem resemble the beginning of the *Odyssey*? I proposed in the last chapter at least one respect in which the Proteus episode was classifiable as epic: in respect of being an ambitious emulation of Homer, the originator and exemplar of the epic mode. To that extent, at least, the Proteus passage might correspond to the *Siegeslied* of the prologue to Book 3.

The poet offers us a timetable. The future epic will occur *mox*, after he has completed his sojourn in the *Dryadum siluae saltusque* (40). As Thomas admits, this description of his intermediate activities is not unquestionably valid of the entire remainder of the *Georgics*.[12] Certainly, Virgil's terms here imply that the victory he will enjoy will not be constituted by the pastoral content of Book 3 and the first half of Book 4, but by something subsequent to it. But that need not rule out the conclusion of Book 4. Where precisely, then, does the agricultural poem (40–5) end and the poem on the *ardentes pugnae* of Caesar (46–8) start? It is at least unclear whether the agricultural work includes the *Aristaeus*. *Siluae saltusque* are the habitat of herds, as Virgil proceeds to make clear (43–5). They are also the haunt of bees (4.53). But they are not obviously where most of the action of the *Aristaeus* takes place, and certainly not where Aristaeus' capture of Proteus does, very much an *ardens pugna* (4.401–2, 425–8). There are thus no very pressing grounds to prohibit our understanding the victory as in some sense coextensive with (part of) the *Georgics*; and by contrast there are some fairly strong reasons why we might understand it this way.

At 22–3, for example, Virgil imagines the ritual sacrifices which will conclude his triumphal procession to the Capitol: *iam nunc sollemnis ducere pompas | ad delubra iuuat caesosque uidere iuuencos*. The expression *caesi iuuenci* recalls the transgressive sacrifice at the end of Book 2 (537), and I talk about this connection in my next chapter. It recurs twice more in Virgil's corpus: once at the end of *Aeneid* 8 – Octavian's triple

---

[12] Thomas (1988) ad loc.

triumph of 29 BC – where much of the terminology of Virgil's prediction is picked up, especially with reference to the sacrificial victims (719, *ante aras terram caesi strauere iuuenci*). But in addition the *Aristaeus* is of course centrally concerned with the slaughter of bullocks, which is the means by which Aristaeus ultimately reconstitutes his bee-swarm. Furthermore, Aristaeus' killing of the bullocks takes place precisely *ad delubra* (4.541), at shrines to the Nymphs, and the terms in which Virgil chooses to describe the practice of *bugonia* at the start of its aetiological myth (4.284–5) are the same again: *quoque modo caesis iam saepe iuuencis | insincerus apes tulerit cruor*. The evocation of triumphal ritual in the prologue to Book 3 thus seems to double as the anticipation of the details of the *Aristaeus*, and it is a strong encouragement to associate what is predicted at the opening of Book 3 with what happens towards the end of Book 4.

A similar suggestion could be made about Caesar's *ardentes pugnae* at 3.46, which at least faintly foreshadow Aristaeus' attack on Proteus (cf. 4.425–8), and about the expression *Tithoni prima ... ab origine* (48), which Servius reasonably interprets as a reference to the *mundi principium*, the beginning of the world, the reasoning being clearer in Servius *auctus*, who glosses the expression *ab infinito infinitum, quia Tithoni origo non potest comprehendi*. Tithonus is as old as time, as it were. The expression *prima ab origine* establishes the scope of the future epic as the totality of historical time. The same expression is re-employed at 4.286,[13] and there also, as I shall later suggest, it indicates the total comprehensiveness of the narrative that follows.

The prologue to Book 3 anticipates Virgil's composition of epic poetry, but there is still room, I have suggested, to understand that prediction as fulfilled by what happens at the end of Book 4. Besides the epic quality of the poem predicted, however, a number of critics cite Virgil's words at 3.10, *modo uita supersit*, as proof that the reference is to the *Aeneid*: the expression suggests, as Thomas says, 'a future project, not

---

[13] See pp. 98–101 below.

completion of the present task'.[14] The expression has interesting parallels, though. Wimmel compares it to two other contexts in contemporary poetry, *Ecl.* 4.53–4, *o mihi tum longae maneat pars ultima uitae | spiritus et quantum sat erit tua dicere facta!*, and Prop. 2.10.20, *seruent hunc mihi fata diem!*[15] Wimmel claims to see a distinction between Virgil's expression in the *Georgics* and Propertius': Virgil's apparently firm undertaking is rendered by the later poet distant and unreal. But is there really a distinction, or is it just that we happen to know Virgil did go on to write an epic and Propertius did not? In each instance a poet envisaging writing some kind of panegyrical epic prays that time for the task be vouchsafed him. It is apparently a conventional motif, related to the *tempus erit* topos,[16] but also to a convention regarding the proper age of the composer of 'serious' literature. Epic is a genre for the mature man: as Propertius writes in the same poem (2.10.7), *aetas prima canat Veneres, extrema tumultus.* We might compare Prop. 3.5.19–48, where old age is specified as the appropriate time for natural philosophy (cf. 47, *exitus hic uitae superet mihi*), and Tacitus' undertaking at *Hist.* 1.1.4 to tackle the *uberior securiorque* historical material of the reigns of Nerva and Trajan in old age, *si uita suppeditet.* The motif is thus a standard element in this type of *recusatio*, and I would suggest that Virgil is quite deliberately equating his prologue with this kind of composition-deferring passage: Thomas in fact comments on the passage that 'it is tempting to look at the lines as a *recusatio* ... and if the *Aeneid* did not exist that is how they would doubtless be read'.[17] It would be quite in the character of this poem to play with the conventions of the *recusatio*; and simultaneously with generic conventions. The *Georgics* is a poem which plays extensively on its own generic identity. At the close of *Georgics* 1 and 4, as we have seen, there are references to the *Hymn to Apollo* (the Euphrates

---

[14] Thomas (1988) ad loc. Cf. Mynors (1990) ad 10–11; Wilkinson (1969) 323; Miles (1980) 181.
[15] Wimmel (1960) 180, 199.
[16] See Stat. *Theb.* 1.16–33, *Ach.* 1.14–19.
[17] Thomas (1988) ad 3.1–48.

parallels) which are hard to interpret except as expressions of generic affiliation. The prologue to Book 3 rejects Callimachean themes, but in doing so, as Thomas has pointed out,[18] closely imitates the structure of *Aetia* 3 and uses Callimachean programmatic terminology,[19] as if implying that the poet of the *Georgics* is still anchored in the Callimachean mode and that this poem at least, if not the predicted epic to come, is 'Callimachean' in ethos. Yet throughout the poem there are examples of programmatic statements which appear to hover nervously between orthodox Callimacheanism and the imagery of epic. Thomas claims that 'in every programmatic utterance of the poem Virgil characterizes his position as transitional',[20] and in Book 4, as we have seen, there is emulation of the Homeric poems. Throughout the *Georgics*, in fact, we are confronted with the problem of how to categorize it. Does it owe its affiliations to Callimachean poetry, which at first sight a four-book poem ostensibly modelled on the *Works and Days* should, or perhaps also to epic? The prologue to Book 3, I would suggest, contributes to this dilemma: from the viewpoint of Book 3 the prologue may seem to describe a different poem – perhaps, like Propertius' epic, one which will never in fact be written – but then from the viewpoint of Book 4 certain coincidences between this prologue and the conclusion of the poem may occur to the reader, and it may well appear (in retrospect) to describe the achievement of the *Georgics*.[21]

---

[18] Thomas (1983b) 101.

[19] See, e.g., Thomas (1988) ad 3.11 and 19–20.

[20] Thomas (1988) 1 2. Even the description of Virgil's current, agricultural project at the end of this prologue has a rather more elevated feel than we might expect: *haud mollia iussa* (41: for the programmatic implications of *mollis*, see Hinds (1987) 141 n. 58), *uocat ingenti clamore Cithaeron* (43).

[21] Another line of enquiry leading to a similar conclusion might be provided by Thomas (1983a) esp. 179–80. Thomas investigates the motif of the ecphrastic description which makes reference to its own centrepoint in such a way as to construct a parallel between the work of art described and the poem in which it appears. Thus the *in medio* of the description of the Shield of Aeneas (*Aen.* 8.675) not only refers to the shield itself but also occurs in the centre of Virgil's *description* of the shield. Thomas then gives a further example where the double reference appears to take in the *whole* poem: the prologue to Book 3. At 16 Virgil states of his temple that *in medio mihi Caesar erit templumque tenebit*. As Thomas says, the

II

At the core of the imagery of this prologue, as Buchheit emphasizes, is a parallelism between poet and ruler.[22] As he makes clear, this is a thread which runs right through the poem, from the prologue to Book 1, where Octavian is requested to *join* the poet in pitying the directionless farmer, *ignarosque uiae mecum miseratus agrestis*, to the end of the *laudes Italiae* (2.170–6), where poet and general – in their disparate fields – both serve the greater glory of their homeland.

In the prologue to Book 3, as in the instance from the *laudes*, the poet's assimilation of his own activities to those of the ruler is in fact a special case of a common poetic convention whereby the poet 'is described as doing what he describes being done',[23] as implicated, in other words, in the very processes he depicts. This is a conceit employed repeatedly (indeed consistently) in the *Georgics*: at 3.284–94, for instance, where Virgil pictures himself dragged over the heights of Parnassus by the same impulse, *amor*, which he has just described driving mares over similarly arduous terrain (3.269–79).[24] In the prologue to Book 3, however, both motifs reach something of a climax. Virgil imagines himself celebrating Octavian's martial successes, and he simultaneously conceives of himself as a military victor in his own right: there is complete assimilation of the (triumphant) poet and the poet's theme, his triumphant ruler.

The blend of triumphal and epinician imagery in the prologue has been thoroughly analysed, by Thomas and Buchheit especially,[25] and I have nothing to add. All *I* want to do is emphasize this one aspect of the passage, the degree to which

temple 'which itself appears in the centre of the *Georgics*, will have as its own centerpiece the triumphant Octavian'. Thomas does not seem to consider how this bears upon the identification – or otherwise – of the temple with the *Aeneid*. But if we take one obvious step further than Thomas it clearly does: Caesar occupies the centre of the temple just as Caesar, in his temple, occupies the central point of the *Georgics*. Temple and *Georgics*, in this respect, are identical.

[22] Buchheit (1972) esp. 146–8.
[23] Hardie (1985) 85; Lieberg (1982).
[24] Gale (1991) 421.
[25] Thomas (1988) ad locc.; Buchheit (1972) 99–103.

Virgil's and Octavian's triumphs pass beyond being merely complementary, and become practically indistinguishable. The engravings and statuary of the temple established by the triumphant Virgil illustrate not his but Octavian's triumphs, and the statue of Apollo (36) is appropriate both to a temple celebrating Octavian's successes, such as the real temple of Apollo on the Palatine (see Prop. 2.31), and to one constructed by a triumphant poet: Thomas explains the literary resonance of the epithet *Cynthius*.[26] The figure of *Inuidia* (37), again, who will be consigned to Hades after the victories, is a bane of *both* the politician and the poet:[27] they will each attain sufficient success in their disparate fields to banish her. Finally, Buchheit brings out the subtle ambiguity of 46–8, where Virgil recapitulates his undertaking to praise Octavian:

> mox tamen ardentis accingar dicere pugnas
> Caesaris et nomen fama tot ferre per annos,
> Tithoni prima quot abest ab origine Caesar.

But the time will come when I shall gird myself to tell of the blazing fights of Caesar, and carry his name in story through as many years as separate Caesar from the original birth of Tithonus.

Not only does Virgil, predictably, depict his *mimesis* of military action as the real thing (*accingar*); he also leaves it unclear whether it is Caesar's, or his own, name which will live for ever as a consequence of it.[28] It is both, of course. The poet's celebration of his patron's military successes will bring himself, also, comparable honour: both will gain everlasting glory from the undertaking. The poet's triumph will entail precisely giving expression to the triumphs of Octavian.[29]

The exact nature of Virgil's forthcoming victory is not too hard to decode. The triumph was the most elevated ritual

---

[26] Thomas (1988) ad loc.
[27] See Mynors (1990) ad loc., who cites Lucr. 5.1125–6 for the role of *Invidia* in politics; for its significance to literature see Thomas (1988) ad loc.
[28] Buchheit (1972) 146–7.
[29] Significantly, the depiction of Augustus' triumph of 29 at *Aen.* 8.714–28 is closely related to Virgil's triumph in the prologue to *G.* 3. The *ipse* overseeing the triumphal celebrations at *G.* 3.21 is Virgil, at *Aen.* 8.720 Augustus: the epic poet is a *triumphator* and the triumph is the epic topic *par excellence*. On the connections between the writing of epic/history and the triumph see Quint (1993) 31–4.

observed by the Romans.[30] Virgil has chosen the most hyper-
bolic metaphor available to describe his future undertaking.
Furthermore, for the ancients subject-matter, as well as style,
dictated the genre of poetry undertaken. There was only one
genre in which the martial/heroic/panegyrical nature of Virgil's
anticipated commission could properly be described; and that
was the genre inaugurated and dominated by the figure
of Homer. As Horace (*Ars P.* 73–4) famously put it (with
specific reference to metre), *res gestae regumque ducumque et
tristia bella | quo scribi possent numero, monstrauit Homerus.*
For Latin poets of the Neoteric period and after, Homer was
above all the representative of the martial and encomiastic
poetry against which they defined their own 'Callimachean'
compositions. Conventionally, as in the prologue to *Ecl.* 6,
writing Grand Epic is considered identical to writing war
poetry and panegyric – Homer *is* war poetry, *is* panegyric,
and *vice versa* – and can be considered (by the same token) to
entail an invidious attempt to rival Homer. Thus in Propertius
1.7 Ponticus' foolishness is to attempt to emulate Homer,
which, since his chosen genre is martial epic, it is implied he
cannot fail to do (1–4):

> dum tibi Cadmeae dicuntur, Pontice, Thebae
> armaque fraternae tristia militiae,
> atque, ita sim felix, primo contendis Homero,
> (sint modo fata tuis mollia carminibus)

Whilst you are telling of Cadmean Thebes, Ponticus, and the grim arms of
warfare between brothers, and, gods preserve me, competing with the pre-
eminent Homer (if only the fates are gentle to your songs)

When Virgil imagines himself bringing the Muses home captive to Italy it is an extremely assertive claim, far more so, for
example, than its forerunners in Lucretius (1.921–50, 4.1–25).
Lucretius receives from the Muses an *insignis corona* of a kind
never bestowed before; Virgil captures and enslaves the Muses
and forcibly relocates them to Italy. Wimmel understandably
finds Virgil's mode of expression 'überstark'.[31] It can only

---

[30] Livy 30.15.12: *neque magnificentius quicquam triumpho apud Romanos ... esse.*
[31] Wimmel (1960) 180.

mean one thing: a writer of hexameter poetry with a martial/ panegyrical theme in mind can only imply by this an undertaking to emulate the poet who simultaneously represents martial/heroic poetry *par excellence* and also, as we have seen, was conventionally considered – like the Muses – to contain the seeds of all Greek written culture: Homer.[32] The appropriation of the Greek Muses is an act of identical significance to the appropriation of the poetry of Homer: both represent the whole of Greek literary culture. What appears to be Virgil's programme here is neatly summarized by Hardie:[33]

> The *Aeneid* is at one level a colossal exercise in definition, seeking to define the Roman epic as the new *Weltgedicht* through an act of appropriation or of literary imperialism, whereby the world of Greek culture and literature (understood as the realization of what was always potentially present in Homer) is pressed into the service of the new age in Rome ...

For Hardie the vehicle of this 'literary imperialism' is, as we can see, the *Aeneid*. His description, however, is a remarkably accurate account of what I believe to be the programme of the Proteus episode: namely, the appropriation of the Greek literary tradition (represented by its traditional originator and source, Homer) as a prerequisite of an adequate celebration of the heroic achievements of Octavian. This – or something very similar – is also what is predicted (in terms of the abduction of the Muses to Italy) in the prologue to Book 3. There would appear to be a further allusion in this prologue – with similar implications – to Ennius' *Annals*,[34] which it was the poet's original intention to end with an account of his patron M. Fulvius Nobilior's campaign in Aetolia, his triumph in 187 BC and his founding of the temple *Herculis Musarum* (or else his addition of a portico of the Muses to the pre-existing temple of *Hercules Magnus Custos*)[35] at the end of Book 15.[36] Nobilior was thus responsible for introducing the cult of the

---

[32] On the close association of Homeric inspiration with the Muses see Skiadas (1965) 75–86.
[33] Hardie (1993) 1–2.
[34] Hardie (1993) 105.
[35] For the various possibilities see Newlands (1995) 216 n. 22.
[36] Skutsch (1985) 144–6, 553, 649–50.

Muses to Rome, and as a tangible token of this housed in his new institution statues of the nine Muses which he had plundered from what had been the site of Pyrrhus' palace at Ambracia (Livy 38.9.13). *Inde Musas Fulvius Nobilior Romam transferret*, writes Pliny (*HN* 35.66). So like Virgil in the prologue to Book 3 Fulvius literally relocated the Muses to Italy. Clearly Fulvius' military achievements parallel Ennius' aspirations as an epic poet to Romanize Homer. Virgil thus apparently assimilates his future project to Ennius' impersonation of Homer.[37]

What I wish to suggest, of course, is that Virgil's prediction of a poetic triumph in Book 3 is satisfied (or might be considered satisfied: generic ambiguity persists to the end, as I shall later suggest) by the emulation of the Ocean poet, Homer, which I have argued occurs at the end of Book 4. But equally clearly the appropriation of the Homeric source is only one dimension of the victory predicted: Virgil's poetic victory was to be to give adequate glory to – to panegyrize – the victories of Octavian. If the *Proteus* is anywhere near adequately to answer the requirements of the prologue to Book 3 I need also to establish that the referent of Virgil's Homeric emulation is the triumphant Octavian.

This may seem simply bizarre: the referent of 4.387–529 is Proteus, after all. But perhaps the problem can be stated another way. I hope by now that I have established that intensive emulation of Homer occurs at 4.387–529. But to establish the fact of imitation is only half the problem. The proper form and the proper meaning of the Homeric text – the two issues are at root indistinguishable – was the single most contentious issue of Hellenistic interpretative criticism. We thus require to know not merely that Homer has been emulated, but in addition *which* Homer (or *which* Proteus, more strictly) has been emulated out of several current in later antiquity, the rela-

---

[37] The further parallel with the end of *Aen.* 8 – a patron's triumph and foundation of a temple to a god with literary associations – is also suggestive at the end of a passage (The Shield) which is analogous to a poem: Hardie (1993) 105. Cf. n. 29 above.

tively 'literal', 'self-sufficient' texts – give or take the odd excision – of the Alexandrian scholars, or one of a number of 'allegorical' readings which made of Homeric myth a highly intellectual prefigurement of later philosophical doctrine, and of Homer himself a philosophical sage. How, in other words, is the Proteus-emulation to be read?

III

... the tendency to turn even the most *doctus* of poets into a modern research scholar (did Virgil really study the Alexandrian commentaries on Homer?) can perhaps be taken too far.

So writes Gransden in his review of the book which offers, in Most's words, 'the strongest case so far for a systematic use by Virgil of Stoic cosmological doctrines': Hardie's *Cosmos and Imperium*.[38] As Gransden's comment implies, no matter how cogent the argumentation there remains a considerable degree of scepticism regarding the suggestion that the Homer confronting the aspiring epic poet in Virgil's time and cultural context could have been the poet of natural philosophy posited by allegorists. The scepticism amongst critics perhaps largely derives, as Most suggests, from an ingrained contempt for the (as far as moderns are concerned) non-canonical works which employ allegorical criticism. Yet as Most proceeds to show, Cornutus, author of the allegorist[39] *Epidrome*, can be placed right at the centre of the Neronian literary milieu. Persius' fifth satire testifies to the respect he commanded, and Macrobius (*Sat.* 5.19.3) called him *tantus uir, Graecarum etiam doctissimus litterarum*. More cogently, Hardie's readings of the Shield of Aeneas through (the allegorized) Shield of Achilles have the virtue of being extremely germane to the acknowledged preoccupations of their context; and I shall argue in due course that the issues addressed by allegorical

---

[38] Hardie (1986); Gransden (1988) 26; Most (1989) 2043.
[39] Or perhaps better, 'etymologist', with Long (1992) 54. The methodologies are anyway closely related.

exegesis of Homer's *Proteus*, also, are far too akin to those of the *Aristaeus* to be coincidental. Furthermore, in the case of the Homeric emulation constituted by Virgil's Proteus episode we may be fortunate enough to have an explicit signpost to the kind of reading of Homer required.[40]

A preliminary qualification. Interpretation of Virgil's cosmological allegory has tended to assume two things: first that the leading light of Homeric allegoresis in Pergamum, Crates of Mallos, was a Stoic; and secondly, following on from the first assumption, that his interpretations of the Homeric text were couched in a reasonably orthodox form of Stoicism. Recently Long and Porter have raised doubt on both counts.[41] Porter points out that Crates is only called a 'Stoic philosopher' once, by the *Suda*; and Long argues that when the Stoics interpreted Homeric myth it was not meant as an interpretation of Homer's (intended) meaning but of the underlying meaning of the myths Homer employed, of which Homer himself need not have been aware. The idolatry of Homer as (himself) a cosmologist is then – according to this argument – not orthodox Stoicism. Nevertheless in the remainder of this chapter I assume that the physical doctrines believed to be presented allegorically in Homeric myth are generally Stoic in nature. The significant point here is that the 'idolatrous' allegorists of Homer – particularly Crates and Ps.-Heraclitus – were extremely influenced by the doctrines of Stoic physics, as indeed were technical writers in general,[42] and the allegories they read, consequently, were focally Stoic in nature. My main concern in this chapter is the allegory of Proteus preserved by Ps.-Heraclitus. Of the doctrines underlying this allegory Buffière writes that Ps.-Heraclitus must have read them 'dans quelque traité stoïcien, plus ou moins teinté d'orphisme ou de pythagorisme'.[43]

---

[40] For the entire remainder of this chapter, as is inevitably the case with treatments of Homeric allegory, I am profoundly indebted to Buffière (1956) esp. 86–8 (on Ocean) and 179–86 (on Proteus).

[41] Long (1992); Porter (1992).

[42] Long (1992) 47, 66.

[43] Buffière (1956) 181.

IV

At 380–3, I argued,[44] Virgil gives notice that his poem is entering a 'Homeric' section:

> et mater 'cape Maeonii carchesia Bacchi:
> Oceano libemus' ait. simul ipsa precatur
> Oceanumque patrem rerum Nymphasque sorores,
> centum quae siluas, centum quae flumina seruant.

His mother said: 'take up goblets of Lydian Bacchus; let us pour an offering to Ocean'. Then she at once prays to Ocean, father of all things, and the sister Nymphs, who protect a hundred forests and a hundred rivers.

In my last chapter I explained Homer's soubriquet 'Ocean' as being derived from the passage in *Il.* 21 where it is stated that in Ocean all watercourses have their source. I quoted a representative passage from Dionysius of Halicarnassus;[45] Romm, similarly, cites Quintilian. But as Romm points out the identification of Homer and Ocean had other origins – and broader implications – as well: 'Beyond this, however, Ocean also formed an analogue for epic poetry because of its grandeur and immense scope.'[46] For Ocean as an image of poetic grandeur Romm cites Ps.-Longinus (*Subl.* 35.4), and we might recall the references to epic as the open sea which we noted above.[47] The related notion of what Romm describes as the 'immense scope' of Homeric epic may be illustrated from the *Georgics* itself. At 2.39 the poet seems to countenance embarking on the open sea, an obvious reference to epic. Immediately, however, he retracts (42): *non ego cuncta meis amplecti uersibus opto*, 'It is not my desire to embrace everything in my poetry.' Epic, Virgil implies, is a genre whose scope is nothing short of universal. The epic poet contains (*amplecti*) within his poetry literally everything. The notion in play here is the status of epic as what Hardie has termed a 'totalizing form'.[48] Epic, the grandest literary genre, and Homer its primogenitor, countenance the entirety of existence. Now the

---

[44] See pp. 33–6 above.   [45] See p. 32 above.   [46] Romm (1992) 181.
[47] See p. 48 n. 85 above.   [48] Hardie (1993) 3.

implications of this generic expectation are immense and various. The genre which took the whole of existence as its subject also claimed to contain within its ambit all other genres, a notion we have already encountered in this book and shall encounter again. But the perceived universality of Homer's genre also fed into the notion that his text conveyed – in a veiled fashion – ultimate truths about the underlying physical processes of the universe; and this conception of epic is of focal importance to the remainder of this chapter.

The physical Ocean marked the boundary of the world. In a strong sense it came to *define* that world. Thus, for example, when Crates of Mallos interpreted Homer's shield of Achilles as a κόσμου μίμημα, 'image of the world', it was largely because the shield was rimmed by a depiction of Ocean.[49] Similarly, Smith discusses one of the most extensive exercises in Julio-Claudian monumental propaganda known: the recently excavated Sebasteion at Aphrodisias,[50] an elaborately decorated temple complex dedicated to Aphrodite Prometor and the Julio-Claudian emperors. The mode of propaganda is allegorical: a series of reliefs from the north portico depicting more or less outlandish *ethne* (peoples) – apparently recreating monuments of a similar nature known from written sources to have existed at Rome as early as Augustan times[51] – represent the comprehensiveness of Roman dominion. At the very east end of the north portico were discovered two 'universal' reliefs, Day and Ocean, probably to be understood as coordinated with Night and Earth respectively, perhaps at an equivalent point at the west end. Smith offers a plausible interpretation of the decoration of the monument:

It seems clear that in the Sebasteion the selection of outlandish peoples was meant to stand as a visual account of the extent of the Augustan empire, and ... to suggest that it is coterminous with the ends of the earth ... This

[49] Romm (1992) 14.
[50] Smith (1988); cf. Smith (1987). The building was probably started under Tiberius and completed under Nero: Smith (1987) 90.
[51] Serv. *auct.* ad *Aen.* 8.721; Pliny, *HN* 36.39. Similar representations seem to have adorned the Forum of Augustus (Vell. Pat. 2.39.2); and images of *ethne* conquered by Augustus were carried in procession at his funeral: Smith (1988) 71–4.

meaning is complemented by the universal allegories of time and place in the storey above. Combined, the allegories and the *ethne* stated that the Roman empire extends from furthest west to furthest east, from the rising to the setting sun, from Day to Night, bounded only by Ocean.[52]

Ocean, then, can stand for the world. But what Romm well displays is that in addition to being geographically liminal and definitive of the world Ocean could also represent the *origins* of the world: 'Ocean could represent the outer limits of both geographic space and historical time at once.'[53] Romm quotes a *sententia* of Artemon referring to Ocean preserved in Seneca the Elder's *Suasoriae* (1.11): . . . ἀλλ' εἴτε γῆς τέρμα, εἴτε φύσεως ὅρος, εἴτε πρεσβύτατον στοιχεῖον, εἴτε γένεσις θεῶν, ἱερώτερόν ἐστιν ἢ κατὰ ναῦς ὕδωρ, '. . . but whether it is the limit of the earth, the boundary of nature, the oldest element or the origin of the gods, it is water too holy for ships'. Artemon bundles up together a number of views of Ocean – geographical and cosmological – because they are not really distinguishable. Ocean represented a mysterious and rather vaguely conceived 'margin of existence' which might be spatial or temporal: Ocean might stand at the edge of the contemporary world or else, as it were, at the edge of historical time. It defined the world in its synchronic or diachronic totality. For as well as constituting the geographical margin of the world (Artemon's γῆς τέρμα) Ocean was also felt to be the element from which the world originated (πρεσβύτατον στοιχεῖον). Descriptions of the contemporary, geographical Ocean, as Romm shows, reflected this notion of the originality of Ocean. It was treated as 'a vestige of a primary stage in cosmic evolution'.[54] In it – as, for example, in the report of the explorer Pytheas of Massilia[55] – the elements formed an undifferentiated jelly too soft to walk upon but too thick to sail through. As such Ocean corresponded to Anaximander's *apeiron*, the boundless, formless 'welter of elements from which the universe had been formed'.[56] Ocean not only surrounded the world, then, but gave rise to it in the first place.

[52] Smith (1988) 77.   [53] Romm (1992) 26.   [54] Romm (1992) 23.
[55] Polyb. 34.5.3–4 = Strab. 2.4.1 = Pytheas fr. 7a Mette; Romm (1992) 22–3.
[56] Romm (1992) 11.

Clarifying this state of affairs will take us back to *Georgic* 4. Virgil's first mention of Ocean at 380–3, given the proximity of *Maeonii*, inevitably called to mind the figure of Homer and his traditional status as the source of Greek culture. But the second, *Oceanum ... patrem rerum*, though (as we shall see) still intimately associated with the person of Homer, points us towards this notion of Ocean as the physical origin of the world. Servius *auctus* notes ad 380: *et Oceanum patrem rerum secundum physicos dixit, qui aiunt omnium rerum elementum aquam esse: in quibus Thales primus*, 'and he calls Ocean "father of things" in accordance with the natural philosophers, who state that the first principle of all things is water: Thales first of all'. Servius is rehearsing a view at least as old as Aristotle that two Homeric descriptions of Ocean at *Il.* 14.201 and 302 (a repeated line), Ὠκεανόν τε θεῶν γένεσιν καὶ μητέρα Τηθύν, and 246, Ὠκεανοῦ, ὅς περ γένεσις πάντεσσι τέτυκται, anticipated the theory of the Presocratic Thales that the entire physical universe originated from the element of water.[57] At *Metaph.* 983b18–32 Aristotle, in a discussion of first causes, mentions Thales' theory of the primordial nature of water, offers some explanation for Thales' view, and then says,

εἰσὶ δέ τινες οἳ καὶ τοὺς παμπαλαίους καὶ πολὺ πρὸ τῆς νῦν γενέσεως καὶ πρώτους θεολογήσαντας οὕτως οἴονται περὶ τῆς φύσεως ὑπολαβεῖν· Ὠκεανόν τε γὰρ καὶ Τηθὺν ἐποίησαν τῆς γενέσεως πατέρας, καὶ τὸν ὅρκον τῶν θεῶν ὕδωρ, τὴν καλουμένην ὑπ' αὐτῶν Στύγα·

Some think that even the ancients who lived long before the present generation, and first framed accounts of the gods, had a similar view of nature; for they made Ocean and Tethys the parents of creation, and described the oath of the gods as being by water, to which they give the name of Styx.

Behind οἱ παμπάλαιοι, clearly, lies Homer, and *Il.* 14.201; behind τινες probably Plato, *Tht.* 152e. The view which Aristotle here reports with such caution becomes in later times a staple of those interpreters – at Pergamum above all – who read Homer allegorically, as a poet primarily concerned not with the deeds of heroes but with natural philosophy, the

[57] Farrell (1991) 271.

study of the fundamental processes of the universe. We have
met part of the motivation for this interpretation of the
Homeric text already: a poet as incomparable as Homer must
necessarily treat of equally superlative themes, and the greatest themes available to a poet, conventionally, were those of
natural philosophy.[58] But Pergamene Homeric scholarship
might also be seen to be, like Alexandrian athetesis, an attempt to ensure that no lapse of taste was imputed to a figure
in whom by this stage so much of Greek national identity and
cultural pride was invested.[59] Each, in their way, sought to
establish τὸ πρέπον as the touchstone of the Homeric canon.
But where Alexandria athetized, Pergamum allegorized,[60] interpreting passages which risked rejection by Ptolemaic critics
on grounds of impropriety as disguised accounts of fundamental scientific processes. In the case of Ocean, as will turn
out to be the case more generally, it is the author known as
Ps.-Heraclitus who gives the fullest treatment of the issue. At
chapter 22 of the *Quaest. Hom.* he begins by citing the conventional view that it was Thales who originated the theory
that water was the primordial element of the universe, the element that the universe came from (and that the universe still,
essentially, is); but then disputes that view (22.3–10):

Θάλητα μέν γε τὸν Μιλήσιον ὁμολογοῦσι πρῶτον ὑποστήσασθαι τῶν
ὅλων κοσμογόνον στοιχεῖον τὸ ὕδωρ· ἡ γὰρ ὑγρὰ φύσις, εὐμαρῶς εἰς ἕκαστα
μεταπλαττομένη, πρὸς τὸ ποικίλον εἴωθε μορφοῦσθαι. τό τε γὰρ ἐξατμι-
ζόμενον αὐτῆς ἀεροῦται, καὶ τὸ λεπτότατον ἀπὸ ἀέρος αἰθὴρ ἀνάπτεται,
συνιζάνον τε τὸ ὕδωρ καὶ μεταβαλλόμενον εἰς ἰλὺν ἀπογαιοῦται· διὸ δὴ τῆς
τετράδος τῶν στοιχείων ὥσπερ αἰτιώτατον ὁ Θάλης ἀπεφήνατο στοιχεῖον
εἶναι τὸ ὕδωρ.
Τίς οὖν ἐγέννησε ταύτην τὴν δόξαν; οὐχ Ὅμηρος, εἰπών·
    Ὠκεανός, ὅσπερ γένεσις πάντεσσι τέτυκται
                                                    (*Il.* 14.246)

---

[58] Innes (1979).
[59] The description by Lamberton (1986) 15 of one of two primary motives for
allegoresis, 'the desire to defend Homer against his detractors', applies as well to
the Alexandrians; the common desire of Hellenistic critics to establish the 'propriety' of the *genuine* Homeric text is well documented by Schlunk (1974) esp. 8–
35.
[60] On occasion quite literally: the Shield of Achilles was athetized by Zenodotus and
allegorized by Crates: see Pfeiffer (1968) 240.

φερωνύμως μὲν ὠκεανὸν εἰπὼν τὴν ὑγρὰν φύσιν παρὰ τὸ ὠκέως νάειν, τοῦτον
δ᾽ ὑποστησάμενος ἁπάντων γενεάρχην;
    Ἀλλ᾽ ὁ Κλαζομένιος Ἀναξαγόρας, κατὰ διαδοχὴν γνώριμος ὢν Θάλητος,
συνέζευξε τῷ ὕδατι δεύτερον στοιχεῖον τὴν γῆν, ἵνα ξηρῷ μιχθὲν ὑγρὸν ἐξ
ἀντιπάλου φύσεως εἰς μίαν ὁμόνοιαν ἀνακραθῇ.
    Καὶ ταύτην δὲ τὴν ἀπόφασιν πρῶτος Ὅμηρος ἐγεώργησεν, Ἀναξαγόρᾳ
σπέρματα τῆς ἐπινοίας χαρισάμενος ἐν οἷς φησίν·
        Ἀλλ᾽ ὑμεῖς μὲν πάντες ὕδωρ καὶ γαῖα γένοισθε
                                                        (Il. 7.99)
πᾶν γὰρ τὸ φυόμενον ἔκ τινων εἰς ταὐτὰ ἀναλύεται διαφθειρόμενον, ὡσπερεὶ
τῆς φύσεως ἃ δεδάνεικεν ἐν ἀρχῇ χρέα κομιζομένης ἐπὶ τέλει.

Take Thales of Miletus: the common opinion is that he was the first to
propose water as the creative element of the universe: for liquid, being of
such a nature as to be readily moulded into any shape, has the property of
great mutability. That part of it which evaporates becomes air, and the most
rarified emanation from air catches fire, becoming ether; and water when it
settles down and changes into mud becomes earth. And so Thales declared
that of the four elements water was, as it were, the most original.

But who was the author of this theory? Was it not Homer, when he said:
        Ocean, the source of all there is,
aptly terming liquid 'Ocean', a name deriving from 'flowing quickly', and
making Ocean the origin of all things?

Anaxagoras of Clazomene, Thales' pupil and successor, added to water a
second element, *earth*, so that the blend of wet and dry might create from
contrary substances one homogeneous mixture.

But this again is ground which Homer ploughed first, graciously giving
Anaxagoras the germ of his theory in the words:
        May you all become water and earth!
For every living thing, when it decomposes, resolves itself into the same
elements from which it came, as if nature were reclaiming its debt and
taking back at the end what it had lent at the outset.

Two cosmogonical theories are here cited: the position conventionally attributed to Thales that there is a single fundamental substrate of the physical universe – water – and the
later view (attributed erroneously by Ps.-Heraclitus to Anaxagoras rather than its real author Xenophanes) to the effect
that the universe was constructed out of the harmonious
union of *two* elements, water and earth. Both theories are
attributed to Homer, without any particular concern for the
consistency of the great sage's thinking.

Ps.-Heraclitus is only the most comprehensive of a large
number of authors to whom this interpretation of Homer as

providing the πρόφασις of Thales' and Xenophanes' cosmogonical theories was familiar: similar readings of Ocean are
found in Ps.-Plut. *De Vita et Poesi Homeri* B93, Stob. *Ecl.*
1.10.2 and 4, Sext. Emp. *Math.* 10.313–18, Plut. *De Is. et
Os.* 364d, Ps.-Probus, *Comm. in Vergili Bucolica* 6.31 (p. 21,
14K), and numerous scholiastic notes.[61] The broad currency
of the idea and, in addition, striking resemblances between the
accounts contained in these texts make a common source
more than likely, as Diels argues.[62] His plausible conclusion is
that there was a single source of the passages in Ps.-Probus,
Sextus, Ps.-Heraclitus, Stobaeus and Ps.-Plutarch, namely an
anonymous allegorist, predating Vitruvius, who at *De Arch.* 8.
praef. 1 seems to display knowledge of the same source. Mette
canvasses a connection with Crates of Mallos, first head of the
library at Pergamum.[63]

Whether or not we can confidently trace these accounts
back to Crates himself is actually of limited importance.
There can be little doubt that, if not Crates himself, then certainly one of his successors in the Pergamene school was responsible for giving philosophical respectability and currency
to a tradition which, as the reference in Aristotle shows, considerably predated them. Virgil's expression *Oceanumque
patrem rerum* thus does two things. It confirms the relevance
of Homer at this point in Virgil's narrative, since it is a clear
reference to a Homeric context. But it also foregrounds a
particular approach to the Homeric text. This context in the
Iliad can be shown to have been a celebrated piece of evidence
for the view that Homer was a poet whose real, underlying
theme was natural philosophy.

The cosmogonical Ocean of the allegory, then, is very
commonly found in ancient writings.[64] It also appears to have
enjoyed a precedence amongst the many Homeric episodes
allegorized in this way. This can be seen from the two texts
which *list* allegories of Homer, Ps.-Heraclitus' *Quaest. Hom.*
and the stultifyingly compendious *De Vita et Poesi Homeri* of
Ps.-Plutarch.

---

[61] For a comprehensive list, see Mette (1936) 192–9.
[62] Diels (1929) 88–95.   [63] Mette (1936) 48–50.   [64] Buffière (1956) 86.

Ps.-Heraclitus' technique in the *Quaest. Hom.* is to take instances from the Homeric poems which seem to contravene Plato's strictures on acceptable poetry, and then establish, through allegory, that the *real* meaning of the passages makes them models of propriety. The assumption is always that Homer is incapable of impiety.[65] At chapter 21 Ps.-Heraclitus raises the problem of the Homeric passage describing the abortive revolt against Zeus by the Olympians, and his rescue by Thetis and Briareus (*Il.* 1.399–406). On Ps.-Heraclitus' terms the superficial meaning of this story is definitively ἀπρεπές: gods do not do such an unexemplary thing as conspiring against their brother, husband or father, and it is highly irregular also for Zeus to be rescued by figures as humble as Thetis and Briareus. If the superficial meaning of the passage is the *real* meaning, then, Homer is indeed liable to all Plato's sanctions, and more. But in fact rather than being the specimen of ἀσέβεια and ἀπρέπεια it *prima facie* appears to be, the Briareus myth is an allegory concerning the primordial material of the universe. For Homer, it transpires, in addition to the expertise Ps.-Heraclitus has so far attributed to him in epidemiology (6–16, on the plague in *Il.* 1) and psychology (17–20, on Athena's calming of Achilles' anger, *Il.* 1.194–222), was also the originator of all physical theory (22.1–2).[66] Ps.-Heraclitus then proceeds to cite evidence in support of this statement; and the *very first* passage he cites is the allegory of Ocean as a prefiguration of Thales' theory of the primordiality of water.

At *De Vita et Poesi* B93 Ps.-Plutarch begins his demonstration of Homer's physical knowledge, and once again he cites the Ocean allegory first of all:

ἀρξώμεθα τοίνυν ἀπὸ τῆς τοῦ παντὸς ἀρχῆς καὶ γενέσεως, ἣν Θαλῆς ὁ Μιλήσιος εἰς τὴν τοῦ ὕδατος οὐσίαν ἀναφέρει· καὶ θεασώμεθα εἰ πρῶτος Ὅμηρος τοῦθ᾽ ὑπέλαβεν, εἰπών
> Ὠκεανός θ᾽ ὅσπερ γένεσις πάντεσσι τέτυκται.

---

[65] As Ps.-Heraclitus memorably puts it (1.1), πάντα γὰρ ἠσέβησεν, εἰ μηδὲν ἠλληγόρησεν.
[66] καὶ τῶν φυσικῶν κατὰ τὰ στοιχεῖα δογμάτων εἰς ἀρχηγὸς Ὅμηρος (22.2).

Let us begin, then, from the start and origin of everything, which Thales the Milesian refers to the substance of water; and let us investigate whether Homer was the first to hold this belief, in the words,
Ocean, who is the origin of all things.

We must assume this allegory had primacy also in the sources these authors were using. It thus seems fair to say that Ocean was a very prominent example in the ancient world of natural-philosophical allegoresis of Homer, one in fact capable of representing this entire mode of Homeric exegesis.

We saw above the proximity of the conceptions of Ocean as margin and Ocean as source. The point has relevance also for depictions of Ocean in visual art. The Great Altar of Zeus, at Pergamum, was ringed by a frieze depicting Gigantomachy in terms quite possibly indebted to Cratetan methods of criticism.[67] It is a fairly firm conjecture that Ocean (with, perhaps, his wife Tethys) occupied one end of the frieze on the southern side of the northern projecting wing, up against the grand stairway:[68] an appropriate location indeed, as Simon notes, for a god commonly conceived as 'der Ringstrom an den äussersten Enden der Erde';[69] but a position not inappropriate, either, particularly given the necessarily linear format of the monument, for a figure representing the chronological beginnings of Creation.

So Ocean can represent both the margins of the world and the origins of the world. But he can also represent Homer, the *Weltdichter*. I would like to conclude this section by showing how very close Ocean as an image for the physical universe and Ocean as an image of the poet of that universe might become. If we think back to Virgil's *recusatio* of epic at 2.39–46, and in particular 2.42, *non ego cuncta meis amplecti uersibus opto*, once again the image of Ocean seems to underlie Virgil's imagery. This will be clearer if we compare Virgil's expression of the comprehensiveness of the epic genre with two other quotations from Latin hexameter poetry. The first quotation is Catullus' description of the physical Ocean

---

[67] Hardie (1986) 28.
[68] For the conventional reconstruction of the frieze, see Pollitt (1986) 96–7.
[69] Simon (1975) 8 (see also 10); Kähler (1948) 50.

(64.30), *Oceanusque, mari totum qui amplectitur orbem*, 'and Ocean, who embraces the whole world with sea'. The second is Silius' summary of the poetic power and scope of Homer (*Pun.* 13.788–9), *carmine complexus terram, mare, sidera, manes | et cantu Musas et Phoebum aequauit honore*, 'embracing earth, sea, stars and dead in his poetry he rivalled the Muses in song and Phoebus in glory'. Homer is Ocean, then, because he is the source of all other literature, and because of a less tangible sense of his surpassing greatness, but also because of what was perceived as the limitless scope of his poetry. Homer offered a total vision of existence; like Ocean he thus *encompasses* the world. It seems true to say that these different reasons for the name were not really distinguished: Homer as Ocean is a poet in command of a poetic and physical totality.

Strabo provides a useful parallel here. Strabo, naturally enough, begins his *Geography* with Homer – claiming him as the founder of geography (1.1.2) – and with Homer's geographical conception of Ocean (1.1.3). (This is clearly comparable to the primacy of Homer's cosmological conception of Ocean in the works of Ps.-Heraclitus and Ps.-Plutarch.) Essentially, according to Strabo's account, Homer conceives of Ocean as forming the margin of a circular world (1.1.7, quoting *Il.* 14.200–1):

καὶ ἄλλως δ' ἐμφαίνει τὸ κύκλῳ περικεῖσθαι τῇ γῇ τὸν Ὠκεανόν ὅταν οὕτω φῇ ἡ "Ηρα·
> εἶμι γὰρ ὀψομένη πολυφόρβου πείρατα γαίης
> Ὠκεανόν τε θεῶν γένεσιν

In another way, too, Homer indicates that Ocean surrounds the earth in a circle, when Hera says:
> For I am going to see the limits of the bountiful earth,
> and Ocean, father of the gods[70]

Later, at the end of his treatment of Homer's Ocean, Strabo summarizes his argument (1.1.10): ὥσπερ οὖν τὰ ἔσχατα καὶ τὰ κύκλῳ τῆς οἰκουμένης οἶδε καὶ φράζει σαφῶς ὁ ποιητής ...

---

[70] In this same context Strabo uses the Shield of Achilles – rimmed by Ocean – as evidence for Homer's view that Ocean surrounds the earth, a clear gesture in the direction of Crates' interpretation of the shield as an image of the world: Romm (1992) 14.

'in the same way as the poet knows and clearly explains the extremities of the world and what surrounds it ... '. The phrase τὰ κύκλῳ corresponds to Ocean (compare κύκλῳ περικεῖσθαι τῇ γῇ τὸν Ὠκεανόν). But it is noticeable that Strabo's description of the physical Ocean (as delineated by Homer) comes exceptionally close to Strabo's description of *Homer himself*. We might compare the last quotation with a description of the sage Homer and his geographical knowledge which precedes it (1.1.2): οὐ γὰρ ἂν μέχρι τῶν ἐσχάτων αὐτῆς περάτων ἀφίκετο τῇ μνήμῃ κύκλῳ περιιών, 'otherwise he would not have attained to the uttermost boundaries of the world, *going round it in a circle* in his description'. The expression τῇ μνήμῃ κύκλῳ περιιών is strange and significant. To say that Homer 'encircles' the world intellectually is to bring Homer's poetic activity into very close proximity to the geographical phenomenon of Ocean encircling the world. The resemblance to Virgil's *amplecti* (of the comprehensiveness of epic) and Catullus' *amplectitur* (of the physical Ocean) is striking. The two conceptions – of physical entity and poet – seem to coalesce: in a double sense Homer *cuncta amplectitur*.[71]

I have suggested that it is primarily Ocean in the aspect of the *origin* of the world that is indicated in Virgil's *pater rerum*. To conclude this section I would like to raise the possibility that just as the physical margin of the world, Ocean, and the poet of that world, the Ocean-like Homer, become somewhat hard to distinguish, so also with Ocean *pater rerum*. I have argued that the first naming of Ocean at *G.* 4.381 must call to mind the figure of Homer. But when the name is repeated in the following line coupled with *pater rerum* it is hard not to refer that expression to Homer as well. But how could Homer be described as *pater rerum*?

---

[71] This passage would tend to belie Lamberton's assertion that the articles by Long (1992) and Porter (1992) yield a picture of Stoic readings of Homer 'not unlike that of Strabo': Strabo, according to Lamberton, unlike authors such as Ps.-Heraclitus, does not treat Homer as 'a visionary sage whose every word is privileged': Lamberton and Keaney (1992) xix–xx. His position is not borne out by Strabo 1.1.2. Comparable to Strabo's description of Homer is Epicurus' all-encompassing flight of the mind at Lucr. 1.72–7, *atque omne immensum peragrauit mente animoque*, a flight which by implication Lucretius is also engaged upon. See p. 98 below.

Hardie has sought to backdate to the time of Virgil the concept that the epic poet is analogous to or even identical with the divine demiurge, the creator of the world, something which Lieberg considers classical antiquity never consciously developed.[72] Hardie interprets the Shield of Aeneas, in the light of Crates' allegoresis of the Shield of Achilles, not only as another κόσμου μίμημα – the universe in this case being equated with Roman imperial dominion – but also as an image of epic poetry itself:

> Like the poetic temple of the *Georgics*, the Shield is at the same time an image of the power of the Roman state and its great men and of the power of the epic poet; the cosmological component further suggests that the activities of both *princeps* and poet are analogous to those of a divine demiurge.[73]

The epic poet creates an image of the entire world. By a natural development of Lieberg's motif (whereby the descriptive activity of the poet is equated with the activity described)[74] he can easily become *creator* of the world. For comparison Hardie cites Macrob. *Sat.* 5.1.19, who draws an 'analogy between Virgil's epic and the divine creation as an image for Virgil's comprehensive use of all varieties of eloquence':[75] here the epic impulse to comprehensiveness again entails both a universality of theme – the whole universe – and a literary universality: epic employs all modes of speech.[76]

To summarize: the figure of Ocean *pater rerum* might denote the physical source of all existence, but might also depict the, as it were, chronicler of that totality, Homer. Some of the implications of the vast status which Virgil attributes to the Homer he is emulating will emerge as this book progresses. For now, though, I want to concentrate on just one manifestation of the 'totalizing impulse' of epic. If Homer is the poet of everything, of the universe, then the themes of his poetry, as we have seen, will be the physical fundamentals of the universe. One of the things the invocation of *Oceanus pater rerum*

---

[72] Lieberg (1982) 172–3; Hardie (1985).   [73] Hardie (1985) 87.
[74] See p. 17 above.   [75] Hardie (1985) 95 n. 2.
[76] See pp. 183–4 below.

achieves, I suggest, is to set a cosmic agenda, so to speak, for the Homeric episode which follows this encounter with Ocean. In short, it encourages us to read the *Proteus* as physical allegory.

V

Proteus is a creature of Ocean: both literally, as a sea god, and also as a figment invented by Homer. But Ocean and Proteus also have other things in common: both belong to the notoriously interchangeable family of marine divinities, and both are to a greater or lesser degree identifiable with the sea.[77] Furthermore, Homer's Proteus, like Homer's Ocean, was a favourite object of allegorical interpretation. Fully one fifth of (what survives of) Ps.-Heraclitus' treatment of the *Odyssey* is given over to the underlying meaning of the outlandish myth of Proteus. And as we shall see, the dominant allegory of Proteus, and our allegory of Ocean, are very similar: both represent the physical Creation. Proteus is another Homeric sea god who became an allegorical figure for *the source*.[78]

Proteus was a leading candidate for allegoresis. As we have

---

[77] See Cornutus (*Theol. Graec.* 23) on Nereus: ὁ δὲ Νηρεὺς ἡ θάλαττά ἐστι. His interpretation is based on the description γέρων ἅλιος which is applied to both Nereus (Hes. *Th.* 1003) and Proteus (*Od.* 4.384). Both figures are prophetic and shape-shifting. For their interchangeability, with each other and with other 'Old Men of the Sea', see West (1966) ad *Th.* 233 and Dion. Byz. (fl. *c.* AD 175) 49: τοῦτον [sc. γέροντα ἅλιον] οἱ μὲν Νηρέα φασίν, οἱ δὲ Φόρκυν, ἄλλοι δὲ Πρωτέα ... Virgil's Proteus noticeably shares the characteristics of the sea: he is *caeruleus* (388), his eyes blaze *lumine glauco* (451). It was a standard Stoic approach to divinities which were closely associated with a real physical phenomenon to identify them with it. Hence Cornutus' interpretation of Nereus (above), and see also Feeney (1991) 135–6 on Neptune in *Aen.* 1, Varro *apud* August. *De civ. D.* 7.16, p. 294, and p. 233 below. On Ocean as the sea, see p. 48 n. 84 above.

[78] Cf. Farrell (1991) 258–72, who also offers an allegorizing reading of the *Aristaeus*. By such allegoresis, Farrell argues, Virgil assimilates Homeric epos to the didactic epos of Hesiod, Aratus and Lucretius, which has been his main model during the poem: thus all the diverse models of the poem are contained within the didactic matrix. Henceforth my argument will recurrently parallel Farrell's conclusions, particularly regarding allegoresis of Proteus and the literary-generic relation between the Proteus and Orpheus episodes: see Farrell (1991) 320–4, and pp. 80, 181–2, 184 below. Whereas Farrell's focus is at all times strictly literary-generic, however, my emphasis is on the political and propagandistic dimension of the poetic-generic issues Virgil raises.

seen, a primary impulse behind both the Cratetan and Aristarchean model of Homeric criticism was to rescue the good name of the cultural icon of Greece, Homer. And if Crates and Aristarchus represent the iconodoulic tendency, the great iconoclast was Plato. In the *Republic* he outlined a Utopian state governed in accordance with the highest order of goodness and knowledge. It is a community where the status of poets is at best equivocal: they are either to be limited to composing edifying didactic verse, or else excluded from the state entirely.

One of the greatest errors of poetry, according to the *Republic*, is the misrepresentation of God. God is perfectly good, and as such neither has the need nor possesses the requisite deceitfulness to change shape (*Resp.* 381d1–9, quoting *Od.* 17.485–6 and a line from a lost play of Aeschylus):

Μηδεὶς ἄρα, ἦν δ' ἐγώ, ὦ ἄριστε, λεγέτω ἡμῖν τῶν ποιητῶν, ὡς-
θεοὶ ξείνοισιν ἐοικότες ἀλλοδαποῖσι,
παντοῖοι τελέθοντες, ἐπιστρωφῶσι πόληας·

μηδὲ Π ρ ω τ έ ω ς καὶ Θέτιδος καταψευδέσθω μηδείς, μηδ' ἐν τραγῳδίαις μηδ' ἐν τοῖς ἄλλοις ποιήμασιν εἰσαγέτω Ἥραν ἠλλοιωμένην, ὡς ἱέρειαν ἀγείρουσαν-
Ἰνάχου Ἀργείου ποταμοῦ παισὶν βιοδώροις·
καὶ ἄλλα τοιαῦτα πολλὰ μὴ ἡμῖν ψευδέσθων.

So we cannot have any poet saying that the gods
disguise themselves as strangers from abroad
and wander round our towns in every kind of shape;
we cannot have falsehoods told about the transformations of Proteus and Thetis, or poets bringing Hera on the stage disguised as a priestess begging alms for
the lifegiving children of Inachus, river of Argos.
We must stop all falsehoods of this kind.

Plato was an extremely influential figure, but as Buffière says, 'plus un mythe est attaqué, mieux il est défendu'.[79] The very fact that its propriety had been called into question (by Plato, no less) effectively ensured that Homer's transformation of Proteus would be interpreted as allegorical. But furthermore, the Homeric tale of Proteus was intrinsically susceptible to

[79] Buffière (1956) 168.

allegoresis. To start with, as a scholiast puts it, Proteus' name, with its intimation of primordiality, seems almost designed for allegory (Σ *Od.* 4.384, M. and E.): τὸ δὲ Πρωτέως ὄνομα εἰς τὴν ἀλληγορίαν ἐπιτήδειον. And since much (particularly Stoic) investigation of concepts began from etymology (literally, the discovery of the true meaning of a word by consideration of its origin)[80] this was no doubt a significant catalyst. Fundamentally, however, as Farrell suggests, the myth of Proteus was far too vivid and strange *not* to find itself regularly redeployed in this fashion.[81] At any rate, this suitability was extensively exploited by the ancients.

Σ *Od.* 4.384 (M. and E.), besides citing the interpretation I set out below, record an interpretation whereby Proteus represents τὸν πρὸ τοῦ ἔαρος καιρόν, the time of the year after which the earth begins to produce flowers. In his role of *precursor to generation* this Proteus closely parallels the three allegories that had the greatest currency in the ancient world, the Pythagorean, the Neoplatonic and the Stoic-influenced Pergamene. I shall in fact suggest further on that within the terms of the imagery of the *Georgics* three models of renewal – spring, foundation and Creation – are practically interchangeable. Farrell has pointed out the proximity of the notions of spring and Creation in Homeric allegoresis,[82] and Proteus is a good example of this. The (unstated) implication of a scholiast's account of Proteus as the time μεθ' ὃν ἄρχεται ἡ γῆ εἴδη ποιεῖν βοτανῶν καὶ γενῶν, 'after which the earth begins to create the varieties of plants and crops', is that Proteus' subsequent metamorphoses represent the proliferation of life (the growing of plants) at the onset of spring. Proteus premetamorphosis is the dead earth of winter, on this interpretation, just as according to the cosmogonical allegory I discuss below he is the inert matter of the universe from which spring

---

[80] Most (1989) 2027.
[81] 'Proteus, more perhaps than any other Homeric character, lends himself to allegorical interpretation': Farrell (1991) 266.
[82] Farrell (1991) 271–2. Virgil himself of course relates spring to Creation at 2.336–42. Cf. Dio Chrys. *Or.* 36.54–7, who describes the conditions of the newly-recreated universe as the ἱερὸς γάμος of Zeus and Hera, the mythical scheme which Virgil relates to spring (2.325–6).

the elements of the differentiated cosmos. The two interpretations are clearly closely akin: in both cases the core
notion is of an initially inert substance – wintry earth, cosmic
matter – from which emerges the variety of elements or plants.
Significantly, Virgil's description of *bugonia* at 4.295–314 (and
especially 305–7) bears a striking resemblance to the scholiastic spring-allegory of Proteus. The beating to a pulp of the
bullock occurs before the growth of flowers, the implication
being that the creation of bees by *bugonia* is equivalent to the
growth of flora at the start of spring.[83]

According to the Neoplatonic Proclus, Proteus, an angelic
mind in the procession of Poseidon, incorporates all the forms
of the world: ἔχων καὶ περιέχων ἐν ἑαυτῷ τὰ εἴδη πάντα τῶν
γενητῶν;[84] in both Pythagorean and Stoic-influenced allegory, similarly, he represents the cosmos in potentiality.
For Pythagoreans Proteus was the Monad, the Number One:
Proteus 'contains the properties of all things just as the monad
contains the combined energies of all the numbers'.[85] From
numbers, according to Pythagoreans, everything else in the
universe was composed. For the Pergamenes, similarly, he is an
image of the primitive matter out of which the cosmos is born,
and his metamorphoses represent the Creation. Once again
the fullest account of the allegory is given by Ps.-Heraclitus,
an account which though in details somewhat eclectic undoubtedly derives from what is in essence, as Buffière states, a
Stoic treatise.[86]

The discussion of Proteus fills chapters 64–7 of the *Quaest.
Hom.* The author begins his interpretation by pointing out

---

[83] This despite the fact that according to Columella (9.14.6) Democritus and Mago,
as well as Virgil (Columella is thinking, presumably, of G. 4.425–8, and forgetting
305–7), give the time for *bugonia* as the thirty days between the summer solstice
and the rising of Sirius: Bettini (1991) 208. Perhaps confirming a vegetative
dimension to *bugonia*, Ovid's descriptions of *bugonia* at *Fast.* 1.363–80 and *Met.*
15.364–7 both differ from Virgil's in a significant respect: the bullock from which
the bees emerge is in Ovid's accounts buried in the ground (note the agricultural
associations of the *scrobis* in which the *Met.* bull is interred). The ox is also buried
in the account by Antig. Car. *Hist. Mir.* 19.23: Bettini (1991) 209.
[84] *In R.* 1.112.28–9; see Lamberton (1986) viii and 226–7.
[85] Iambl. *Comm. Math.* 7.20–3, and the translation of Lamberton (1986) 37.
[86] Buffière (1956) 181, (1962) 125 n. 4.

those elements of the story which mark it out as obviously allegorical: with its unfeasibly miserable protagonist living a life divided between land and sea, to whom even the pleasure of sleep is denied since he must bed down with his seals, and whose own daughter betrays him – not to mention his transformations – the myth is simply too absurd to be taken at face value (64.4): ποιητικοὶ καὶ τεράστιοι μῦθοι δοκοῦσιν, εἰ μή τις οὐρανίῳ ψυχῇ τὰς ὀλυμπίους Ὁμήρου τελετὰς ἱεροφαντήσειε, 'they would appear to be fanciful yarns, unless some divine intelligence is to initiate us into Homer's Olympian mysteries'. Ps.-Heraclitus obliges.

Homer's story of Proteus, according to Ps.-Heraclitus, represents the imposition of order (κόσμος) on the universe after Chaos. At one time everything was a shapeless or muddy soup (65.3–6):

οὔτε γὰρ γῆ τῶν ὅλων ἑστίᾳ κέντρον ἐπεπήγει βέβαιον οὔτ' οὐρανὸς περὶ τὴν ἀίδιον φορὰν ἱδρυμένος ἐκυκλεῖτο, πάντα δ' ἦν ἀνήλιος ἠρεμία καὶ κατηφοῦσα σιγή, καὶ πλέον οὐδὲν ἦν κεχυμένης ὕλης· ἄμορφος γὰρ ἀργία, πρὶν ἡ δημιουργὸς ἁπάντων καὶ κοσμοτόκος ἀρχὴ σωτήριον ἑλκύσασα τῷ βίῳ τύπον τὸν κόσμον ἀπέδωκε τῷ κόσμῳ· διεζεύγνυ τὸν μὲν οὐρανὸν γῆς, ἐχώριζε δὲ τὴν ἤπειρον θαλάττης, τέτταρα δὲ στοιχεῖα, τῶν ὅλων ῥίζα καὶ γέννα, ἐν τάξει τὴν ἰδίαν μορφὴν ἐκομίζετο· τούτων δὲ προμηθῶς κιρναμένων ὁ θεὸς ⟨...⟩ μηδεμιᾶς οὔσης διακρίσεως περὶ τὴν ἄμορφον ὕλην.

The earth, the hearth of the universe, did not have a firm and fixed core; and the sky did not turn, established in its eternal course; everywhere was sunless desert and dark silence; nothing existed but confused matter; all was formless inertia, until the first maker of all things and begetter of the universe provided protection to life and gave to the cosmos the stamp of order.[87] It detached the sky from the earth and separated the land from the sea; and the four elements, root and seed of all things, attained, in turn, their proper form. God, blending these elements with care ⟨...⟩,[88] as there was no distinction in the shapeless matter.

The ὕλη, matter, as the Homeric scholia make rather more clear than Ps.-Heraclitus, is represented by Proteus. The demiurge, at first an abstract demiurgic ἀρχή but later called ὁ θεός, corresponds to Proteus' daughter *Eido*thea, so called according to Ps.-Heraclitus because she gave *form* to everything:

[87] A rough translation: the text looks corrupt.
[88] See Buffière (1962) 124 for suggestions as to the content of this lacuna.

79

Eidothea is Providence, one of the many manifestations of the Stoic θεός, though this is a role which might as well (as we shall see) have fallen to Menelaus. And the first event of the new universe, the birth of the elements, is further represented by Proteus' transformations. His various metamorphoses represent the four elements (66.3–6):

διὰ μὲν οὖν τοῦ λέοντος, ἐμπύρου ζῴου, τὸν αἰθέρα δηλοῖ. δράκων δ' ἐστὶν ἡ γῆ· τὸ γὰρ αὐτόχθον αὐτοῦ καὶ γηγενὲς οὐδὲν ἄλλο πλὴν τοῦτο σημαίνει. δένδρον γε μήν, ἅπαν αὐξανόμενον καὶ τὴν ἀπὸ γῆς ὁρμὴν μετάρσίαν ἀεὶ λαμβάνον, συμβολικῶς εἶπεν ἀέρα. τὸ μὲν γὰρ ὕδωρ εἰς ἀσφαλεστέραν ὧν προηνίξατο δήλωσιν ἐκ τοῦ φανερωτέρου παρεστήσεν εἰπών·
γίνετο δ' ὑγρὸν ὕδωρ.

By the lion, a fiery animal, he denotes ether. The snake is earth: this is clearly the reason why it is called 'of the land' and 'earth-born'. With the tree, constantly growing and always receiving an upwards impulse from the earth, he figuratively meant air. Water – as confirmation of his earlier hints – he presented more clearly, with the words
he became liquid water.

'Pour mener la raisonnement au but fixé d'avance, notre auteur doit torturer un peu les mots,' indeed.[89] Quite naturally, scholars have not been hasty to posit so wilful a misreading of the *Odyssey* as an influence on Virgil: Farrell was to my knowledge the first. He goes so far, though, as to call it a 'fairly obvious case'.[90] I suggested earlier that one of the strongest arguments in favour of cosmic allegory is always how germane the allegory proves to be to the explicit preoccupations of the Virgilian context: and in a passage which is centrally occupied with the concepts of source and rebirth this reading of Proteus as the Creation is surely, as Farrell argues, far too apt to be coincidental. This argument from pertinence is supported, I believe, by closer study of Virgil's text, and I return to this question later. For now, though, it would perhaps be profitable to establish that this allegory had a currency outside the work of specialists such as Ps.-Heraclitus.

The *Quaest. Hom.* was perhaps composed in the first century AD.[91] Its reading of Proteus is less extensively in evidence in the other allegorist works than Ocean was: the version re-

---

[89] Buffière (1962) 72.   [90] Farrell (1991) 266.   [91] Buffière (1962) ix–x.

corded (without conviction) by Eustathius (1503.6–13) interprets Proteus in precisely the same way as Ps.-Heraclitus – as ἡ πρωτόγονος ὕλη – but makes of Eidothea a figure rather more Peripatetic than Stoic: for him she represents Aristotelian κίνησις, the movement from potential to actualization; here more specifically the passage of matter towards form.[92] Buffière considers it an earlier, because less elaborate, version,[93] a pre-existing Peripatetic interpretation later accommodated to (what we must presume was) the dominant, Stoic-coloured reading.

But the allegory also finds its way into more mainstream works, both in the same form as Ps.-Heraclitus' and in a slightly divergent form. When Sextus Empiricus employs the allegory (*Math.* 9.5) its terms are reversed – Eidothea becomes matter, Proteus the first cause which acts upon it. This clearly complicates the situation somewhat. Although on the one hand in natural-philosophical allegoresis the Proteus myth always represents Creation, nevertheless certain of the details are contested: not only the interpretation of Eidothea, but in Sextus even the otherwise firm identification of Proteus with primordial matter; and Buffière believes Sextus may well have been recording a fairly widespread interpretation of the figure.[94] But it can be established, I think, not only that a natural-philosophic reading of Proteus seeped into the very mainstream of ancient literary culture, but in addition that this popularized version was closely akin to the Proteus/ matter equation recorded by Ps.-Heraclitus.

To begin with, so far as it goes, the scholia favour the Heraclitean version,[95] which at least provides a further indication of what we have concluded already, namely that it was

---

[92] Buffière (1962) 124.

[93] Buffière (1956) 183–4.

[94] Buffière (1956) 185. My own suspicion is that Sextus merely reversed the figures out of carelessness. However, another variant along somewhat the same lines is recorded by a scholiast of Aratus: apparently some held that Proteus represented *air*, or the divine *pneuma* which – according to the Stoics – pervades all things, a phenomenon otherwise generally termed Ζεύς. This is also a cosmogonical reading: ὁ γὰρ ⟨Ζεὺς⟩ πάντα ἐστὶ καὶ ἐξ αὐτοῦ πάντα, ὡς ὁ λόγος: Maass (1898) 335.

[95] Buffière (1956) 184 n. 38.

the predominant one. But much more striking evidence of its currency is given by a fascinating passage which concludes Plutarch's homily *De Amicorum Multitudine*. At 96f Plutarch is condemning the man who shares his intimacy among a large number of friends of differing interests. Not for Plutarch the Renaissance man: he is likened pejoratively first to the chameleonic cuttle-fish, then to Proteus. To this extent his usage is conventional: Proteus is regularly used as a figure for moral inadequacy.[96] But hereafter his train of thought becomes rather obscure. I quote in full (97a–b):

Πρωτέως τινὸς οὐκ εὐτυχοῦς οὐδὲ πάνυ χρηστοῦ τὸ ἔργον, ἀλλ' ὑπὸ γοητείας ἑαυτὸν εἰς ἕτερον εἶδος ἐξ ἑτέρου μεταλλάττοντος ἐν ταὐτῷ πολλάκις, φιλολόγοις συναναγιγνώσκοντος καὶ παλαισταῖς συγκονιομένου καὶ φιλοθήροις συγκυνηγετοῦντος καὶ φιλοπόταις συμμεθυσκομένου καὶ πολιτικοῖς συναρχαιρεσιάζοντος, ἰδίαν ἤθους ἑστίαν οὐκ ἔχοντος. ὡς δὲ τὴν ἀσχημάτιστον οἱ φυσικοὶ καὶ ἀχρώματον οὐσίαν καὶ ὕλην λέγουσιν ὑποκειμένην καὶ τρεπομένην ὑφ' αὑτῆς νῦν μὲν φλέγεσθαι νῦν δ' ἐξυγραίνεσθαι, τοτὲ δ' ἐξαεροῦσθαι πήγνυσθαι δ' αὖθις, οὕτως ἄρα τῇ πολυφιλίᾳ ψυχὴν ὑποκεῖσθαι δεήσει πολυπαθῆ καὶ πολύτροπον καὶ ὑγρὰν καὶ ῥᾳδίαν μεταβάλλειν. ἀλλ' ἡ φιλία στάσιμόν τι ζητεῖ καὶ βέβαιον ἦθος καὶ ἀμετάπτωτον ἐν μιᾷ χώρᾳ καὶ συνηθείᾳ· διὸ καὶ σπάνιον καὶ δυσεύρετόν ἐστι φίλος βέβαιος.

Such varied adaptation were the task of a Proteus, not fortunate and not at all scrupulous, who by magic can change himself often on the very instant from one character to another, reading books with the scholarly, rolling in the dust with wrestlers, following the hunt with sportsmen, getting drunk with topers, and taking part in the canvass of politicians, possessing no firmly founded character of his own. And as the natural philosophers say of the formless and colourless substance and material which is the underlying basis of everything and of itself turns into everything, that it is now in a state of combustion, now liquefied, at another time aeriform, and then again solid, so the possession of a multitude of friends will necessarily have, as its underlying basis, a soul that is very impressionable, versatile, pliant, and readily changeable. But friendship seeks for a fixed and steadfast character which does not shift about, but continues in one place and in one intimacy. For this reason a steadfast friend is something rare and hard to find.[97]

---

[96] Serv. ad G. 4.400; Clem. Alex. *Paed.* 3.1.1; Philo, *Ebr.* 36 (where the description of Proteus' transformations may also carry cosmological associations). This strong association of Proteus with degeneracy should not necessarily be resisted, of course, in connection with Virgil's treatment either.
[97] Translated by Babbitt (1928).

The ease with which Plutarch moves from Proteus to natural philosophy would seem to indicate how strong the association of Proteus and primordial ὕλη was in Plutarch's lifetime and circles. He does not even need to signpost the connection: we must assume that this is because it was familiar to his readership.

This passage of Plutarch can be placed roughly at the turn of the first and second centuries AD. But similar knowledge of the Proteus allegory in non-allegorist literature can be traced back somewhat further. In the *Legatio ad Gaium* 80 Philo again uses Proteus in the standard ethical way, but as with Plutarch in his elaboration of a moral *exemplum* he displays familiarity with the natural-philosophic allegory. He is damning the proclamation of his own divinity made by the emperor Gaius. He began, says Philo, by identifying himself with the minor deities – Dionysus, Hercules and the Dioscuri – covetously assuming the costume, insignia and honours not just of one but of all of them at different times, 'remodelling and recasting the substance of a single body into manifold forms' Αἰγυπτίου τρόπον Πρωτέως, ὃν εἰσήγαγεν Ὅμηρος μεταβολὰς παντοίας ἐνδεχόμενον εἰς τε τὰ στοιχεῖα καὶ τὰ ἐκ τούτων ζῷα καὶ φυτά, 'in the manner of Egyptian Proteus, whom Homer depicted admitting every kind of metamorphosis both into the elements and the animals and plants which they make up'. The technical term στοιχεῖα, 'elements', points to natural philosophy, and Philo's explicit reference to the physical doctrine of the primacy of the elements (τὰ ἐκ τούτων ζῷα καὶ φυτά) makes it clear that here also allegoresis of Proteus is involved.[98] And once again the offhand manner in which he introduces natural philosophy implies that the interpretation was a commonplace. Philo was an Alexandrian. The embassy to Rome which he records in this work took place in AD 39–40, and he died in 45. Seventy years after the

---

[98] The version recorded by Eustathius also seemed to interpret Proteus' transformations as a representation not only of the elements but also of animals and all other constituents of the universe (καὶ οὐ στοιχεῖα μόνον, ἀλλὰ καὶ ζῷα καὶ ἕτερα τὰ κατὰ κόσμον, 1503.11–12). Cf. as well Lucian, *Dem. Enc.* 24.

publication of the *Georgics*, then, the Stoic-coloured interpretation of Homer's Proteus as a covert description of the
Creation enjoyed extensive currency well beyond the special-
ized exponents of allegory. And one thing we can be sure of is
that it was not Ps.-Heraclitus or his like that made it so, but a
critic who in all likelihood belonged to the school of Pergamum initiated by Crates, a hundred years before Virgil's
Proteus was composed.

VI

We have already considered the (currently contentious) issue
of the philosophical sources underlying cosmological allegoresis of Homer.[99] I have suggested that they are profoundly
influenced by Stoic doctrine whether or not the allegorists
themselves could be termed orthodox Stoics; and it is of some
importance to my broader argument that this should be so. In
the case of the allegory transmitted by Ps.-Heraclitus we have
a model of Creation which is undeniably strongly influenced
by Stoicism; but it could not be called *orthodox* Stoicism. It is
my contention, however, that Virgil's allegory does reflect
closely (more closely than Ps.-Heraclitus) the cosmogonical
doctrines of Stoicism. Consequently what I now want to do is
sketch the Stoic model of creation so as to compare it with the
details of Virgil's passage, in such a way as to establish the
essentially Stoic derivation of Virgil's imagery at this point.
To this end I shall also, following Lapidge, try to give some
idea of how the concepts of Greek Stoicism found expression
in Latin.[100]

Cosmology was, as Lapidge says, the very cornerstone of
the Stoic system:[101] if the ultimate goal of Stoicism was a life
in harmony with φύσις, then, necessarily, understanding the
nature of φύσις was a first priority. Its nature, as understood
by the Stoics, was essentially material. The universe consisted

[99] See p. 62 above.
[100] Lapidge (1989) esp. 1385–92; Lapidge (1978). The whole remainder of this section is deeply indebted to these two articles.
[101] Lapidge (1978) 161–2.

of a single substance (οὐσία) possessing two aspects or 'principles' (ἀρχαί), one active (τὸ ποιοῦν) and one passive (τὸ πάσχον), in Cicero's Latin *efficiens* and *id quod efficitur* (*Acad. Post.* 24): the passive principle was identified as matter, ὕλη (*materia, Acad. Post.* 24), the active as θεός (*deus, Acad. Post.* 29). We are by now quite familiar with them both: the Stoic θεός, as we have seen, was synonymous with Providence, but also with Fate, Ζεύς, λόγος, νοῦς and Nature. In Cicero's account the essential nature of the active principle, corresponding to the *materia* of the passive, is *uis* (*Acad. Post.* 24).[102] It, or he, was fiery in nature, for Zeno a πῦρ τεχνικὸν ὁδῷ βαδίζον εἰς γένεσιν, 'workmanlike fire going methodically about the business of creation'. Cicero renders πῦρ τεχνικόν as *ignis artificiosus* (*Nat. D.* 2.57). For Chrysippus the active principle was a fiery πνεῦμα. In both systems this principle permeates the cosmos. Chrysippus' πνεῦμα, as in Stoic accounts of the human body (a common analogy), held all parts of the cosmos together in tension; and this latter doctrine gave rise to one of the most persistent metaphors of Roman Stoicism: the cosmic *bond* or δεσμός.[103] Allegorists, predictably, interpreted the golden δεσμός with which Zeus bound and punished Hera (*Il.* 15.18–20) as this cohesive 'pneumatic tension' of Chrysippus.[104] The Latin translation was generally *uinculum* or *foedus*.[105] Lapidge cites the Stoic Balbus in Book 2 of Cicero's *De Natura Deorum*:[106]

Balbus accurately describes Stoic cosmology in Chrysippus' terminology, and it is not surprising that he should also make reference to the metaphor of cosmic binding: all things in the universe are held together, he explains, as if by a certain 'chain' or 'bond' – *quodam uinculo circumdato colligantur* (II.115), where *uinculum* corresponds exactly to Chrysippus' δεσμός.

---

[102] *In eo quod efficeret uim esse censebant, in eo autem quod efficeretur materiam quandam*; the cohesion of this *materia*, he goes on to say, depends on the *uis* of the active principle: see *Acad. Post.* 28 (*illa uis*), 29 (*quam uim animum* [i.e. νοῦν] *esse dicunt mundi*).

[103] On this see specifically Lapidge (1980).

[104] Cornutus, *Theol. Graec.* 17; Ps.-Heraclit. *Quaest. Hom.* 40; Lucretius, at 2.1154, also seems to show an acquaintance with (non-Stoic) allegoresis of the same passage.

[105] Manilius 2.60–6, 3.47–58; *Aetna* 230; Lapidge (1980); Lapidge (1989) 1394–7.

[106] Lapidge (1980) 819.

If the active principle was fiery, the essential property of the passive, though much less clear-cut, would appear to have been conceived of as liquid. We are told that Zeno offered an etymological interpretation of Hesiod's πρώτιστα Χάος (*Th.* 116) as a derivation ἀπὸ τοῦ χέεσθαι, 'from its being liquid' (*SVF* 1.103). *SVF* 1.104 confirms that Zeno believed Hesiod's Chaos to have been simply water. We must conclude, with Lapidge, that the passive ὕλη of the universe was commonly depicted as moisture or water.[107]

The two ἀρχαί of the universal substance, θεός and ὕλη, were normally considered distinguishable only theoretically: but the creation of the world was conceived of as the moment when the action of θεός (or synonyms) first came into contact with formless ὕλη and made of it the universe of the elements. Crucially, however, this Stoic Creation was not a one-off. Once created the universe was in a perpetual state of decline, and periodically the structure of the universe would be dissolved and the world would suffer ἐκπύρωσις, dissolution by the fiery principle.[108] But the fire that destroyed in the very process of destroying created a pristine new universe. Dissolution and (re)generation, in other words, were in Stoic doctrine cyclical occurrences. In fact in Stoic cosmological theory destructive violence was not merely allowed for in the process of renewal: the process actually entailed it. Without the prior destruction there was no creation. As Schofield says of the Heraclitean doctrines apparently employed by Chrysippus in his *On Nature*, 'the cosmic order is a function of change and conflict'.[109] This scheme of chaos engendering order, war engendering peace, and death life, is one we shall encounter again. But clearly the cyclical nature of the Stoic model of creation made it a potentially ideal vehicle for Augustan propaganda, with its ideology of renewal and also – I shall later suggest – its pressing need to place a positive gloss on

---

[107] Lapidge (1978) 165.
[108] A (seemingly) later development of the theory postulated an alternation between dissolution by fire (*ecpyrosis*) and destruction by flood (*cataclysmos*): see Ps.-Heraclit. *Quaest. Hom.* 25.5; Sandbach (1975) 79; Zeller (1892) 168–9.
[109] Schofield (1991) 80.

the violent chaos which accompanied the establishment of the new regime. Foreshadowing the common model of the *Aeneid*,[110] a political renewal could easily be redescribed as *cosmic* renewal.

But this is to jump the gun a little. The question now is, are there details of Virgil's Proteus incident over and beyond those inherited from the *Odyssey* which might confirm that one of the poet's intentions in the episode is to represent a specifically Stoic Creation?

VII

Seneca summarizes the Stoic theory of Creation as follows (*Ep.* 65.2):

Dicunt, ut scis, Stoici nostri duo esse in rerum natura, ex quibus omnia fiant, causam et materiam. materia iacet iners, res ad omnia parata, cessatura, si nemo moueat. causa autem, id est ratio, materiam format, et quocumque uult uersat, ex illa uaria opera producit.

Our Stoic philosophers, as you know, claim that there are two things in the universe from which all things come into being, cause and matter. Matter lies inactive, a substance with the potential for anything but which will do nothing if no one sets it in motion. Cause, however, that is reason, gives shape to matter and turns it in whatever direction it will, and produces from it diverse artefacts.

A kinship between this account and Aristaeus' forceful assault on the sleeping Proteus, an assault which brings about his metamorphoses, may already be evident. The parallels in detail between Virgil's *Proteus* and Stoic theory, at any rate, seem strong enough to establish my case. To start with, Ross has pointed out the extensive elemental colouring of the capture-scene. It occurs, pointedly, *not* in the cave where Proteus is sleeping but in the blazing midday sunshine, in a physical context emphatically bereft of water (401–3).[111] The second scene-setting passage, in the authorial narrative, is if

---

[110] Hardie (1986) *passim*.

[111] Ross (1987) 224–6; Thomas (1988) ad 4.401, 425–8: for Ross this heat is an image of the power of intellect, the triumph of which he believes Aristaeus' mastery of Proteus to represent.

anything even more explicit on this point than Cyrene's prediction (425–9). In both cases the point involves an otherwise rare departure from the Homeric model. I shall quote them both:

> ipsa ego te, medios cum *sol accenderit aestus*,
> cum *sitiunt* herbae et pecori iam gratior umbra est,
> in secreta senis ducam.

> iam rapidus *torrens sitientis Sirius* Indos
> *ardebat* caelo, et medius *sol igneus orbem*
> *hauserat*; *arebant* herbae, et caua flumina *siccis*
> faucibus ad limum *radii tepefacta coquebant*,
> cum Proteus ...

Terms for aridity predominate: *sol, accenderit, aestus, sitiunt, torrens, sitientis, Sirius, ardebat, sol igneus, hauserat, arebant, siccis, radii, tepefacta, coquebant*.[112] The main source of the heat is the sun: ἐκπύρωσις was conceived of as activated by the sun, as if the sun was actually the controlling, fiery principle of the cosmos, the deity which destroys and creates.[113] In addition Aristaeus' very name seems to carry connotations of dryness.[114] But if the assault and the assailant are asso-

---

[112] O'Hara (1996) 35–6, 288 suggests an implied etymology at 425 (*torrens ... Sirius*), the name Sirius having been glossed by Aratus (*Phaen.* 328–32) as related to σειριάω, 'to be scorching'.

[113] See Long and Sedley (1987) II 275; I 278: 'The present world-order will end in a total conflagration activated by the sun'; Mansfeld (1979) 154–5; Cic. *Acad. Pr.* 126; *SVF* 1.499. Relevant here is the common assimilation of Aristaeus to Apollo, who for allegorists is often simply the sun: see Ps.-Heraclit. *Quaest. Hom.* 7, Cornutus, *Theol. Graec.* 32. Aristaeus was particularly close to Apollo Νόμιος: see Ap. Rhod. *Argon.* 2.506–7, and Farnell (1896–1909) IV 123–4, 360–1, who quotes Pind. *Pyth.* 9.63–5, and Serv. ad *G.* 1.14, *Aristaeum inuocat, id est, Apollinis et Cyrenes filium, quem Hesiodus dicit Apollinem pastoralem. Pastoralis* is a translation of Νόμιος. Farnell also cites an inscription from Ceos, a location particularly associated with Aristaeus (*G.* 1.14–15), containing a private dedication τῷ 'Απόλλωνι 'Αρισταίῳ. Richard Hunter has suggested to me further grounds for equating Aristaeus and Apollo. The strange initial attribution of divinity to Aristaeus (*quis deus ...*, 315) recalls, amongst other Homeric contexts – see Thomas (1988) ad loc. – *Iliad* 1.8, τίς τ' ἄρ σφωε θεῶν ἔριδι ξυνέηκε μάχεσθαι, to which the answer is Apollo, who at this point in Homer's narrative bears a particularly close likeness to Aristaeus as the *cause of plague*. In *Aen.* 4, also, Aeneas is likened to this plague-bringing Apollo: compare *Il.* 1.46 and *Aen.* 4.149 and see Lyne (1987) 124–5. In each case the plague in question is closely related to the phenomenon of *amor*.

[114] Ross relates *Aristaeus* to *arista*, the latter being a word commonly derived *ab ariditate*: see Ross (1987) 34–8; Serv. ad *G.* 1.8 and Maltby (1991) s.v. *arista*.

ciated with fiery heat, their object, Proteus, obviously has a correspondingly aqueous quality: he is a denizen of the sea who appears to share some of its properties – he, like it, and like Tiber at *Aen.* 8.64, who is also in some sense identical with his element, is *caeruleus* (388). Thus far, at any rate, the imagery of the passage seems to be in close accordance with Zeno's model of a fiery active principle and liquid passive.[115]

I referred in Chapter 1 to a few departures from the *Odyssey* model in Virgil's *Proteus* which given the otherwise near total correspondence of the passages seemed to carry a great deal of significance. One of these was Virgil's addition of chains, *uincula*, to the purely manual force exerted over Proteus by Menelaus. These, though extraneous to the Homeric account, are also obviously an extremely appropriate addition if the passage at issue is an allegory for the imposition of order on chaos in the cosmic arena: if Proteus represents formless matter, and his transformations the genesis of the four elements, the *uincula* with which Aristaeus exerts control over him seem neatly to parallel the cosmic δεσμός by which Zeus, λόγος or the active principle of Stoic theory ensures the continuing order of the universe.

In Chapter 1 I also suggested that an important conceptual link existed in the *Georgics* between *uinculum*, 'chain', and *uis*, 'power, violence', which stressed even further the violent force of Aristaeus' assault on Proteus. *Vis*, I suggested, is one of the central preoccupations of the *Georgics*. In the Proteus episode this theme reaches its summation: Aristaeus brings to bear *uis* and *uincula* (399; cf. 396, 398, 405, 409, 412 and 439) on Proteus; the latter is thus the object of *uis*, and finally, at the last, *uictus* (443) and compelled *ui multa* (450) to speak. A central message of the *Aristaeus*, as I shall suggest in my next chapter, is the constructive potential of violence. Here Aristaeus' (heavily emphasized) violence is a necessity if he is to capture

---

[115] As Lapidge (1978) 165–6 points out, the notion that creation occurred from the paradoxically creative conflict between heat and wet was of very wide currency in the ancient world. The description of *bugonia* at 295–314 reflects this. The bees are created by the *umor* of the bullock's flesh *heating up* (*tepefactus* ... | *aestuat*, 308–9). Cf. the similar *discors concordia* at Ov. *Met.* 1.430–3.

Proteus. Paradoxically constructive violence was also a central feature of the Stoic cosmogony, as we have seen, and we may well be tempted to think back to Cicero's account of Antiochus of Ascalon's stoicizing physical theory at *Acad. Post.* 24-9, according to which the passive *materia* of the cosmos was given coherence by the power, *uis*, which was the characteristic possession of the active principle, the *animus mundi*. Once again, in his fulfilment of a role so rigidly and pointedly *passive* in nature Proteus would seem to correspond closely to the infinitely malleable substrate he was interpreted to be by the allegorists.

The wielder of *uincula*, the embodiment of *uis* – in other words, the equivalent in Virgil's scheme to the active, demiurgic principle in the Creation, be it Fate, Providence, θεός or, in particular, Zeus – is Aristaeus. Neither the implication that he is divine nor the identification with Zeus which would result if we felt able to apply this allegory to the Proteus episode is unparalleled. We need only think of 4.315, *Quis deus hanc, Musae, quis nobis extudit artem*, which besides defining Aristaeus as a god also relates his achievement as cultural *artifex* to the actions of Jupiter at 1.122-3, who *primusque per artem | mouit agros curis acuens mortalia corda* with the ultimate aim that (133-4) *uarias usus meditando extunderet artis | paulatim*.

There is not a lot of information surviving about the figure of Aristaeus. What there is, however, shows clearly that the identification of Aristaeus with the supreme god is not Virgil's invention: Pindar suggests at *Pyth.* 9.63 that Aristaeus is both Zeus and Apollo; and Servius, at *G.* 1.14, states of Aristaeus, *nam apud Arcadas pro Ioue colitur*.[116] The Christian apologist Athenagoras (second century AD) confirms that Aristaeus was

---

[116] A connection between Aristaeus and Arcadia is pointed up in the first mention of Aristaeus in the *Aristaeus* (283, *Arcadius magister*). There are parallels in Nonnus (13.277) and Servius (ad *G.* 1.14), who precedes his statement about the worship of Aristaeus as Zeus with the information, derived from Pindar (fr. 251 Snell), that Aristaeus migrated to Arcadia from Ceos. Arcadia was also an important location for the worship of Apollo Νόμιος, whose connection with Aristaeus is asserted at Pindar, *Pyth.* 9.63ff. and Servius ad *G.* 1.14: Cic. *Nat. D.* 3.57.

associated with *both* Zeus and Apollo.[117] A scholiast of Apollonius relates him to both, but more closely to Zeus.[118] If for no other reason the identification with Zeus would have been familiar to Virgil's contemporaries since it featured in an episode of Callimachus' *Aetia* which was popular enough to stand for Callimachus' entire opus (Ov. *Rem. Am.* 382): the *Acontius and Cydippe. Aet.* fr. 75.30–7 Pf. traces the ancestry of Acontius back to the priests of 'Zeus Aristaeus the Icmian'. The myth told how Aristaeus put an end to a plague which afflicted the island of Ceos as a consequence of the heat of Sirius. Aristaeus built an altar to Zeus Icmaeus, god of rain, after which Zeus caused the Etesian Winds to blow for forty days after the rise of the Dog-Star (cf. Ap. Rhod. *Argon.* 2.516–27). Aristaeus and Zeus apparently became indistinguishable and were worshipped as one. Clearly the detail of plague and the elemental colouring of the myth have a resonance in *G.* 4, and indeed the story is gestured at in 425, *iam rapidus torrens . . . Sirius.*[119]

As *artifices*, anyway, both Jupiter and Aristaeus correspond to the underlying metaphor of the Stoic δημιουργός, and also for that matter to Zeno's πῦρ τεχνικόν, which, we recall, Cicero translated as *ignis artificiosus*. The verb *extundere* (315) – with its resonance of workmanship – appears only once more in Virgil's works, at *Aen.* 8.665, where it describes the activity of Vulcan, another demiurgic figure.[120]

What this tells us about the depiction of Octavian in the poem I shall consider later. But for now I turn to the culmination of the tale of Proteus, and of the Stoic-coloured allegoresis of it: Proteus' transformations. These were supposed to represent the differentiated elements of the recreated universe,

---

[117] *Pro Christ.* 14, Κεῖοι Ἀρισταῖον· τὸν αὐτὸν καὶ Δία καὶ Ἀπόλλω νομίζοντες.

[118] Σ *Argon.* 2.500: Ζεὺς Ἀρισταῖος ἐκλήθη καὶ Ἀπόλλων Ἀγριεὺς καὶ Νόμιος. In other words, Aristaeus is the cult-name of Zeus when he is closely related to Apollo Nomius.

[119] The description of the effects of Sirius at *Aen.* 3.141–2 significantly refers back to this passage. Compare *G.* 4.427 and *Aen.* 3.142.

[120] Thomas (1988) ad loc.; Hardie (1986) 340.

and indeed Virgil's version is more explicitly elemental.[121] But in Chapter 1 I isolated Virgil's versions of the metamorphoses, along with the innovatory *uincula*, as notable diversions from his Homeric model. I suggested at the time that the creatures which occupy the place of Homer's lion and panther – the tigress and lioness – establish a link with the great portrayal of a world afflicted by destructive violence, the 'fire of love' at 3.242–83.[122] In this passage *amor*, as Ross points out, is equated with *fire*, and as such is seen to dominate all other elements. At 3.242–8 we are told,

> omne adeo genus in terris hominumque ferarumque
> et genus aequoreum, pecudes pictaeque uolucres,
> *in furias ignemque ruunt*: amor omnibus idem.
> tempore non alio catulorum oblita leaena
> saeuior errauit campis . . .
> . . . tum saeuus aper, tum pessima tigris

Every race on earth, of men and animals, and the race of the sea, herds and colourful birds, rush headlong into madness and fire. Love is the same for all. At no other time does the lioness, forgetful of her cubs, roam more savagely over the plains . . . Then the boar is savage, then the tigress is at her worst.

Love, portrayed as fire, controls all creatures of the three remaining elements, earth, water and air;[123] the world thus depicted is hence one experiencing a radical imbalance of the elements. The first *exemplum* of this fundamental elemental disharmony is the lioness, closely followed by the boar and tigress. Similarly at 432–4 the snake, inhabitant of earth and water (430), is turned savage by the parching effects of heat, which cracks the earth and evaporates his watery habitat (432). The treatment of snakes blends, as we have noted, with the description of plague which follows; and plague, like the maddened snake, is an embodiment of the destructive power of fire. Once again creatures of every other element succumb

---

[121] Cf. Thomas (1988) ad 409–10 on Virgil's change of the metamorphoses into water and a tree in Homer's longer description to fire and water, which 'better suits the emphasis on extremes of the various elements in the second half of the book'.

[122] Ross (1987) 157–67, 177–83.

[123] Ross (1987) 164.

to the *sacer ignis* (566) of disease, in the sea, on the earth and in the air (541–7).[124] Proteus' transformations can represent the elements, then, but there is a further point: when the actions of Aristaeus are compared to the effects of *amor* – and indeed of plague[125] – the result is to suggest the paradoxically constructive power of what had seemed earlier in the poem to be merely destructive. Stoic theory postulated an alternation in world-history between elemental balance and the domination of the other elements by the fiery principle which destroyed but also recreated the universe. Virgil's adaptation of the Proteus episode thus (I would suggest) deliberately recalls a scene of elemental disharmony, of the tyranny of a single element, fire, over all others, of what might justly be called an *ecpyrosis* by the *sacer ignis* of love and plague. Virgil points up the paradoxical quality of *ecpyrosis*: that which destroys simultaneously creates; violence which appeared arbitrary is purposeful.[126]

VIII

From here it is only a short step to seeing reflected in the demiurgic renovator of the cosmos Octavian himself: as Hardie makes clear, the whole tenor of the 'universal' imagery pervading the epic *Aeneid* is to identify the political with the cosmic, the national with the global, *urbs* and *orbis*.[127] The common ground between the Octavian of his own propaganda, initiating a new age, and a Zeus-like cosmic monarch recreating absolutely everything, is self-evident; and it would certainly not be the first occasion such a connection was made, even in this poem. On two occasions in particular, appropriately in the prologue and the epilogue, Virgil makes

---

[124] Ross (1987) 182.
[125] See p. 106 below.
[126] Compare Gransden (1976) 39–40 on the potential of fire either to destroy or create in *Aen.* 8. It is creative, according to Gransden, when brought under the control of a figure like Hercules. Aristaeus' constructive use of otherwise destructive forces places him in a similar demiurgic light.
[127] Hardie (1986) 364–6.

the ultimate propagandistic statement (which Thomas some-how manages to construe as ambivalent)[128] that Octavian is identifiable with Jupiter. At 1.24–42 Octavian appears to have taken Jupiter's place in the introductory prayer,[129] in the latter's absence; and at 4.559–61 Virgil pays Octavian a highly subtle compliment with the same implication:

> haec super aruorum cultu pecorumque canebam
> et super arboribus, Caesar dum magnus ad altum
> fulminat Euphraten

I sang this song on the care of fields and herds and on trees whilst great Caesar lightened at the deep Euphrates

The verb *fulminat*, unprecedented as a description of anyone's activity but Jupiter's,[130] points us towards Callimachus' cele-brated epigram in the *Aetia* (fr. 1.20 Pf.), βροντᾶν οὐκ ἐμόν, ἀλλὰ Διός. Octavian's thundering, by contrast, is entirely ap-propriate, since (it is implied) he is analogous to Jupiter.[131] And besides the start and end of the poem, in the middle as well (3.13–16) we find a temple being built to be occupied by Caesar.

IX

There are perhaps other reasons why we might expect allegory in the *Aristaeus*. Damien Nelis has pointed out the verbal similarities between *G.* 4 and the first book of the *Aeneid*.[132] In particular he has demonstrated the 'highly allusive and subtle connections'[133] which occur between the song of Cly-mene in the *Georgics* (345–7) and the song of Iopas at *Aen.* 1.742–6. Both Virgilian songs, he argues, are related to the

---

[128] Thomas (1988) ad 4. 560–1.
[129] Thomas (1988) ad loc.
[130] Thomas (1988) ad loc.
[131] On thunder/lightning as the peculiar weapon of Jupiter (and as a token of the epic genre), see Ov. *Am.* 2.1.11–18; and see pp. 214–15 below.
[132] Nelis (1992a), Nadeau (1984) also noted the similarities, though his conclusions were somewhat different.
[133] Nelis (1992a) 10.

much allegorized 'Lay of Demodocus' concerning the affair of Ares and Aphrodite at *Od.* 8.266–366, Clymene's song explicitly (she tells a variant of Demodocus' story)[134] and Iopas' both through its context (Dido's banquet, during which Iopas sings, is modelled on the banquet of Alcinous, the context of Demodocus' 'lay')[135] and via the mediation of Apollonius' song of Orpheus at *Argon.* 1.496–511, which as Nelis argues elsewhere is a 'de-allegorized' version of Demodocus' song unveiling the 'true' meaning – as explicated by allegorists such as Ps.-Heraclitus (69) – of the superficially blasphemous Homeric myth.[136] Demodocus' song was interpreted by allegorists as a prefiguration of Empedocles' theory that the universe originated from a constant struggle between the contrary cosmic principles of Love and Strife, identified, respectively, with Aphrodite and Ares. When Apollonius starts Orpheus' song with a cosmogony by νεῖκος (498), Nelis suggests, he is gesturing at the allegorized version of the Homeric song.

Apollonius' song of Orpheus fuses aspects of the song of Demodocus with references to the Shield of Achilles, the other Homeric passage commonly interpreted as an allegory of Empedoclean *Neikos* and *Philia*.[137] The song of Iopas, besides imitating Orpheus' song, also alludes to these two Homeric contexts.[138] Lines 742, 744 and 745 of Iopas' short song recall *Il.* 18.484, 486–7 and 489. *Aen.* 1.742 also recalls *G.* 2.478, and *Aen.* 1.745–6, *quid tantum Oceano properent*

---

[134] The variant seems subtly to gesture at the original. The amatory associations of *cura* (345) point to Hephaestus' unrequited *love* in Demodocus' song: Hardie (1986) 83; *dolos* (346) perhaps also suggests the δόλος much in evidence in the *Odyssey* passage; see *Od.* 8.276, 282, 317. As Farrell (1991) 271 suggests, the song of Clymene seems deliberately to evoke both the cosmological preoccupations of epic and the love theme of recent, Neoteric poetry, the effect being to assimilate these two (conventionally incompatible) modes of poetry. This, as both Farrell and I argue, is an important part of the programme of the Aristaeus: see p. 184 below.

[135] Farrell (1991) 259.

[136] Nelis (1992b).

[137] Nelis (1992b) 158: compare, in particular, *Argon.* 1.496 and *Il.* 18.483.

[138] Nelis (1992a) 11–12.

se tingere soles | hiberni, uel quae tardis mora noctibus obstet,
are repeated verbatim from *G.* 2.481–2,[139] the context of the
poetic dilemma between the themes of agriculture and natural
philosophy.

If its position in this network of cosmogonical songs
is a strong indication that Clymene's song has a natural-
philosophic dimension, then this is perhaps confirmed by the
final detail of Virgil's description. The *amour* of Mars and
Venus, it turns out, is only one of a catalogue of *amores*
described by Clymene from Creation on: *a … Chao* (347).
This reference to the beginning of the universe, Nelis argues,
makes it clear that Virgil and his readership were fully aware
of the allegorical reading of Demodocus' song. Clymene's
song is termed by Hardie a 'cosmic overture', presenting the
theme of the *Aristaeus* – generation or creation – in a general
form as a prelude to the detailed treatment of the issue which
follows.[140] We can perhaps add that the *nature* of this theme
is also anticipated: it is a specimen of natural philosophy,
apparently indebted to the allegoresis of Homer.

Finally Farrell, working along similar lines to Nelis, has
argued that other Homeric references in the *Aristaeus* also
should be interpreted in terms of allegorical (and specifically
natural-philosophical) exegesis of Homer. Virgil models Aristaeus' encounter with Cyrene on Achilles' two meetings with
Thetis, Farrell suggests, because each Homeric episode introduces a passage – the insurrection against Zeus (*Il.* 1.396–
406) and the Shield of Achilles (*Il.* 18.478–613) – which were
interpreted as allegories of Creation. Virgil's episode, Farrell
continues, also introduces an allegory of Creation: the Proteus
episode. Farrell considers that the allusions in Clymene's song
to another allegorized passage, the affair of Ares and Aphrodite, and the cosmogonical Ocean references at 381–2 have a
related function, namely to alert the reader to an allegorical
dimension in the poetry which follows.[141]

---

[139] Farrell (1991) 259. [140] Hardie (1986) 83–4.
[141] Farrell (1991) 258–72.

X

Another text from earlier in the *Georgics* which I have tried to relate to the *Aristaeus* is the prologue to Book 3. The requirement for a *poetic* victory, I argued, was quite adequately fulfilled by the emulation of Homer undertaken by Virgil in his Proteus episode; but I suggested that the passage as a whole would not comply with Virgil's prediction in the prologue unless in the process of emulating Homer Virgil also honoured Octavian: the victory which he predicts for himself was precisely to involve giving adequate glory to the triumphs of Octavian. My interpretation of the Proteus episode, I wish to argue, meets these criteria: Virgil's victory, the appropriation of the Homeric source, is simultaneous with – is in fact the very same undertaking as – his depiction of a figure who broadly reflects the person and achievements of Octavian figuratively bringing about the recreation of the cosmos. Virgil finds the style – Grand Epic – to eulogize Octavian, and eulogizes him, all at the very same time. We find in the *Proteus* the two figures, ruler and poet, in the same close association we have seen throughout the work: Virgil a poet who has now mastered the highest genre of poetry, the Homeric poetry of war, power and natural science; and Octavian the ultimate object of that style of poetry, the summit of Stoic cosmology, the demiurge, θεός, Jupiter. The parallel and potentially conflicting requirements of an epic poet – to panegyrize and to deal in cosmic subjects – dovetail in the assimilation of the object of praise, Octavian, and the greatest power of the universe, Jupiter: a process elucidated at length by Hardie with regard to the *Aeneid*.[142]

The whole is clearly an excellent example of Godo Lieberg's assimilation of poet and subject.[143] Virgil is engaged in a parallel programme to the *princeps*, achieving a renewal on Roman terms in the poetic field (by emulating Homer in the Latin language) just as Octavian is in the military and

---

[142] Hardie (1986) *passim*.   [143] Lieberg (1982).

political by subjugating the world to Roman order. But I have tried to push the analogy a little further. Lieberg's achievement has been to establish the prevalence – in Virgil's poetry especially – of a conception of poetry as sorcery, capable of conjuring up its own reality. Similar schemes are discernible elsewhere in poetry of this period. Thus Lucretius, for example, establishes an identification of his poem and the universe it describes: the *DRN* is a microcosm.[144] It is on this analogy – the identification of artistic depiction and real action – that I have suggested Homer might be understood as *pater rerum*. Homer, as the poet of unlimited range – the poet of the universe, the *Weltdichter* – is also, through the magic power of poetry, the *creator* of what he describes, namely the creator of the universe. He is himself – without mediation – *pater rerum*. Virgil's appropriation of Homer's universal poetic power is thus closely comparable to Aristaeus/Octavian's appropriation of the creative power of the *physical* universe. He is the Homeric *poeta creator* to the Jupiter-like Octavian.

XI

I have thus attempted to read the *Aristaeus*, and in particular the Proteus episode, in terms of two passages elsewhere in the *Georgics*: the prologue to Book 3 and the song of Clymene. In each I identified the theme I see as central to the meaning of the *Aristaeus*: creation, beginning, source. The relevance of this theme has been widely recognized.[145] I now wish to suggest another passage which may foreshadow the theme.

At 285–6 Virgil presents the following preamble to the coming myth: *altius omnem | expediam prima repetens ab origine famam*. 'I shall unfold the entire tale in greater depth, starting from the very beginning' would be a reasonable provisional translation. But Thomas has divined a hidden agenda

---

[144] Schrijvers (1970) 64. On the Lucretian microcosm see further Schiesaro (1994).

[145] Nelis (1992a) 15–16, for example, locates the essential similarity between *G.* 4 and *Aen.* 1 in the shared theme of *renewal*.

behind the *altius* of 285;[146] and it transpires that the rest of the sentence, also, is open to variant interpretation. Ostensibly it is an undertaking not to treat the myth of the *Aristaeus* superficially. But Hinds has recently demonstrated the prismatic suggestiveness of the term *origo* with reference to Ovid's account of the 'creation' (or αἴτιον, or even 'etymology') of the Hippocrene.[147] Here in Virgil's text we might be tempted to share Thomas' view that there is at least one sense of *origo* in operation beyond that of the 'beginning' (of the story): perhaps here, as at *Ecl.* 6.72 (and *Met* 5.262),[148] *origo* carries the implication of *aetiology*, the narrative mode especially associated with Callimachus.[149] Such suspicions are fully confirmed as the myth develops: the ensuing story concerns the αἴτιον of *bugonia*.

So the (apparently) well-established aetiological associations of the word[150] broach the semantic issue, so to speak. But can we tease out other implications of the expression?

The polysemy of *origo* was clearly valued by Latin authors, as Hinds has established. Alongside its use to render the Greek αἴτιον, for instance, is a common assimilation of the word to the Greek γένεσις, 'coming-to-be'. In Cicero's *Timaeus*, for example, it corresponds in at least three places to γένεσις in the Platonic original.[151] Γένεσις, of course, was a word with a broad field of reference. In these cases the sense picked up by *origo* is that of a specifically cosmic coming-to-be – the creation of the universe – rather than, for example, an individual's birth (which is the primary sense of the word at *G.* 3.48). This usage of *origo* can easily be paralleled elsewhere. Lucretius, Virgil, Ovid and Seneca all talk of Creation as the *origo mundi*,[152] and in the bilingual so-called Philoxenus

---

[146] Thomas (1988) ad loc.: 'it should perhaps be taken "in a higher mode", an entirely legitimate characterization of the style of the rest of the book'.

[147] Hinds (1987) 4–6; on *origo* and other aetiological phraseology in Ovid's *Met.* and *Fasti* see Myers (1994) 63–7.

[148] Hinds (1987) 4–5.

[149] Thomas (1988) ad loc.

[150] Hinds (1987) 5 calls it 'quasi-technical'.

[151] 3, = 28a; 9, = 29d; 29, = 38c.

[152] Lucr. *DRN* 5.548; Virg. *G.* 2.336; Ov. *Met.* 1.3; Sen. *Q Nat.* 3.29.3.

glossary *origo* is equated with ἀρχαιογονία, another term commonly used of the Creation.[153] Here we may be reminded of the allegoresis of the capture of Proteus as the Creation.

Elsewhere it is the foundation of political units which is rendered by *origo*, another sense very germane to the preoccupations of the *Aristaeus*. Thus Cato's *Origines* dealt with the κτίσεις of the Italian *ciuitates*. Similarly Donatus' *Vita* of Virgil (80) explains that the *Aeneid* tells of *Romanae simul urbis et Augusti origo*. There is also a wealth of examples where *origo* is essentially synonymous with *fons*,[154] connoting an aquatic source of some kind, commonly a spring. Thus in Pliny's contribution to the long-running debate concerning the source of the Nile (*HN* 5.10.51) the river is *incertis ortus fontibus*, but as far as King Juba of Numidia could ascertain, *originem ... in monte inferioris Mauretaniae ... habet*. Parallels with the source of the river Peneus are tempting, but perhaps also something more. A passage of Quintilian which employs the image of Homer as Ocean offers quite a similar expression. The word *ortus* is clearly cognate with *origo*, and as Cicero's phrase *ortus mundi* shows (*Tim.* 3) close also in meaning. Quintilian writes (*Inst.* 10.1.46), *hic enim, quemadmodum ex Oceano dicit ipse omnium amnium fontiumque cursus initium capere, omnibus eloquentiae partibus exemplum et ortum dedit*, 'in the same way as in his own account it was from Ocean that the courses of every river and spring took their beginning, so he gave to every department of rhetoric a model and a source'. Again, then, an allusion to Virgil's imitation of Homer, source of all poetry, is not impossible.[155] So a couple more interpretations of the phrase *prima ab origine*, alongside *origo*-αἴτιον, seem available: *origo*-κτίσις, *origo*-πηγή and *origo*-γένεσις can also be seen as motifs which occur in the *Aristaeus*. The same phrase also provides further

---

[153] Clearly, also, if *origo* is easily assimilated to words cognate with γίγνομαι, this may be another respect in which *origo* looks to the βουγονία, the γένεσις of bees from a βοῦς.

[154] Hinds (1987) 4–6; Hor. *Carm.* 4.14.45.

[155] We may note that Virgil undertakes to trace back all *fama* from its first origin: on the connections of *fama* to the compositions of poets see Hardie (1986) 275.

grounds for assimilating Virgil's predicted commission in the prologue to Book 3 and the *Aristaeus*. At 3.46–8 Virgil undertakes to extend his own and Caesar's[156] fame as far into the future as Caesar is from the 'first origin of Tithonus': *et nomen fama tot ferre per annos | Tithoni prima quot abest ab origine Caesar*. The expression is the same as at 4.286. Thomas understands a reference to Troy, Tithonus' homeland, and thus to the plot of the *Aeneid*. Servius, however, picks up on another indubitable implication of the expression. Tithonus is of inconceivably great age: his *origo*, then, according to Servius is figuratively equivalent to the *mundi principium*, and indeed this is also the reference of the expression *prima ab origine* when it first appears in the poem at 2.336. If Servius is correct, 3.48 seems to anticipate the cosmogonical doctrines of the *Aristaeus*, and also seems strongly to assimilate the prediction of the prologue to Book 3 and the end of Book 4.

But what *prima ab origine* at 4.285–6 might also do is foreshadow the universal scheme which I have suggested is introduced by the mechanism of Ocean, *pater rerum*, a figure who encompasses the entire universe, the source of everything there is. During the *Aristaeus* both protagonist and poet appear to be engaged with a totality: the poetic universality represented by Homer, and the physical represented by the cosmological allegoresis of his poetry, stretching back to the origins of the entire universe.[157]

---

[156] For the dual reference see p. 97 above.

[157] Other occurrences of the phrase *prima ab origine* seem to parallel this 'totalizing' force: at Lucr. 5.548; at *Aen.* 1.372, where it is interestingly coupled with the word *annales* (as pointed out to me by Debra Hershkowitz); at *Aen.* 1.753, just before Aeneas' narrative and just after the song of Iopas, like the song of Clymene a 'cosmic overture' (Hardie [1986] 66) providing for what follows it a universal framework; at *Met.* 1.3: see Myers (1994) 6; at Luc. 6.611, spoken by Erictho, who has 'at [her] disposal a complete grasp of history and time, a kind of ideal model of the universal epic': Hardie (1993) 108; Masters (1992) 179–215.

PART TWO

MIRABILE DICTU

It is good for the world that such things should be done. The old heart of the earth needed to be warmed with the red wine of the battlefield. Such august homage was never before offered to God as this, the homage of millions of lives given gladly for love of country.

Pádraic Pearse, December 1915, in *Political Writings and Speeches* (Dublin, 1952), 216.

CHAPTER 3

OX AND PARADOX

I

I have argued in my previous chapter that Aristaeus' capture of Proteus has propagandistic implications over and above those commonly recognized by critics. Through Proteus, I suggested, Virgil relates Octavian's acquisition of power in Rome to the creation of the universe and specifically to the dissolution and rebirth – ἐκπύρωσις and παλιγγενεσία – periodically experienced, according to Stoic cosmological theory, by the physical universe. I offered a number of reasons for supposing that the allegorical interpretation of Homer's Proteus episode preserved for us in the *Quaest. Hom.* and elsewhere was relevant also to Virgil's episode, reasons gleaned, in particular, from the work of Hardie, Farrell and Nelis. But ultimately, perhaps, the most cogent grounds for reading Virgil's Proteus allegorically are those of pertinence: like Farrell I consider the central theme of the allegory of Proteus – cosmogony – simply too germane to the preoccupations of the *Aristaeus* to be coincidental. What I want to investigate next is whether the particular (Stoic) model of cosmogony which I have argued Virgil employed in this context might yield other illuminating parallels to the events described in the *Aristaeus*. Is a general shared theme of 'rebirth', in other words, the limit of the resemblance between *bugonia* and Stoic cosmogony?

As many critics have noted, *bugonia* is a particularly uncompromising version of regeneration. A bullock must be killed from which the new swarm will be created, and it must be killed in a singularly brutal fashion.[1] Virgil's version of the

---

[1] Cf. pp. 12–13 above.

capture of Proteus, similarly, I have suggested, seems actually to advertise the high degree of violence it requires of Aristaeus.[2] Furthermore, the processes of *bugonia* are described in terms apparently deliberately designed to assimilate them to the destructive phenomena of plague and passionate love in Book 3.[3] How can we explain this heavy emphasis on the (destructive) violence of Aristaeus' actions?

My first point would be that in the Stoic theory of creation, at any rate, violence is far from being a straightforwardly *bad* thing. At the core of it is a striking paradox: destruction and creation are actually inseparable. The Stoic palingenesis, as we have seen, was part of the same process as the annihilation of the pre-existing cosmos. In fact the fire which destroyed the previous universe simultaneously set in place the conditions for a new one to be born. *SVF* 1.98 summarizes the theory succinctly: κατά τινας εἱμαρμένους χρόνους ἐκπυροῦσθαι τὸν σύμπαντα κόσμον, εἶτ' αὖθις πάλιν διακοσμεῖσθαι, 'at certain fated times the whole universe is completely consumed by fire, and then it is again made into an ordered universe'. Chaos, on this Stoic model, was not a contradiction of order so much as a *prerequisite* of it, a *sine qua non*. In Seneca's memorable formulation (referring to his *two*, alternating principles of destruction, conflagration and flood),[4] *utrumque fit, cum deo uisum ordiri meliora, uetera finiri. aqua et ignis terrenis dominantur; ex his ortus, ex his interitus est*, 'each will happen when it seems best to god for better things to begin and old things to end. Water and fire dominate earthly things: from them is the origin, from them the destruction' (*Q Nat.* 3.28.7). Cosmic order for the Stoics, as Schofield has put it,[5] was a *function* of change and disorder, cosmic peace a function of violence. Total dissolution by fire was a necessary precursor of an ordered new world.

---

[2] Pp. 44–6 above. See, for example, Ross (1987) 218–19 on the 'extraordinary' violence of *bugonia*.
[3] Miles (1980) 253. Compare *G.* 3.271–2 (love) and 484–5 (plague) with 4.301–2, 308–9 and 555. And see Thomas (1988) ad 4.301–2, 308–9.
[4] See p. 86 n. 108 above.
[5] Schofield (1991) 80, and see p. 86 above.

Now Florus relates the Civil War between Caesar and Pompey to the Stoic dissolution of the cosmos (*Epit.* 2.13.3–4):[6]

Caesaris furor atque Pompei urbem Italiam, gentes nationes, totum denique qua patebat imperium quodam quasi diluuio et inflammatione corripuit, adeo ut non recte tantum ciuile dicatur, ac ne sociale quidem, sed nec externum, sed potius commune quoddam ex omnibus et plus quam bellum.

The frenzy of Caesar and Pompey affected Rome, Italy, tribes, nations, ultimately the whole extent of the empire as if with flood and conflagration, to the extent that it is not correctly termed only a civil war, nor a war between allies, nor even a foreign war, but rather a war sharing all these characteristics and something more than a war.

Subsequently Florus uses the imagery of cosmic *order* to describe the rule of Augustus (*Epit.* 2.14.5–6): *imperii corpus, quod haud dubie numquam coire et consentire potuisset, nisi unius praesidis nutu quasi anima et mente regeretur*, 'the body of the empire, which without doubt would never have been able to enjoy coherence and harmony if it were not controlled by the will of a single ruler, as if by its soul and mind'. In fact, as we have seen, cosmic order was according to Stoic theory a function of the periodic disorder which the universe underwent. In the process of asserting that order the active principle destroyed the previous instantiation of the universe. There is in other words (strictly speaking) a missing link here, and it is a missing link which I wish to suggest the imagery of the *Georgics* furnishes. Whilst Florus equates civil war and cosmic *disorder* on the one hand, and Augustan peace and cosmic *order* on the other, Virgil, I shall argue, presents the Civil Wars as a catastrophic cosmic dissolution, as Florus does, but yet as a destruction which is the necessary prerequisite of the restoration of order. A provisional explanation is thus offered of the strange description of *bugonia* which seemed to replicate the highly destructive principles – love in particular – figured in Book 3: the phenomenon which destroyed the farmer's concerns in Book 3 recreates them in Book 4. Virgil

---

[6] Hardie (1986) 383. Comparable is Lucan's assimilation of civil war to cosmic catastrophe, on which see Lapidge (1979).

is arguing the paradoxical power for good of highly destructive events, chief of which at this time in his readers' minds must have been the Civil Wars. Like the Stoic cosmogony, he seeks to suggest, these were a paradoxical process whereby destruction brought about creation. Miles arrived at a similar conclusion from his consideration of the extreme violence of the process of *bugonia*:

The *bugonia* extends these ideas further with the paradox that destruction is actually a necessary condition for creation, that life is impossible without death. In the *bugonia* that paradox is expressed precisely and vividly: in order to achieve his end the beekeeper must perform a particularly brutal and repugnant sacrifice.[7]

II

At 2.536–7 Virgil presents two events which marked the catastrophic disappearance of the Saturnian or Golden Age and the onset of the debased Iron Age. These events are the accession to power of Jupiter and the first consumption of beef: *ante etiam sceptrum Dictaei regis et ante | impia quam caesis gens est epulata iuuencis*, 'before the dominion of the Cretan king and before an evil race feasted on slaughtered oxen'. The detail about eating oxen is derived by Virgil from Aratus, *Phaen.* 132. At 96–136 Aratus discusses the constellation Virgo or Astraea. She is often identified with Justice, Aratus informs us, and he proceeds to relate the story of her catasterism. During the Golden Age, and also during the Silver Age (though less willingly), Justice-Astraea dwelt on earth, amongst humans. With the onset of the Bronze Age, however, the corruption of the human race became such that Justice abandoned it and took refuge in the heavens (129–34):

> ἀλλ' ὅτε δὴ κἀκεῖνοι ἐτέθνασαν, οἱ δ' ἐγένοντο,
> χαλκείη γενεή, προτέρων ὀλοώτεροι ἄνδρες,
> οἳ πρῶτοι κακόεργον ἐχαλκεύσαντο μάχαιραν
> εἰνοδίην, πρῶτοι δὲ βοῶν ἐπάσαντ' ἀροτήρων.
> καὶ τότε μισήσασα Δίκη κείνων γένος ἀνδρῶν
> ἔπταθ' ὑπουρανίη.

---

[7] Miles (1980) 254; cf. 284.

But when they [sc. the Silver Race] too were dead, and when, more ruinous than those who went before, the Race of Bronze was born, who were the first to forge the dagger of the highwayman, and the first to eat the flesh of the ploughing-ox, then indeed Justice, loathing that race of men, flew up to heaven.

Why should eating plough-oxen have had such catastrophic consequences? The explanation lies in the proverbial intimacy of the ox's relationship with the farmer. We find numerous references in ancient texts to a pre-eminence among domestic animals attributed to the ox which is such as to accord oxen a status almost equivalent to humans. According to Varro (*Rust.* 2.5.3; cf. Columella 6 *praef.* 7), killing an ox had in the past been a capital offence. The ox was the *socius hominum in rustico opere*, 'the partner of mankind in agricultural work', and as such equivalent to, and as inviolable as, a human fellow-worker. Similarly, Pliny the Elder cites a case where a man who killed an ox, his *socium ... laboris agrique culturae*, 'partner in work and agriculture', had been punished just as if he had killed his farm-labourer (*HN* 8.180; cf. Val. Max. 8.1 *damnat.* 8). Ovid also has Pythagoras make much of this close relationship between man and ox (*Met.* 15.120–42). Aelian makes the point explicit, stating that in Athens it was not permitted to sacrifice a plough-ox, ὅτι καὶ οὗτος εἴη ἂν γεωργὸς καὶ τῶν ἐν ἀνθρώποις καμάτων κοινωνός, 'because it also was a farmer and partner in human labours' (*VH* 5.14; cf. *NA* 2.57).[8]

This is why Aratus specifies the plough-ox, βοῦς ἀροτήρ,[9] as the victim of the crime; and there would seem to be the same implication of the intimacy of farmer and plough-ox, and thus the near-fratricidal nature of the ox's demise, in the *Georgics*. Repeatedly in the poem (1.45, 65, 210; 2.206, 237 and 357; 3.50, 515) Virgil presents cattle in their role as plough-animals. Just prior to the description of their consumption Virgil depicts these *meriti iuuenci*, 'deserving oxen',

---

[8] For other statements of the inviolability of oxen see Ampolo (1980) 46; Habinek (1990) 222 n. 22.
[9] Aratus' phrase is the same as that at Hes. *Op.* 405, the famous passage where Hesiod appears to equate wife and plough-ox in importance for the farmer.

as one of the easy responsibilities of the idyllic farmer's life (514–15), almost as members of the family: *patriam paruosque nepotes | sustinet,* . . . *armenta boum meritosque iuuencos,* 'He sustains his fatherland and little grandsons, . . . his herds of cattle and deserving oxen.' It is with the ox also, naturally, that Virgil goes furthest in the poem (with the possible exception of the bee) in the process of assimilating beast to man delineated by Gale.[10] In Book 3, in particular, during his discussion of the husbandry of cattle, and in the set pieces concerning *amor* and the plague, the 'anthropomorphizing vocabulary'[11] Virgil employs of oxen serves to equate their experiences closely with those of humans. Gale describes how when the death-by-plague of the plough-ox is depicted (515–30) – a clear reflection of the transgressive killing of the plough-ox at an equivalent point of Book 2 – the emotions of the dying bull's yoke-fellow, on which Virgil concentrates, seem to coincide with those of the ploughman, the *tristis arator* (517–18): *it tristis arator, | maerentem abiungens fraterna morte iuuencum,* 'sadly the ploughman goes, unyoking the mourning ox from his brother's death'.[12] The ox is practically human, practically a workmate, practically here a brother to the ploughman. Of Virgil's description of the killing of oxen Mynors says, 'as an example of *impietas,* we could not ask for better'. *Impietas* is a 'failure in a sense of obligation, duty, respect, etc.':[13] the plough-ox deserves all respect for his fellowship, yet instead is slaughtered and eaten.

The consequences of the act are proportionate to its wickedness. In Virgil's model here, Aratus, the eating of plough-oxen marks the final sundering of relations between the human and divine spheres – the departure of Justice – and the consequent end of the Silver Age, an era not as idyllic as the Golden Age but infinitely preferable to the Bronze Age which ensued. In the *Georgics* the consequences of the action

---

[10] Gale (1991).

[11] Gale (1991) 417. Outside Virgil the terms *iuuenca* and *iuuencus* are also found used directly of young *people*: see Hor. *Carm.* 2.5.6, 8.21.

[12] Gale (1991) 422.

[13] *OLD* s.v.

are more dramatic: the eating of the oxen concludes the Golden, Saturnian Age and directly ushers in the Iron (536–40). It marks the pagan Fall from Grace of the human race.

And that would rather seem to be that – catastrophe, full stop – except that, as we have already seen,[14] this is not the only instance in Virgil's corpus of the expression *caesi iuuenci*. The same expression in fact occurs three more times in Virgil's works, at *G.* 3.23, 4.284 and *Aen.* 8.719, and – strikingly – on each subsequent occasion it signifies something unequivocally positive. Thus at *G.* 3.22–3, *iam nunc sollemnis ducere pompas | ad delubra iuuat caesosque uidere iuuencos* ('even now it is a joy to lead the solemn procession to the sanctuary, and see the oxen slaughtered'), the identical expression, *caesi iuuenci*, is recontextualized to denote the sacrifices on the occasion of Virgil's imagined poetic victory or triumph, a scene undoubtedly largely based on the triple triumph celebrated by Octavian on his return from the East in 29 BC. Another occurrence of the phrase, at *Aen.* 8.719, *directly* describes the events of the triple triumph: *ante aras terram caesi strauere iuuenci*, 'before the altars slaughtered oxen strewed the ground'. But perhaps the most striking reoccurrence of the expression is in *G.* 4. At 281–6 Virgil introduces his description of the remedy for the total extinction of a bee-swarm by disease. What this remedy turns out to be is of course *bugonia*, a process whereby an ox is slain and its flesh pummelled to liquefaction. From this flesh emerges a new swarm of bees. At 284–5 the process is summarized in advance: *quoque modo caesis iam saepe iuuencis | insincerus apes tulerit cruor*, 'it is also time to reveal the notable discovery of the Arcadian master, and the method whereby often in the past the corrupt gore of slaughtered oxen has engendered bees'. Thus – by slaughtering oxen – is the bee-swarm which had been destroyed by disease triumphantly restored by Aristaeus at the end of the poem. In this way are the fractured relations between the divine and human realms restored (534–6), and everything apparently put to rights. In short *this* ox-

---

[14] See pp. 52–3 above.

slaughter has the precisely opposite effect of the ox-slaughter which estranged Justice at the end of Book 2. Whilst one was the archetypal calamity, this is the ultimate solution.

III

Suetonius records the emperor Domitian's hysterical response to the first instance of the expression *caesi iuuenci* in *G.* 2 (*Dom.* 9.1):

inter initia usque adeo ab omni caede abhorrebat, ut absente adhuc patre recordatus Vergili uersum:
> impia quam caesis gens est epulata iuuencis
edicere destinarit, ne boues immolarentur.

To begin with Domitian was so repelled by all bloodshed that during the absence of his father, recalling the line of Virgil
> before an evil race feasted on slaughtered oxen
he planned to issue the edict that no oxen should be sacrificed.

Domitian, then, (quite rightly) discerned a connection between the instance of cattle-slaughter which marked the end of the Golden Age and the *sacrifice* of cattle. Furthermore, Habinek shows how Virgil assimilates *bugonia* to sacrifice. As he points out, there are two quite different descriptions of *bugonia* (4.295–314, 538–58). The first, according to Habinek, is an 'account of bees born from the blood of oxen that have been smothered', the second is one 'of bees born from the victims of a conventional Greco-Roman blood sacrifice'.[15] Virgil, Habinek concludes, is relating the consequences of *bugonia* to the effects of conventional sacrifice. (He actually considers Virgil's description of *bugonia* an *aetion* of sacrifice; and this is certainly Ovid's line at *Fast.* 1.362–80, where he may or may not have felt that he was innovating.) Habinek's reading is in essentials unquestionably right. Thomas has fiercely attacked his conclusions,[16] but his criticisms are only partially cogent. Thomas does nothing, for example, to account for the divergence between the first and second descriptions of *bugonia*. Even if – as Thomas does establish – the details of Aristaeus'

---

[15] Habinek (1990) 210.   [16] Thomas (1991).

ritual do not correspond quite as closely to conventional ox-sacrifice as Habinek suggests, nevertheless there is no question that the terms of the second description – altars, sanctuaries, vows, placation –[17] are at least very strongly *reminiscent* of sacrificial practice, more so at any rate than they are of the first description of *bugonia*.[18] However, where I think Thomas is correct to take issue with Habinek is when he disputes Habinek's suggestion that *every* example of ox-slaughter in the *Georgics* is straightforwardly sacrificial. The instance in Book 2 is not specifically a sacrifice: it remains ox-slaughter in general. Neither in Aratus nor in Cicero's translation of Aratus (*Nat. D.* 2.159, *et gustare manu uinctum domitumque iuuencum*) nor in the *Georgics* is the mythical instance of ox-slaughter which initiated the current, debased age particularized as sacrifice. Let us consider: at *G.* 3.22–3 and *Aen.* 8.719 the slaughter of oxen has to be carefully contextualized to yield a denotation of sacrifice, and *bugonia* has to be re-described in terms strongly redolent of sacrificial procedure for the connection to be felt. Ox-slaughter is thus not auto-matically sacrificial. Habinek I think senses this, and cites the supposedly religious overtones of the verb *epulor*. But as Thomas makes clear *epulor* does not do the specifying work Habinek needs it to.[19]

So on the one hand – *pace* Habinek (and *pace* Suetonius/ Domitian for that matter) – the cattle-slaughter in Book 2 is not a specifically sacrificial event. But on the other hand – *pace* Thomas this time – the repetition of the phrase *caesi iuuenci* clearly serves to assimilate the instances of construc-tive cattle-slaughter (sacrifice and *bugonia*) to an appalling crime at the dawn of the Iron Age. What, then, is Virgil's point?

A small deviation is in order. Habinek, we have seen, in-terprets 2.537 as strictly sacrificial. In this he is followed by Elsner, who in a discussion of the Ara Pacis Augustae argues that the sacrificial imagery of the Ara, far from propagating

---

[17] Habinek (1990) 212.
[18] Bettini (1991) 209 also considers the second *bugonia* essentially sacrificial.
[19] Habinek (1990) 222 n. 23; Thomas (1991) 214–15.

unproblematically Augustan ideology (as it was presumably designed to), in fact 'frames the emperor in a context of ideological uncertainties and contradictions'.[20] In support of his argument Elsner cites Habinek's interpretation of the repeated phrase *caesi iuuenci* at 2.537 and 3.23 as positive and negative evaluations of sacrifice: 'In Virgil's *Georgics*, "two interpretations of ox-slaughter – as impious crime and unifying ceremony – are balanced at the very centre" in the form of the sacrifices at II.536–7 and III.22–3.'[21] In his treatment of the sculptural decoration of the Ara, Elsner makes much of the 'ironic' fact that 'death itself must be the prophylactic barrier to death'.[22] The overwhelming emphasis of the monument on death is always liable, according to Elsner, to undercut any affirmative propagandistic message which it might be intended to disseminate. But my question is: is this a remotely adequate analysis of the institution of sacrifice? *Can* its significance be so easily subverted? Surely in fact to suggest that an onlooker might deconstruct the sacrificial imagery of the Ara in terms of 'the problematic of dying and the implicit negation by which death ... undermines life'[23] is rather like imagining a Catholic analysing (and finding wanting) the central paradox of the Eucharist in terms of 'the problematic of dying'. It is not so much that it does not or would not happen; it is simply that the 'problematic of death' is precisely the point both of the central Christian mystery and (to all appearances) Greco-Roman sacrifice. Miraculously and mysteriously life results from Christ's (or the sacrificial victim's) death. The supposed efficacy of sacrifice is (precisely) a paradox, and it is from this paradoxicality, presumably, that sacrifice, in its Christian and pagan forms, has derived its religious force: *credo quia absurdum*. Both the leading contemporary theorists of sacrifice, Girard and Burkert,[24] insist upon the focally paradoxical nature of the procedure. For Girard sac-

[20] Elsner (1991) 61.
[21] Elsner (1991) 58, citing Habinek (1990) 215.
[22] Elsner (1991) 58.
[23] Elsner (1991) 60.
[24] Girard (1972); Burkert (1972); see also the short expositions of their theories presented in Hamerton-Kelly (1987).

rifice is a form of socialized, constructive violence – a 'violence sainte, légitime'[25] – which engenders a general social and religious harmony: 'l'ordre, la paix et la fécondité'.[26] The 'étonnant paradoxe'[27] is that only (sacrificial) violence can put an end to violence.[28] Similarly, Burkert talks of the paradox embodied in the ritual that 'im Erlebnis des Tötens wird die Heiligkeit des Lebens erfahren'.[29] My interpretation of the repetition of the *caesi iuuenci* expression consequently follows a middle path between Habinek/Elsner and Thomas. What I suggest Virgil is doing here is not establishing an irresoluble antithesis between different attitudes to sacrifice, but in fact deliberately drawing out this paradoxical quality of sacrifice. Cattle-slaughter is an act of the utmost impiety; that same cattle-slaughter is a solution. And if we ask why Virgil is so emphatic about the paradoxicality of sacrifice an explanation is readily to hand. Throughout the *Georgics* disastrous events are presented which are clearly designed to reflect the recent cataclysmic Civil Wars. When Virgil depicts the slaughter of cattle as one such appalling event, but subsequently presents cattle-slaughter as constructive, he is implying the potential of the Civil Wars also – in a manner analogous to the miraculous processes of sacrifice – to be constructive.[30]

Burkert's discussion of the Athenian *Buphonia* may offer an instructive parallel here. This festival, in honour of Zeus 'of the City' (Διὶ Πολιεῖ), was held on the highest point of the Acropolis on the fourteenth day of the month of Skirophorion, in midsummer, and was thus the last major festival of the Athenian year.[31] The legend of its *aetion*, recorded by Porphyry (and perhaps traceable back to Theophrastus),[32] describes how in the time preceding the practice of blood-

---

[25] Girard (1972) 42.
[26] Girard (1972) 77.
[27] Girard (1972) 59.
[28] Girard (1972) 45: 'on ne peut pas se passer de la violence pour mettre fin à la violence'.
[29] Burkert (1972) 49.
[30] For the continuation of the theme of constructive destruction into *Aeneid* 8, where the fourth instance of *casei iuuenci* occurs, see Morgan (1998).
[31] Burkert (1972) 153–61.
[32] For Porphyry's sources see Burkert (1972) 155.

sacrifice one Sopatros (elsewhere Thaulon) slew a bull which interfered with a sacrifice involving inanimate offerings (*Abst.* 2.29–30). Drought ensued, and the Pythia was consulted. Her instructions to the Athenians were not to atone for the 'crime' but *repeat* it, and also eat the victim sacrificed in this fashion. Furthermore, in the course of the very same sacrifice in which the victim would die, the Pythia said, it would be resurrected, and this process was symbolized in the historical form of the ritual, Porphyry tells us, by the exhibition of the stuffed hide of the dead ox. For Burkert this ritual is a means for society to renew itself through periodic dissolution. Here, at the end of the agricultural year, the paradoxical logic of sacrifice demanded that the victim be 'der Arbeitsgenosse des Bauern',[33] the *socius hominum in rustico opere* (Varro, *Rust.* 2.5.3), the plough-ox.

The *aetion* of sacrifice preserved by Porphyry dramatizes both the guilt associated with the slaying of the workmate and also the sense of resolution offered by the institution of sacrifice, here represented by the mysterious Pythian command to reiterate the original infringement and the equally counter-intuitive resurrection of the sacrificed animal – a reification, apparently, of the intangible benefits conferred by sacrificial killing. It is this paradoxical quality, I suggest, that Virgil is seeking to convey through his repetition of the *caesi iuuenci* expression: ox-slaying is an action of the utmost impiety, equivalent to fratricide, equivalent to civil war, so transgressive that it alienated the gods and ended the Golden Age; but miraculously this action becomes an act of piety by which relations with the divine (the *pax deorum*)[34] are restored.

IV

An interpretation similar to the foregoing interpretation of the *caesi iuuenci* expression is also available, I now want to suggest, for a parallel sequence of imagery in the *Georgics* concerned with the figure of Romulus.

---

[33] Burkert (1972) 161.   [34]Fowler (1911) 171.

In its original context (2.536–40) the slaughter of cattle constitutes the transgression which brings the Golden or Saturnian Age to an end. The earlier, pristine way of life is exalted (532–5) as that enjoyed by the 'ancient Sabines' (532) and *Remus et frater* (533), and as the manner in which Etruria and Rome grew great. The reference to Rome (534–5), *scilicet et rerum facta est pulcherrima Roma, | septemque una sibi muro circumdedit arces*, clearly has strong ktistic overtones. Line 534 might in fact mean 'Rome was made the finest thing on earth', or 'Rome, the finest thing on earth, was created'. 535 refers to the process of foundation more unequivocally, and is particularly pointed after the reference to *Remus et frater*. According to the familiar legend Romulus and Remus, his twin, both laid claim to the honour of founding the new city, each favouring different hills for their site: the Palatine and the Aventine, respectively; from his hill each took the auguries. A dispute ensued as to whom the auguries favoured in which Remus perished (by the hand either of Romulus himself or of a subordinate), commonly after a derisive leap over Romulus' nascent city-wall. The removal of Remus – according to a dominant reading of the myth – allowed a single, unified city to be built, and the suggestion of plurality resolved into unity in Virgil's *septem . . . una* (535) surely reflects this.[35] It would seem from Cicero (*Rep.* 2.11) that if Romulus did

---

[35] Thus in Ennius' *Annales* the singularity of Romulus after the death of Remus (54–5 Sk.) is kind of guarantee of the stability of Rome (90–1 Sk.) Cf. Ov. *Met.* 14.808–9, reading with Hardie (1993) 6 *et* not *nec*, on the stable singularity of Romulus and Rome after the death of Ovid's Remus-substitute, Titus Tatius. The myth of Romulus' killing of Remus is more than once linked with the notion – proverbial in Rome, Hardie (1993) 6 – of the inherent instability of joint monarchy and thus the desirability of true monarchy. Lucan's *exemplum* of Remus' death is employed to illustrate the apophthegm (1.92–3), *nulla fides regni sociis, omnisque potestas | inpatiens consortis erit*, an echo of Ennius (fr. inc. 169b V.), *nulla sancta societas | nec fides regni est*. Ovid (*Ars Am.* 3.563–4) gives the notion an ironic twist, applying it to love affairs. A related expression, *insociabile regnum*, is employed by Quintus Curtius (10.9.1) and Tacitus (*Ann.* 13.17), perhaps suggesting it was proverbial. Tacitus, like Lucan, relates the phrase to *antiquae fratrum discordiae*, prominent among which must be the archetypal fratricide of Remus. Tacitus is describing reaction to Nero's killing of Britannicus, suggesting that the myth continued to be used (as I shall argue it is in the *Georgics*) to justify the violence of the *princeps*. Dion. Hal. 1.85.6 similarly talks of ἀκοινώνητος φιλαρχία in connection with Romulus and Remus.

not himself build a city which encompassed the seven hills it was at any rate he who put in train the process toward the enclosure of the seven hills by the Servian Wall (in fact a construction of the fourth century, but commonly attributed to Servius Tullius, sixth king of Rome).[36] The city of seven hills was created under his auspices, as it were, and as Virgil himself puts it at *Aen.* 6.781–4 (repeating *G.* 2.535 *verbatim* but for a change of tense):

> en huius, nate, auspiciis illa incluta Roma
> imperium terris, animos aequabit Olympo
> septemque una sibi muro circumdabit arces,
> felix prole uirum.

Lo! under his auspices, my son, that glorious Rome will make her empire as wide as earth, her spirit as high as Olympus, and, a single city, will enclose her seven citadels with a wall, happy in her progeny of men.

Amidst the idyllic landscape of early Italy, then, we find the foundation of Rome. However, as both Miles and Thomas remark,[37] in the context of repeated references to the *fratricidal* nature of civil war at 496 (*infidos agitans discordia fratres*) and 510 (*gaudent perfusi sanguine fratrum*)[38] the expression *Remus et frater* cannot fail to evoke the mythical fratricide, 'paradigmatic of civil strife',[39] of Remus by Romulus. At *Epod.* 7.17–20 Horace traces the Civil Wars back to the curse (*sacer nepotibus cruor*, 20) of Remus' death. Lucan, similarly, explains the impossibility of sharing absolute power, of which there is no need for foreign or recherché *exempla*: Rome itself was founded on fratricide (1.95): *fraterno primi maduerunt sanguine muri*.[40] With typical variation, Ovid in the *Fasti* (3.202) relates another violent act of Romulus to the Civil Wars, his rape of the Sabine women which led to conflict

---

[36] See Zetzel (1995) ad *Rep.* 2.11.1.

[37] Miles (1980) 162–3; Thomas (1988) ad loc. Cf. Hardie (1993) 6; Dominik (1993) 53.

[38] Compare Lucr. *DRN* 3.72, explicitly describing civil conflict, and Kenney (1971) ad 70–1, 72 and 72–3.

[39] Thomas (1988) ad 533.

[40] On this association see also Ogilvie (1965) 54. As the remainder of my argument will make clear, I dispute his assertion that Virgil was 'at pains to minimize the crime of Romulus by emphasizing the sacrilege of Remus'.

between sons- and fathers-in-law similar to that between Caesar and Pompey.

So the fratricide of Remus by Romulus could be an emblem of civil war, and Virgil works hard in the passage at the end of *G.* 2 to bring out this implication: the description of the Saturnian era gestures, subtly but unmistakably, at a prefigurement of the Civil Wars, the polar opposite of the idyllic existence they enjoyed as a twosome. But there is another dimension to the fratricide, cited equally frequently, and which again Virgil appears keen to alert us to. Buchheit has pointed out the saliency in this proximity of the notion of foundation,[41] and the terms of 534–5 must confirm its relevance. In particular we find Quirinus, reflecting Octavian's role as second founder of Rome,[42] amongst the decorations of Virgil's marble temple (3.27). Romulus as fratricide; Romulus as founder. It can hardly be a coincidence that Romulus' slaying of Remus is typically treated by ancient authors as a prerequisite of the founding of the city of Rome. This at any rate seems to be the implication of Livy's words at 1.7.3, when he tells the story of Remus (*Remum ... interfectum*), then states in the following sentence, *ita solus potitus imperio Romulus; condita urbs conditoris nomine appellata*, 'this was how Romulus obtained sole control; the newly founded city was called by the name of its founder', as if the foundation of the city and the killing of Remus (whereby Romulus attained sole power) were identical. Dionysius of Halicarnassus (*Ant. Rom.* 1.87.4) has Remus killed by Celer, one of the men working on the wall which Remus fatally leaped over. Celer lays him low with a σκαφεῖον, a digging-tool he is using in the activity of building. Aurelius Victor, similarly, has Remus slain with a *rastrum* (*De Vir. Ill.* 1.4); in Ovid's account (*Fast.* 4.843) the murder weapon is a *rutrum*, 'shovel', which is also mentioned in a variant reading of Aurelius' passage. Here it appears that Remus' death is almost literally part of the

---

[41] Buchheit (1972) 77–98. Buchheit argues, amongst other things, for the close interrelationship of the conclusion of Book 2 and the proem of 3.
[42] Serv. ad *G.* 3.27, ad *Aen.* 1.292; Scott (1925) 98.

building process. When Remus has been killed Dionysius continues (*Ant. Rom.* 1.88.1), ἐπεὶ δὲ οὐδὲν ἔτι ἦν ἐμποδὼν τῷ κτίσματι . . ., again as if a living Remus and the foundation of Rome were mutually exclusive.

St Augustine (*De civ. D.* 15.5, p.64), quoting Lucan, compares Romulus to Cain, founder of the 'earthly city'. Just as the 'earthly city' was founded by a fratricide, Cain, so was Rome: *sic enim condita est Roma, quando occisum Remum a fratre Romulo Romana testatur historia*. Once again Romulus' status as founder and as fratricide are inseparable, and Augustine considers this the view of 'Roman history'.[43] Another Christian writer, Tertullian, calls Romulus, succinctly, *fratricida institutor* (*De Spec.* 5). Florus, an author we have had cause before to mine for propagandistic material, goes a step further, not only connecting the killing and the foundation but interpreting the fratricide as a foundational *sacrifice* (*Epit.* 1.1.8): *prima certe uictima fuit munitionemque urbis nouae sanguine suo consecrauit*, 'at any rate he was the first victim, and with his blood made holy the fortifications of the new city'. Closer to Virgil's date Propertius, in an epicizing, politically *engagé* context talks of (3.9.50) *caeso moenia firma Remo*, 'the walls made safe by the slaying of Remus'. Wiseman, similarly, points out that in the passage from Ennius, *Ann.* 1 quoted by Cicero (*Div.* 1.107 = *Ann.* 74–5 Sk.) which describes the foundational taking of the auguries by Romulus and Remus Ennius uses the expression *se deuouet* of Remus:[44]

> in †monte Remus auspicio sedet atque secundam
> solus auem seruat,

74 in monte: in Murco *Sk.* sedet atque *Sk.*: se deuouet atque *B*: se deuoueratq; *V*: se deuouerat quae *AH*

This is a difficult expression, which is emended away by Skutsch (whose text and apparatus are quoted above) but

---

[43] Cf. Tib. 2.5.23–4, *Romulus aeternae nondum formauerat urbis | moenia, consorti non habitanda Remo*, which again implies an identification of the construction of Rome and the elimination of Remus.

[44] Wiseman (1991).

which, if retained, would serve to style Remus a *deuotus*, a sacrifice to the gods of the underworld, a foundational sacrifice ensuring the survival of Rome such as Florus and Propertius seem to envisage.[45] Wiseman relates both text and ideology to the most famous instance of an act of *devotio*, that of the consul P. Decius Mus, who vowed himself and the enemy to the Manes and Tellus to avert defeat by the combined Samnite and Gaul forces at Sentinum in 295 BC (Livy 8.10). Wiseman suggests a connection between the episode of Decius' *devotio* and archaeological remains in the vicinity of the Victoria temple on the Palatine. As Wiseman says,[46] Pensabene[47] identifies a sacred precinct in front of the Victoria temple underneath which lay a grave containing bones and a fourth-century *skyphos*. The Victoria temple was dedicated in 294, one year after Decius Mus's ritual self-sacrifice at Sentinum. Wiseman argues that the grave under the precinct contains the remains of a human sacrifice to which the Romans resorted (as we know they did in 228, 216 and 114) in panic at the dire threat posed to the city by the Gauls. The grave lies beneath the Palatine walls, which were under construction at this time. Wiseman's theory is that the sacrifice was made during the war against the Samnites and Gauls 'to achieve invulnerability for the walls of the Palatine "acropolis"'. *After* victory the grave was subsumed into the precinct of the Victory temple and the altar of the temple was placed above it.[48] The notion that Remus' death was a sacrifice for the protection of Rome perhaps originated at this time. It would seem, at any rate, that Remus as an archetype of *devotio* for the Roman state can count as another of our now burgeoning collection of constructive deaths. Romulus is a fratricide, and that action is equated with civil war, but he is also founder:

---

[45] For the institution of *devotio* – a form of self-sacrifice – see Fowler (1911) 206–9; for a recent article studying its relevance to the *Aeneid* see Leigh (1993); for a more sceptical view see Pascal (1990).

[46] Wiseman (1991) 120.

[47] In Cristofani (1990) 89–90.

[48] Wiseman (1991) 122–3.

in fact the fratricide is effectively the same action as the foundation.[49]

At the end of Book 2, then, cattle-slaughter – which in Book 4 is constructive – is presented as an appalling instance of impiety. Similarly the death of Remus gestured at towards at the end of Book 2 is framed as an unqualifiedly disastrous event, an act equivalent to civil strife: the myth of Romulus and Remus reflects the fratricidal nature of the Civil Wars. But in the immediate context of the ktistic preoccupations of the proem to Book 3 explicated by Buchheit and the depiction of Octavianic power as the *uictoris arma Quirini* (27), the killing of Remus must also be read as a prerequisite of the foundation of Rome.[50] In both cases seemingly unmitigated catastrophe is unveiled as miraculously constructive. The implication for Virgil's contemporaries was that violence in general, though apparently disastrous, had a potential for good.[51] But violence in general had found in recent years a particularly prominent instantiation in the Civil Wars. Virgil

[49] On the ambiguity of the figure of Romulus see also Herbert-Brown (1994) 49–51, who cites the view of Bömer (1957–8) I 27 of 'ein durchaus zwiespältiges Romulus-Bild' in the first century BC between founder and tyrant, although again, as we shall see, I cannot concur with Herbert-Brown's view that 'when [Romulus] is examined in relation to Augustus by authors both ancient and modern, it is only the heroic side which is focused upon' (49) and 'the fratricide ... is carefully dissociated from Augustus' (51).

[50] Cairns (1984) 163–4 similarly reads Propertius' reference to Remus at 4.6.80 (*signa Remi*) both as a precedent for civil war and also as a positive judgement about Augustus' role in it.

[51] These two images of disaster, the death of brothers (of Remus in particular) and the death of oxen (who themselves have almost the status of brothers), seem to be brought together in the scene of the ox's death by plague at G. 3.515–30. Virgil writes, famously, *it tristis arator | maerentem abiungens fraterna morte iuuencum* (517–18). The *iuuencus* mourns the death of his brother, a restatement of the dilemma of the poem, the disaster of fraternal death.

Philip Hardie has alerted me to the similar imagery of Hor. *Epist.* 1.3.30–6. Horace urges reconciliation between Julius Florus and Munatius. In their youthful inclination to anger they are related to bulls or stallions, *indomita ceruice feros* (34), and they are also described – in terms reminiscent of the *Georgics* – as *indigni fraternum rumpere foedus* (35). Finally Horace promises the sacrifice of a heifer in celebration of their return. The line describing the heifer (36) alludes to G. 3.219. Mayer (1994) 275 comments on the allusion, 'Virgil's heifer disturbs the peace of the herd by exciting rival bulls to battle; H.'s will mark the restoration of harmony in Tiberius' *cohors* (itself a sort of *grex*, cf. 9.13) after "bullish" (34) young men are reconciled.' The (paradoxical) movement here from disorder to order through the sacrifice of a heifer is somewhat similar to the scheme adumbrated in the *Georgics*.

is thus apparently seeking to assert that the Civil Wars, also, had constructive potential: like Romulus' slaying of Remus, they will engender a new Rome.

V

There is a more general point to be made here. Having established to his satisfaction that both instances of *caesi iuuenci* at *G.* 2.537 and 3.23 denote sacrifices – positive and negative interpretations thereof, respectively – Habinek continues, 'Does Virgil maintain the balance in *Georgics* 4, or does he tilt it in the direction of sacrifice as a unifying and re-creative social phenomenon?'[52] What interests me about this question is the way that it carries to extremes a very common metaphor in Virgilian criticism: *weighing*. The bad associations of ox-slaughter are envisaged by Habinek as the weights on one side of a pair of scales which may or may not *outweigh* the good associations on the other side. We can compare this passage with a statement on the *Georgics* from Jasper Griffin, specifically referring to Orpheus, which has now become seminal:

For my part I cannot feel that the restoration of bees outweighs the suffering and death of Orpheus and Eurydice, especially in view of the way Virgil has handled the story. An exquisite ambivalence surely prevails.[53]

Note the metaphor again: *outweighs*. Virgil – on this view – is a man in two minds. Positive and negative events happen in his text, and reflect, fairly straightforwardly, attitudes of the poet, though the issue of the poet's conscious design tends to be obfuscated. More recent criticism may prefer 'subvert' to 'outweigh', but the fundamental scheme is the same: images of success on the one hand, images of disaster on the other, with Virgil torn between the two. The model of the ambivalent Virgil has in fact become the orthodoxy, allowing the view to become *de rigueur* that in Virgil we are in the presence of a liberal consciousness somehow stranded in the higher machinery of the Augustan principate. Griffin encapsulates this

---

[52] Habinek (1990) 215.   [53] Griffin (1979) 71; cf. Thomas (1988) I 23.

orthodoxy when he writes, 'Anxiety and hope contend in the *Georgics*.'[54] But its tentacles extend further than Virgil. To pick an example at random, Harrison, towards the end of an interpretation of the Portland Vase,[55] seeks to support his thesis that the decoration of the vase is of ambiguous import with reference to the *communis opinio* regarding the nature of contemporary poetry:

> The designer of the vase ... produced an ambiguous programme, positive and joyful on a superficial view but darker and more subtle on closer investigation, not unlike some of the textures of contemporary Augustan poetry.

The chief weakness of Griffin's approach, in my view, is that in a paradoxical way – given Griffin's stated views on literature and its relation to reality[56] – it fails to give adequate weight in its interpretation of the *Georgics* to the manner in which the poem seeks to engage with contemporary events or attitudes. For Griffin the *Georgics* is essentially mimetic: it depicts a world, the world as perceived by Virgil, radically divided between terrible events and happy events, a dichotomy which yields in the poet (and the reader) a parallel dichotomy between anxiety and hope.[57] According to this version of literary realism the connection which the *Georgics* bears to life takes the form of an insight into the state of the world as filtered through the sentiments of the poet. I have suggested as a replacement model a more functional and reader-orientated approach, one which takes more account of the author's conscious creative design. Perhaps, I wondered, the *Georgics* is a dynamic artefact designed not to represent the poet's (tor-

---

[54] Griffin (1986) 12.
[55] Harrison (1992) 152.
[56] See, for example, Griffin (1985) xiv.
[57] Compare Perkell (1989) 16–17, a more theoretically grounded but nevertheless similarly 'inert' or mimetic interpretation: 'I propose that we need to move towards a more balanced, inclusive view of the poem ... because, as I believe, it is truer to the poem and, not incidentally, to life. As life has joy and grief, so this poem reflects the real tensions of most human experience ... The concept of tension or suspension allows us to see in the *Georgics'* central and unresolved oppositions not just inconsistencies to be normalized or problems to be overcome, but rather an expression or reflection of the poem's deepest vision of the nature of experience.'

tured) state of mind (an obviously Romantic notion) but actively to mould the attitudes of its public.[58]

Perhaps the most striking 'external' feature of this poem is its date: 29 BC. This is one of the most significant dates in Roman history, a turning point for the nation, as it would come to seem, a crucial juncture for Octavian as it must have seemed at the time. Octavian had won another round of the Civil Wars. However, to ensure that this latest of many heralded 'ends' to the Civil Wars should not prove illusory, Octavian needed to follow up that military success with the creation of a stable political order in Rome. It was crucial to the achievement of this latter aim that Octavian conciliated the old ruling class of Rome. This policy would ultimately yield the compromise between autocracy and republican constitutional norms known as the principate, and it is in the context of Augustus' employment of the term *princeps* that Pollini talks of

a new ideology, one of the aims of which was the reconciliation of Rome's nobility, whose cooperation and support were needed to maintain peace and stability within the empire after a century of foreign war and civil conflict.[59]

This policy of rapprochement with the aristocracy reached its culmination in the First Constitutional Settlement of 27 BC, but had its roots much earlier: Octavian was already taking measures to reconcile the Roman aristocracy to his regime in 36 BC. Now the Roman aristocracy was of course by no means a uniform entity. It contained supporters of Octavian, as well as supporters of Antony: men who had presumably looked to benefit from civil war. But nevertheless through the upper class as a whole the typical experience of the previous fifteen years will have been a traumatic one, and this will have been particularly the case for the (still influential) surviving rump of those committed to traditional senatorial government, at whom Octavian's policy of conciliation was especially aimed. Octavian had a problem, then: on the one hand he needed the cooperation of the aristocracy; on the other the

---

[58] See pp. 13–14 above.   [59] Pollini (1990) 336. Cf. p. 4 above.

Civil Wars (in which he had been a prime mover) had caused widespread destruction and suffering, and no group had suffered more than this crucial political elite. Dio elevates this fact into a general rule (52.42.5): οὐδὲν γὰρ οὕτως ὡς τὸ γενναῖον ἐν τοῖς ἐμφυλίοις πολέμοις ἀναλίσκεται, 'for no group is destroyed in civil wars like the aristocracy'. The importance of this demoralization of the Roman upper classes in the first century BC for an understanding of contemporary literature is well recognized by Kenney, with reference to Lucretius' *De Rerum Natura*.[60]

An interesting illustration of Octavian's keenness to reconcile this group is provided by the progressive purges he undertook of undesirable elements in the Senate. The first revision of the senatorial roll was carried out by him in this same year of 29 BC, and it can be interpreted as, at least in part, a gesture in the direction of traditional republican procedure. Those excluded from the Senate are said to be men *post necem Caesaris per gratiam et praemium adlecti* (Suet. *Aug.* 35.1; cf. Dio 52.42.1–4). Amongst those thus expelled will necessarily – it would seem – have been one-time supporters of his own, as well as Antonians.[61] Similar expressions of respect for, and reconstruction of, the pre-war *status quo* are discernible also in regard to the equestrian order.[62] But Octavian had much ground to make up. To many aristocratic Romans in 29 Octavian will have presented a very dubious figure. With the benefit of hindsight later authors would remark on the sharp difference between the mild, merciful Augustus of the principate and the vicious triumvir Octavian. Seneca, for example, after a glowing appraisal of his qualities when *princeps*, adds a proviso (Sen. *Clem.* 1.11.1):

Haec Augustus senex aut iam in senectutem annis uergentibus; in adulescentia caluit, arsit ira, multa fecit ad quae inuitus oculos retorquebat. comparare nemo mansuetudini tuae audebit diuum Augustum, etiam si in certamen iuuenilium annorum deduxerit senectutem plus quam maturam; fuerit moderatus et clemens, nempe post mare Actiacum Romano cruore

---

[60] Kenney (1971) 9.   [61] Sattler (1960) 32–3.   [62] Suet. *Aug.* 40.1.

infectum, nempe post fractas in Sicilia classes et suas et alienas, nempe post Perusinas aras et proscriptiones.[63]

Such was Augustus when an old man, or just on the verge of old age. When young he was hot-headed, he burned with anger, and he did many things which he looked back on with regret. No one will dare to compare the divine Augustus to your [sc. Nero's] mildness, even bringing youthful years into competition with a old age more than mature. Granted he was restrained and merciful – granted, yes, after the sea at Actium had been stained by Roman blood, after his own and others' fleets had been wrecked in Sicily, after the altars of Perusia and the proscriptions.

In 29 BC the *mitis princeps*[64] had yet to materialize. Rome's experience of Octavian at this point – though not unmixed – was still predominantly one of extreme violence and ruthlessness.

The public of ancient literature is notoriously hard to gauge, but it is noteworthy that the target of Octavian's conciliatory offensive – the Roman upper classes – coincides fairly closely with the 'relatively small élite in which high

---

[63] Seneca is referring to the following events of the triumviral period: the battle of Actium (31), naval engagements between Octavian and Sextus Pompey (38 and 36), the siege and capture of Perusia (41–40), and the proscriptions (43). Equally invidious were his involvement in the battle of Philippi (42), of which Velleius says (2.71.1) *non aliud bellum cruentius caede clarissimorum uirorum fuit*, and the subsequent land confiscations. In the expression *Perusinae arae* Seneca is referring to a persistent story, presumably apocryphal, that Octavian sacrificed some of his aristocratic opponents at Perusia before an altar of Divus Julius: see, e.g., Suet. *Aug.* 15. The siege anyway became a 'byword for cruelty': Woodman (1983) ad Vell. Pat. 2.74.4.

For the contrast between Augustus' youth and his principate see further Dio 56.44.1; Stat. *Silv.* 4.1.32 and Coleman (1988) ad loc. Pliny, *HN* 37.10 records that the mature Augustus changed his seal from a sphinx, which he used originally, to an image of Alexander the Great, apparently to avoid the opprobrium associated with his early actions. There are other indications of his desire to distance himself later in life from his younger self, notably his melting down of eighty silver statues of himself, 'brilliant testaments of his "Octavian phase"' (Eder (1990) 102; *RG* 24.2), and his movement away from military titles to civilian: Syme (1939) 311–12. This also had the effect of distancing his style of government from Caesar's: compare Suet. *Aug.* 25.1 and *Jul.* 67.2. Similar considerations must have lain behind his choice of the name 'Augustus' over the more explicitly military 'Romulus' in 27 BC.

[64] Sen. *Clem.* 1.9.1: *diuus Augustus fuit mitis princeps, si quis illum a principatu suo aestimare incipiat; in communi quidem rei publicae gladium mouit*, 'The deified Augustus was a kind *princeps*, if one were to undertake to judge him from his time as *princeps*; but when he shared the state with others he lived by the sword.'

culture flourished'[65] who must have been the main recipients of any propaganda of a literary nature. So at any rate a poem published at this juncture would potentially be an ideal vehicle for Octavian. But if the *Georgics* were propaganda, what form should we expect that propaganda to take? What would be required of an apologist for Octavian in 29 BC? We already know that the achievement of effective propaganda is to co-alesce, as far as possible, with the existing values of its audi-ence, to influence it from within.[66] An effective propagandist cannot ignore the prevailing mood of his public. As Foulkes puts it,[67] the most effective (and hence for inhabitants of the twentieth century elusive and dangerous) type of propaganda is 'the one which succeeds in engaging us directly as partici-pants in its communicative systems'. Turn this around and we might say: it would be little use in 29 BC for an Octavianic propagandist to ignore the Civil Wars, to pretend that they had not happened. If Virgil's agenda *was* propagandistic he would have had to confront the fact of the generally appalling experiences of his readership over at least the previous fifteen years. In fact the single greatest demand on such a propagan-dist at this time would have been to engage with – and, so to speak, neutralize – the violence and destruction that had visited Rome for the previous decade-and-a-half, and Octa-vian's central role in it. What if, then, a central function of the *Georgics* were precisely the *dynamic* one of engaging with the existing attitudes of his readership – that is, the profound pessimism of an elite traumatized by civil war – and negoti-ating the constructive potential of the violence and death the Civil Wars had brought, rehabilitating, as it were, the Civil Wars, and their protagonist Octavian along with them? This *Georgics* would not be an inert reflection of a divided world, or an expression of a poet's profound pessimism, but some-thing of surely much richer significance: an artefact possessing

---

[65] E. J. Kenney in *CHCL* II, 10; for an overview of the relationship between litera-ture and the governing class in the late Republic, see Beard and Crawford (1985) 12–24.

[66] See pp. 7–8 above.

[67] Foulkes (1983) 107.

the dynamic function of moulding the attitudes of its readership in a manner favourable to Octavian.

VI

Romulus was the founder of Rome. Rome was (it was
thought) *called* Rome because Romulus founded it. Thus
(again) Livy 1.7.2–3: *ita solus potitus imperio Romulus; condita urbs conditoris nomine appellata*, 'this was how Romulus
obtained sole control; the newly founded city was called by
the name of its founder'. Virgil's dissection of the Romulus
myth thus goes to the core of the Roman identity. Furthermore, Octavian at this period was engaged in an attempt to
equate the Roman identity and interests with his own. We
know from contemporary sources that Romulus was a figure
with whom Octavian, following the example of Julius Caesar,[68] made strenuous efforts to identify himself. At *Aug.* 7.2
Suetonius famously records how the Senate considered naming him Romulus 'as being himself founder of the city', but
settled on another name – Augustus – partially derived from
Ennius' account of the foundation whilst at the same time
distanced a little from the figure of Romulus.[69] Visual art tells
a similar story. In the Forum Augusti, finally dedicated in 2
BC, in the two exedrae flanking the temple of Mars Ultor,
Augustus placed statues of Aeneas and Romulus. Romulus,
as we can see in wall paintings from Pompeii, was depicted as
the original *triumphator*.[70] The intended parallel with Augustus is clear from the *fasti triumphales* which were affixed to the
triumphal arch of Augustus which stood next to the temple of
Divus Julius. The first triumph recorded in the *fasti* was that

[68] Scott (1925) 82–4; Weinstock (1971) 175–9.
[69] Cf. Dio 53.16.7–8; Florus 2.34.66; Plut. *Rom.* 12 in combination with Scott (1925)
98. Scott discusses at length Augustus' association with Romulus. He suggests
amongst other things (101–2) that the representation of Augustus in the Gemma
Augustea holding a *lituus* is not adequately explained by his membership of the
college of augurs. The *lituus* was closely associated with Romulus, who was the
first to use it (Cic. *Div.* 1.17; Val. Max. 1.8.11), and was commonly designated
'Quirinalis' (eg. Virg. *Aen.* 7.187). It thus appears to establish a connection between Augustus and Romulus.
[70] Zanker (1987) 204–6.

celebrated by Romulus 'in the first year of the state'. 'Was mit dem "Vater der Stadt und der *virtus*" (Prop. 4.10) so stolz begonnen hatte, fand im dreifachen Triumph seine Krönung. So wurde es in die neuen Triumphalfasten eingetragen.'[71] The close association of Romulus with Augustus in the aspect of *triumphator* is of course reflected at *G.* 3.27. Virgil's treatment of Romulus, then, is an extremely searching analysis not only of the nature of Rome as revealed in recent events but also of the role of Octavian in these events. Virgil does not pull his punches: if Romulus is to be condemned as a fratricide, so is Octavian; if Romulus' action is redeemable as a prerequisite of the existence of Rome, so is Octavian's behaviour. I now wish to suggest that the cattle-slaughter motif carries similarly uncompromising implications, both for the nation and for Octavian.

With Romulus and Remus the nationalistic content of the reference is fairly obvious. In discussing his role in the foundation Virgil is addressing a very fundamental component of the Roman self-image. But the choice of oxen to bear so much symbolic weight is perhaps less immediately explicable. The suggestion is often made of the bees that Virgil's anthropomorphism has two levels: they bear a resemblance to the human race in general, but to Romans in particular. The context most cited in this regard is 4.201, which terms the bees *parui Quirites*. In this way the death and rebirth of the bee-colony is closely associated with the recent experiences of the Roman nation. I wish to conclude this discussion of oxen in the poem by considering the possibility that there is a comparable programme of assimilation operating between the Romano-Italian nation and *oxen*.

Italy also, like Rome, had its etymological myths. One etymology of the name *Italia* in particular related it to the country's wealth in precisely the commodity at issue: oxen. One of two common etymologies of the name (the other traced it back to an early king of the territory named Italus) derived it from the word *uitulus* ('calf', 'bullock') or the Greek ἰταλός

---

[71] Zanker (1987) 206.

(a word cited by Hesychius for both Ῥωμαῖος and ταῦρος). At *Rust.* 2.1.9 Varro employs this etymology to illustrate the high esteem in which early peoples held cattle: *denique non Italia a uitulis, ut scribit Piso?*, 'Finally, is not Italy named after *uituli*, as Piso writes?'[72] Later, in his treatment of ox-husbandry (2.5.3, just before one of his two references to *bugonia*), Varro offers a slightly different etymology, but one along similar lines. The ox should be held in particular regard amongst livestock, he says,

> Graecia enim antiqua, ut scribit Timaeus, tauros uocabat italos, a quorum multitudine et pulchritudine et fetu uitulorum Italiam dixerunt. alii scripserunt quod ex Sicilia Hercules persecutus sit eo nobilem taurum *qui* [ut, MSS] diceretur Italus.

> For the ancient Greeks, according to Timaeus, called bulls *itali*, and they employed the name *Italy* as a consequence of the number, beauty and fecundity of its bulls. Others have written that Hercules pursued a noble bull thither from Sicily which was (or so that it [Italy] was) called Italus.[73]

Varro's agricultural treatise is of course a major influence on the *Georgics*;[74] and the substantial role in Italo-Roman self-representation that Varro suggests the ox plays would certainly seem to have a parallel in the *laudes Italiae*. Italy in this description is defined both by what it does contain and by what it does not, and the ox looms large in both categories. The first cited *absence* from the idyllic Italy is that of fire-breathing plough-oxen such as figure in the myth of the Argonauts (140–2); and prominent among the characteristically ideal items that Italy *does* contain are the white oxen of the Clitumnus and the bull, *maxima taurus | uictima*, presented, notably, in its role as the sacrificial victim of the Roman triumphal ceremony willingly leading the procession to the Capitoline (146–8). Similarly in the proem to Book 3, the definitively Roman ritual of the triumph which Virgil imagines

---

[72] *Piso* is the second-century historian L. Calpurnius Piso Frugi; see Forsythe (1994) 83–9.
[73] Cf. Gellius 11.1.1.; Columella 6 *praef.* 7; Paul. Fest. 106 (s.v. *Italia*); Serv. *auct.* ad *Aen.* 1.533: Maltby (1991) s.v. There is a further punning dimension: Varro's interlocutor on the subject of oxen is called Vaccius (2.5.2).
[74] See Thomas (1988) I 11.

himself celebrating after his capture and relocation to Italy of the Muses of Greek literature culminates with bull-sacrifice (23, one of the instances of the *caesi iuuenci* motif). The focal importance of the ox in such defining rituals of the Roman state is made clear by Pliny, who at *HN* 8.183 informs us that bulls provided *uictimae opimae*, 'noble victims', and bull-sacrifice the *lautissima deorum placatio*, 'the grandest means of appeasing the gods'.

Varro offered two etymologies at 2.5.3. The second, though still concerned with cattle, specifically attributes the naming of Italy to Hercules. This etymological *aetion* also finds strong parallels elsewhere. Dionysius of Halicarnassus (*Ant. Rom.* 1.35.1–3), after citing the derivation (attributed to Antiochus of Syracuse) from King Italus, offers an alternative *aetion* from Hellanicus of Lesbos, who told the story that whilst Hercules was driving the cattle of Geryon through Italy on his way home a calf slipped away from the herd, wandered down the entire western seaboard of the country, and then swam across the straits of Messina to Sicily. Going after it, Hercules enquired of the natives along its path whether anyone had seen it, and since they knew little Greek, and referred to the calf in the vernacular as *uitulus* (οὐίτουλος), Hercules christened the territory the calf had traversed Οὐιτουλία, *Vitulia*. Dionysius thus gives a precise mythological context to Hercules' naming of Italy: it occurs during his herding of the cattle belonging to the three-headed Geryon.[75]

Varronian etymology was not an idle intellectual exercise. Words were considered descriptions of the things to which they were applied, and thus by discovering the origin of a word one was also discovering something about the nature of the thing it denoted. Word and thing are inherently connected, on this assumption.[76] If the name *Italia* is established as de-

---

[75] See also Apollod. *Bibl.* 2.5.10, which gives this context in greater detail and also relates the naming of Italy to a *uitulus* which wandered from Hercules' herd.

[76] For a succinct account of the theory see Cic. *Top.* 35–7, where *notatio* (translating ἐτυμολογία) is explicitly stated to be a means of discovering the meaning (*uis*) of a word. He proceeds to illustrate the use of *notatio* by investigating the true nature of the institution of *postliminium*, i.e. the (true) etymology of a term reveals facts about its object.

riving from a word for 'ox', this tells us something about the essential nature of Italy. Hence Varro's insistence that oxen be held in particular esteem as a consequence of this etymology: oxen are, as it were, of Italy's essence.

Taurus, iuuencus, bos and *uitulus* are effectively interchangeable terms in the *Georgics*. For example the victim of *bugonia* (as first described, 295–314) is a *uitulus* (299). Could there then lie behind the choice of *bugonia* (styled as closely approximate to blood-sacrifice) as a conclusion to the poem some such Varronian notion of a special relationship between Italy and oxen? At any rate awareness of this myth of the original naming of Italy would provide an extremely apt backdrop to another episode associated with Hercules' expedition against Geryon which Virgil gave a nodal role in the *Aeneid* – the myth of Cacus in *Aen.* 8, pointedly concerned as it is with the loss (207–8) and the sacrifice (179–83) of oxen.[77] Hardie has illustrated the ktistic and cosmogonical overtones of the Cacus incident in the context of *Aen.* 8 as a whole,[78] and Octavian organized the great triple triumph of 29 BC – with all its implications of cultural renewal – so that the first of its three days coincided with the annual festival of Hercules at the Ara Maxima on 13th August, the festival of which the myth of Cacus was the *aetion*.[79] The name of Italy is explicitly an issue in Book 8,[80] and a contemporary theory linking the actual naming of Italy to this same labour of Hercules may well be of relevance in a passage symbolically addressing the earliest origins of Rome.[81] If indeed there existed at this time such a close symbolic association between things bovine and

---

[77] In which respect it is related to the description of *bugonia*: the lines describing the cattle purloined by Cacus, *Aen.* 8.207–8, are repeated almost *verbatim* from the second, sacrificial description of *bugonia* at G. 4.538 + 540, 550–1.

[78] Hardie (1986) 117–18.

[79] Galinsky (1972) 141.

[80] 329, *saepius et nomen posuit Saturnia tellus.* Cf. 322–1, *Latiumque uocari | maluit, his quoniam latuisset tutus in oris,* and O'Hara (1996) 207 ('Names are prominent in Evander's history of Italy') and 208 ('Evander's concern with names continues').

[81] In the case of Rome, at any rate, the naming of the new foundation is closely bound up with the foundation itself. Thus Livy (1.6.4), *quoniam gemini essent nec aetatis uerecundia discrimen facere posset, ut dii, quorum tutelae ea loca essent, auguriis legerent, qui nomen nouae urbi daret, qui conditam imperio regeret ...* Naming and founding are here effectively synonymous.

the country of Italy, or even between the sacrificial death (as a prerequisite of rebirth) of a *uitulus* and the death and rebirth of Roman *Italia* during the Civil Wars, Virgil's motif can again be seen to reflect more narrowly on Octavian as the ruler and representative of Italy (see especially 2.170–2), who in addition had made such ceremonies as the triumph in which oxen were slaughtered a central means of validating his regime: if ox-slaughter is in one aspect transgressive, so is a ritual Octavian had made his own. If we follow Ahl we might even draw a connection between the *other* half of the *caesi iuuenci* motif and Octavian, between *caesus* and *Caesar*, referring to a fairly widely attested etymology, as for example Pliny, *HN* 7.47, *primus ... Caesarum a caeso matris utero dictus*, 'the first of the Caesars was so called from the cut womb of his mother'.[82] Caesar's very name is *Slaughter*. This may be reading too much into the expression.[83] But we can at least see why many critics have wanted to interpret Virgil as at root a critic of the Octavianic regime. Octavian is thoroughly and uncompromisingly associated with the catastrophe of the Civil Wars. But this perhaps was the challenge Virgil faced: to take the appalling Civil Wars and argue their potential for good; but also to take a protagonist in these wars, a figure thoroughly implicated in the destruction they caused, Octavian, and rehabilitate him as well: Romulus was a fratricide too, and he *had* to be, if Rome was to be founded.

VII

From a process depicted in Book 2 as the original sin, the slaughter of oxen, miraculously derives good: *bugonia* and sacrifice generate a rebirth to peace and order. The context

[82] Ahl (1985) 80–1.
[83] But we might compare Juvenal's fourth satire, on which Gowers (1993) 209 comments that Domitian's 'instincts have always been for cutting up', referring to 37, 130 and the concluding words of the poem, *Lamiarum caede madenti*. Braund (1996) ad loc. writes, '*caede* connects with *conciditur* (130)'. Does *caede* also connect with *Caesar*, the title by which Domitian is referred to at 51 and 135?

for this miracle is carefully delineated, by time and place. It occurs in spring, in Egypt.

It is worth asking what motivated Virgil's choice of Egypt as the location for this form of resolution. One reason might be found in recent geopolitical history. On 1 August 30 BC Octavian defeated the forces of Antony and Cleopatra and entered Alexandria: Antony killed himself, to be followed shortly afterwards by Cleopatra. *Hic finis armorum ciuilium* (Florus, *Epit.* 2.21). In reality the Egyptian campaign was a foregone conclusion, and the final engagement at Alexandria a 'fiasco',[84] but Octavianic propaganda (of this period at least)[85] elevated the skirmish into something far more significant. The last of the three triumphs of 29 BC, the most splendid of them all,[86] commemorated this campaign. Similarly, the *senatus consultum* of 27 BC preserved by Macrobius which renamed the month of *Sextilis* after Augustus in recognition of his many achievements during that month cites as two of those achievements the subjugation of Egypt and the ending of the Civil Wars (which would seem to be understood as the same event).[87] Official calendars subsequently marked the day as a festival:[88] *[Aegypt]us in potestatem po[puli Romani redacta.] ... fer. [ex s. c.] q. e. d. imp. Caes[ar Aug. rem public. tristissimo periculo liberauit]*, 'Egypt brought under the sway of the Roman people ... Holiday by senatorial decree because on that day Imperator Caesar Augustus freed the state from grimmest peril.' In recent history, then, a form of

---

[84] Carter (1970) 232.

[85] Wistrand (1958) 52–5 investigates an apparent contradiction between the emphasis on 1 August, 30 as the decisive event of the war in one strand of Octavianic/Augustan propaganda and the emphasis on the battle of Actium in another. Hor. *Carm.* 4.14.34–40 still marks the day as 'epochal' (54).

[86] Dio 51.21.7, πολυτελεστάτη δ' οὖν καὶ ἀξιοπρεπεστάτη αὕτη ἡ Αἰγυπτία. The triumph was funded by the Ptolemaic treasury, which fell into Octavian's hands with the fall of Alexandria. So much money entered the economy as a consequence of this triumph, in fact, that Rome enjoyed an economic boom, interest rates falling from 12 per cent to 4 per cent and land prices rising steeply: Suet. *Aug.* 41.1; Dio 51.21.5.

[87] Macrob. *Sat.* 1.12.35, ... *et Aegyptus hoc mense in potestatem populi Romani redacta sit, finisque hoc mense bellis ciuilibus inpositus sit ...*

[88] *Fasti Praenestini, AE* 1898, no. 14.

redemption – or so Octavianic propaganda had it – was visited upon Rome which originated in Egypt. But there are also other grounds for Virgil's choice which are more immediately relevant to the topic of this chapter.

We are first alerted to the essentially *paradoxical* nature of *bugonia* at 4.284–5. It is here that it is described in terms reminiscent of the Aratean crime at 2.537: *quoque modo <u>caesis</u> iam saepe <u>iuuencis</u> | insincerus apes tulerit cruor*. From the 'impure', 'corrupt' gore of slaughtered oxen come those perfect animals, bees. The geographical context of *bugonia* is specified by means of a seven-line ethnographical gloss on the name *Aegyptus* (287–94), centred on the river Nile. The passage is designed above all to bring out the miraculous quality of Egypt and its river. In the kind of paradoxical turnaround we should now be expecting from the *Aristaeus*, Egypt is a place where a flood is a piece of good fortune: contrast 1.113–17, 322–34, and 481–3 on the Eridanus.[89] The contrast with the latter instance is particularly striking. The name Eridanus might denote the river Po, or a constellation (Aratus, *Phaen.* 359–66). The constellation Eridanus was closely associated with the Nile: 'Greek authors speculated on the celestial origins of the Nile, identifying it with the constellation of Eridanus, the heavenly river.'[90] This is thus the core of Virgil's presentation of Egypt: as Thomas puts it, it is an exotic place of paradoxical wonders, θαύματα.[91]

---

[89] Cf. Sen. *Q Nat.* 4A.2.10 on the atypical effect *qua* flood of the Nile inundation.

[90] Dwyer (1992) 261; Robert (1878) 177–9. Virgil calls the Eridanus *fluuiorum rex*; the equivalent, ποταμῶν βασιλεύς, is found in Greek sources as an epithet of the Nile: see Cribiore (1995) 101.

[91] Thomas (1988) ad 281–314, 287–94. For Thomas *bugonia, qua* θαῦμα, is an impossibility which cannot 'in *real* terms' (ad 281–314) resolve the problems presented in the poem. I do not consider the criteria of realism and fictionality particularly relevant here. Ross (1987) 216 similarly, states of the *bugonia*, 'a *thaumasion* is worthy of wonder, but is not intended to be believed'. I hope I have established that (avoiding the distancing device of using the Greek term *thaumasion*) the miraculous or *mirabile dictu* was quite likely to inspire belief in Romans: the sacrificial institution was arguably predicated on the miraculous. But in addition, as Hardie (1988) writes in his review of Ross (1987) the 'relationship between poetry and "reality" is more complex than Ross allows'. If we dismiss as 'lies' Virgil's depiction of the Golden Age or his idyllic image of Italy – or *bugonia* – we must do the same with such 'negative' events as the plague of Noricum, the man-eating mares of Glaucus and the myth of *hippomanes*. A similar attempt to drive a

Chomarat has pinpointed the central paradox of the passage, however.[92] At 291 Virgil describes the fructifying effects of the Nile flood: *et uiridem Aegyptum nigra fecundat harena*, 'and it fertilizes green Egypt with black sand'. The collocation *fecundat harena* is within the terms of the *Georgics* a striking oxymoron, since sand functions in the poem as the image *par excellence* of infertility. The *sterilis harena* (1.70), we are told, does not retain the water necessary for germination. At 1.104–10 the industrious farmer is imagined laying low the mounds of 'infertile sand' (*male pinguis arenae*, 107) so that he can introduce the necessary water to his land.[93] The only 'fertile' sand in the *Georgics* is the marvellous incense-bearing sand of Panchaea (*pinguis* again, 2.139), ranked alongside such wonders as the gold-rich river Hermus and the fire-breathing bulls of Colchis.[94] Egypt is another such fabulous location. From the sand of Egypt, paradoxically,[95] comes fertility. In Egypt, according to Virgil, life is born from a substance, barren sand, which is inimical to life. Chomarat comments, 'Dans le domaine des symboles l'Egypte est pour l'espace ce que la saison printanière est pours le temps.'[96] Early spring formed the temporal context of *bugonia*, just as Egypt provided its geographical context. The process takes place at the very first sign of the West Wind, before the growth of flowers and the arrival of the swallow (305–7). As spring is host to the paradox of new life emerging from the

wedge between myth and *praecepta* is attempted by Perkell (1989) with respect to the *Georgics* and Myers (1994) with respect to Ovid's *Metamorphoses*. The latter's distinction between myth and natural philosophy, in particular, seems to take insufficient account of the programme of the *Aeneid*.

[92] Chomarat (1974) 186–7. Chomarat discerns in the *Aristaeus* a general theme of religious initiation encompassing the description of Egypt, Aristaeus' κατάβασις to the watery realm of Cyrene, and the creative collision of heat and moisture in the capture of Proteus.

[93] See also 1.114, *bibula ... harena*; 389, *sicca ... harena*; and 3.493, where sand is associated with the unproductive sacrifice undertaken during the plague.

[94] The word *(h)arena*, like *arista*, was commonly derived *ab ariditate*: see Maltby (1991) s.v. *harena*. The paradoxically fertile combination of (moist) Nile and (arid) sand compares, I would suggest, to the creative conflict of Aristaeus and Proteus (see pp. 88–9 and n. 115 above) and to what is perhaps the central paradox of the poem, the *pinguis arista*, on which see Ross (1987) 32–54, and n. 108 below.

[95] Chomarat (1974) 187: 'cette signification paradoxale'.

[96] Chomarat (1974) 188.

'dead land' of winter (and host also, naturally, to *bugonia*), so
Egypt boasts the miraculous status of a land *fertilized* by sand.

VIII

There is thus a clear analogy between *bugonia* and its physical
context: *bugonia* is a miracle (309, 554), and so is the fructifying power of the Nile flood. But the processes which
brought fertility to Egypt in midsummer, marvellous in
themselves, came to stand in the ancient world for miraculous
processes of much wider reference than the agricultural yield
of the Nile valley. On the one hand the Nile inundation was
considered representative of events in the cosmic arena.
Dwyer explains how this 'transition from the specific natural
phenomenon of the Nile to a generalized cosmogony' was
anticipated in pre-Hellenistic Egyptian religion.[97] Diodorus
(1.12.5–6) asserts that the Egyptians equated Oceanus with (in
particular, the flooding) Nile, since Homer's (by now much
cited) description of Ocean as the origin of the gods (*Il.*
14.201, 302), Ὠκεανόν τε θεῶν γένεσιν καὶ μητέρα Τηθύν, was
also true of the Nile.[98] A token of this conceptual relation
between Nile and Ocean is a commonly held belief in a physical connection. Herodotus (2.21), recording his second explanation of the Nile flood (one that is ἀνεπιστημονεστέρη but
θωμασιωτέρη), states that the river ἀπὸ τοῦ Ὠκεανοῦ ῥέοντα
αὐτὸν ταῦτα μηχανᾶσθαι, 'effects what it does because it
flows from the Ocean'. This is a view 'widely held':[99] the

---

[97] Dwyer (1992) 262–3.
[98] Cf. 1.19.4, 1.96.7. Diodorus betrays some confusion as to whether Ocean (or
Ὠκεάνη) is to be identified with the wet principle generally or specifically with the
Nile, an indication of how easily universalized the processes of the Nile were. See
also Plut. *de Is. et Os.* 364a–d, where Osiris is identified with the Nile, the wet
principle generally, and Ocean (again with reference to *Il.* 14.201, 302: see 364d).
For similar reasons, presumably, the view that all things derive from the element
of water is treated by Vitruvius (8 *praef.* 4) as a particularly Egyptian one. Thales,
the originator of the theory of cosmogony from water, supposedly obtained much
of his knowledge in Egypt: Kirk, Raven and Schofield (1983) 79–80.
[99] How and Wells (1912) ad loc.; cf. Diod. 1.37.7; Luc. 10.255–7. Compare the
'conventional' invocation of the Nile republished by Cribiore (1995). It refers to
Nile as 'the oldest of rivers which queen Tethys begot, or one of the sacred waters
of encircling Ocean'.

Nile acts as it does because its processes are intimately connected with those of Ocean, an equally marvellous thing.[100]
So the events of the Nile flood were easily universalized,[101]
and, in particular, as the location of the Nile flood Egypt had
much to say, it was thought, on the question of cosmogony.
At *Bellum Civile* 10.172–92, during a banquet thrown by
Cleopatra, Lucan has Caesar request knowledge of the Egyptian priest-philosopher Acoreus, knowledge, specifically, of
a natural-philosophical nature to which Caesar as world-
conqueror (and epic protagonist) – there is no one *capacior
mundi*, 'more able to grasp the world', than himself, he says
(183) – claims special right. The scholiast at 175 states (and
modern criticism agrees)[102] that the feast of Cleopatra constitutes *aemulatio* of Virgil by Lucan: Cleopatra entertains
Caesar as Dido did Aeneas at the end of *Aeneid* 1; the speech
of Acoreus in reply to Caesar is equivalent to Aeneas' narrative in *Aeneid* 2 and 3. But there is also a clear equivalence
between the speech of Acoreus with its scientific subject matter and the song of Iopas at Dido's feast (*Aen.* 1.740–7),[103]
which acts, as Hardie has shown, as a 'cosmic overture' to
Aeneas' subsequent tale, anticipating the latent cosmological
content of Aeneas' narrative.[104] Iopas can be seen to 'function as an image of Virgil himself as epic poet',[105] and Acoreus can fulfil a similar function for the epic poet Lucan. For

---

[100] For the 'thaumastic' nature of Ocean in Herodotus' treatment see Romm (1992)
176. See also Tac. *Germ.* 34.3 on Ocean as a mysterious entity in connection with
which 'it seemed more religious and pious to hold beliefs about the acts of gods
than to understand'.

[101] Seneca informs us that the Nile flood failed in the tenth and eleventh year of the
reign of Cleopatra, and that this was interpreted as a sign that Antony and
Cleopatra, 'the two powers of the world', would lose their world dominion (*Q.
Nat.* 4A.2.16). The failure of the Nile thus signifies a failure which has as its arena
the whole world. Contrast the greater than normal flood which occurred when
Vespasian – the future emperor – entered Alexandria during the civil war of AD 69
(Dio 65.8.1), also, apparently, a token of future world control: Liebeschuetz
(1979) 180.

[102] Syndikus (1958) 23–4; Zwierlein (1974) 61–3; Tucker (1975); Schmidt (1986) 190.

[103] Schmidt (1986) ix; Tucker (1975) 19–20: Acoreus' 'reply also may be considered,
in part, to replace the entertainment which was provided at Dido's banquet by
Iopas' songs about the wonders of nature'.

[104] Hardie (1986) 64–6.

[105] Hardie (1986) 56.

our purposes, however, the significant point is how easily the *miracula* (10.196) of the Nile could fill the place occupied in Iopas' song by cosmology. The mystery of the Nile (source and flood, customarily combined) ranked as a similar, epic theme, another 'ultimate' truth.

Further evidence for this is to be found in Ovid (*Met.* 1.422–33) and Diodorus (1.10), both of whom use the Nile flood to illustrate the processes of cosmogony, in the specific form of zoogony, the spontaneous generation of animal life from the primordial ooze. They employ the Nile as an illustration of this process because it was believed that from the flood-waters of the Nile animals were generated.[106] Pliny, similarly, uses the example of the Nile to give credence to other fables of spontaneous generation (Pliny, *HN* 9.179); and Pomponius Mela, perhaps under Pliny's influence, has a similar account (1.9.52). All four authors record the phenomenon supposedly observable during the Nile inundation, of animals – in Pliny and Diodorus the animals are mice, specifically – as yet incompletely formed, still partially mud. Such similarities of detail suggest a common source.[107]

In Diodorus, Ovid and Pliny the extraordinary nature of the Nile zoogony is heavily underlined. In Egypt alone, Diodorus writes, living creatures may be seen coming into being in miraculous fashion (παραδόξως, 1.10.3); for Pliny the spontaneous creation of mice is a miracle 'surpassing everything'; Ovid's emphasis is on the paradoxically creative power of the *crasis* of fire and water, Sirius and Nile, summarized in his oxymoronic formulation *discors concordia* of 433, a paradox which recurs both in *bugonia* (308–9) and, I have argued, in Aristaeus' capture of Proteus. Another place we find the combination is of course in the depiction of violent disease in Book 3.[108] What made the fertilizing of its valley by the Nile especially strange to ancient eyes was the time of its occur-

---

[106] In both cases, also, a connection is made with the myth of Deucalion, a common figure for the cosmic flood or cataclysm, just as Phaethon was a common figure for *ecpyrosis*: see Dio Chrys. *Or.* 36.47–9.

[107] Spoerri (1959) 207 and n. 10.

[108] 482–5. The creative power of the combination of hot and wet is a central concept of ancient science. Varro is typical (*Ling.* 5.61): *causa nascendi duplex: ignis et*

rence: during the reign of the dog star, the hottest and dryest time of the year.[109] In this respect the Nile flood parallels the Etesian winds conjured up by Aristaeus in the Aegean islands, similarly designed to alleviate the scorching effects of Sirius: Koenen suggests that the two myths are connected by Tibullus.[110]

Chomarat further suggests that the emphasis on the four points of the compass in the descriptions both of Egypt and of the *bugonia* hut serves to establish an identification of the two. The *bugonia* room, orientated to North, South, East and West, replays in miniature the miracle that occurs in Egypt as a whole (the flood); but also that which occurs in the *mundus* as a whole in spring.[111] He cites for comparison the Roman conception of every town, and in general every enclosed and sacred space, as a microcosm. Along similar lines, I have pointed out how close Virgil's first description of *bugonia* comes to the allegory of the transformations of Proteus as the onset of spring.[112] It is easy to take a further step still and understand the *bugonia* hut as a microcosm and *bugonia* as a figure for Creation itself.

IX

So much for the Nile flood as a figure for cosmogony. But its universalizability took another form, too. The river came to be equated with Osiris.[113] The story was told of the god that

aqua. The reading of the *Georgics* of Ross (1987) takes its departure from the 'paradox', 'contradiction in terms' (38) represented by one of the central subjects of the poem, the *pinguis arista* of 1.8, *pinguis* having associations of moistness, *arista* of dryness or heat: Ross (1987) 32–54. Agriculture is thus at root paradoxical. For Ross the conclusion drawn is the pessimistic one that conflict is inalienable. My approach would of course be to emphasise the paradoxically creative potential of such conflict.

[109] Koenen (1976) 137.

[110] Tib. 1.7.25–6; Koenen (1976) 140. Koenen posits a reference to the *Erigone* of Eratosthenes, the plot of which is apparently preserved by Hyg. *Poet. Astr.* p. 37,12–p. 38,3 Bunte. See also Call. *Aet.* fr. 75.32–7 Pf. where Ζεὺς ἴκμιος (ἰκμαῖος) is equivalent to Tibullus' *Iuppiter pluuius*.

[111] Chomarat (1974) 187–8.

[112] See above p. 78.

[113] See Bonnet (1952) 527–8. The equation is commonly attributed to 'Egyptian priests': Burkert (1987) 82. According to Heliodorus (9.9.4) the identification of

Seth, god of heat, murdered him, causing the waters of the Nile to diminish and vegetation to wither. Isis, his wife, searched for Osiris, found his body, buried it and raised him to new life: out of his leg poured the Nile flood.[114] Porphyry gives a similar account of the identity of Nile and Osiris in a passage which probably derives from Chaeremon, an Egyptian priest and Stoic of the Neronian period.[115] Plutarch cites the view of 'the wiser of the [Egyptian] priests' (*De Is. et Os.* 364a) to the effect that Osiris is not only the Nile but the principle of moisture generally, and Tibullus also makes the identification of Osiris and Nile in the *genethliakon* for Messalla (1.7.27–8): *te canit atque suum pubes miratur Osirim | barbara, Memphiten plangere docta bouem,* 'The barbarous youth, taught to mourn the bull of Memphis, sing of you and worship you as their Osiris.'

It is here that mystery cult becomes relevant. The combination of Osiris and Apis, the sacred bull of Memphis, yielded Sarapis, the dynastic god of the Ptolemaic regime and god of mysteries widespread in the ancient world,[116] and Nile water continued to play a focal role in these 'Isiac' mysteries as well. Wild describes the fixed 'Nile water containers' to be found in certain sanctuaries of Isis and Sarapis in Hellenistic and Roman times, 'constructed in such a way that at certain times water rose sharply within them or even overflowed. That is, they have been designed to reproduce the phenomenon of "flooding".'[117] The significance of such mini-inundations is clear: 'Each time water rose in these basins, the Egyptian gods demonstrated anew their saving power.'[118] The presence of the god in the form of Nile water, in these basins or other forms,[119] constituted for the pious 'a promise ... of a happier

Isis as earth, Osiris as the Nile and Typhon as the sea was told to the initiated by the 'natural philosophers' and 'theologians' who functioned as priests in Egypt.

[114] Koenen (1976) 137.
[115] Horst (1984) fr. 17D. On Chaeremon see also recently Frede (1989).
[116] Koenen (1976) 140–2.
[117] Wild (1981) 60. The water represented the Nile, as Serv. ad *Aen.* 2.116 states: *nam et in templo Isidis aqua sparsa de Nilo esse dicebatur.*
[118] Wild (1981) 68.
[119] Wild (1981) 103–28.

and better existence beyond the grave'.[120] The mysteries of Isis dramatized a (paradoxical) sequence of mourning generating joy, mourning for the dead Osiris which ended with his discovery in the form of the floodwaters of the Nile, a cue for rejoicing: εὑρήκαμεν συγχαίρωμεν.[121] Through the myth of Osiris, as Burkert puts it, the 'peripety from mournful to joyous festivals was thus correlated to the change of the seasons, "the guarantee of the crops coming back, the elements living, the year replicating itself"'.[122]

Thus the miraculous death and rebirth of vegetation which accompanied the ebb and flow of the Nile, mediated through the mythology of Osiris, became the basis of a mystery cult. Perhaps the most familiar ancient representation of the Nile is the great carpet mosaic from Praeneste, dating (apparently) from the late second century BC.[123] It depicts the whole course of the Nile during the flood-season. Krumme has recently argued that the lower sanctuary at Praeneste (where the mosaic was discovered) should be interpreted as an Iseum, and that the mosaic itself lay in a basin containing the 'Nile water' which was an essential feature of the Isiac cult. The representation of the river lying under the water in the basin would have implied the identity of the water with the sacred water of the Nile. If correct, this is striking confirmation of the powerful mystical and redemptive associations of the river.[124]

X

The mystical associations of the Nile are paralleled by those attaching to *bugonia*. A number of critics have (independently) noted connections between Virgil's bees and mystical

---

[120] Wild (1981) 128.
[121] Firm. Mat. *Err. Prof. Rel.* 2.9. See also Seneca *apud* August. *De civ. D.* 6.10, p. 268, Sen. *Apocol.* 13, Juv. 8.29–30, Lactant. *Inst. Epit.* 18.5–6. A comparison with Vitr. *De Arch.* 8 *praef.* 4 illustrates the cultic assimilation of Nile water and Osiris: the finding of Osiris is the same as the finding of the water.
[122] Burkert (1987) 82, quoting Tert. *Adv. Marc.* 1.13.5.
[123] Ling (1991) 7.
[124] Krumme (1990) esp. 164–5. I was alerted to this article by Kathleen Coleman.

religions of redemption. Wormell, Chomarat, Bettini and Farrell all compare Virgil's *bugonia* to the words of Porphyry at *Antr.* 18–19, where he states that bees symbolize the souls of the dead, specifically those that were to be reborn and to live just lives.[125] He also brings this interpretation into connection with *bugonia*. That some such symbolic application of bees was familiar to Virgil is suggested by his use of bee imagery to describe the just souls awaiting rebirth at *Aen.* 6.707–9.[126] Such an interpretation of *bugonia* might also give further point to Ovid's pentameter summary of the ritual (*Fast.* 1.380), *mille animas una necata dedit*. At any rate Aeneas of Gaza (*Theophr.* 155) gives a very similar description of *bugonia* in a context referring to the reincarnation of souls,[127] and Servius *auctus* ad *Aen.* 1.430 preserves an interesting aetiological explanation of the Greek word μέλισσα, 'bee', concerning what Bettini calls a 'variant of *bugonia*'. Servius tells how Ceres confided to an old woman named Melissa the secrets of her mysteries, and forbade her to reveal them. Certain women tried to extract the secrets from her, and failing, ripped her to pieces. From her dismembered body Ceres made bees be generated.[128] Taken together, the evidence suggests that Virgil's bees, like his emphasis on the location in Egypt, will have carried strong overtones of the doctrines of mystery cult, and also (incidentally) will have invested sacrificial ritual – with which *bugonia* is so closely connected in the *Aristaeus* – with similar associations: the effect of sacrifice and of mystery cult are to some degree conflated.

[125] Chomarat (1974) 189; Bettini (1991) 198–9; Farrell (1991) 262–4; Wormell (1971) 430–1.
[126] Norden (1916) ad loc.: Farrell (1991) 263–4. For further references to the notion of bees as images of the soul, see Bettini (1991) 304–5 n. 4.
[127] Bettini (1991) 212.
[128] Bettini (1991) 215. For the redemptive significance of dismemberment in mystery cult, see my next chapter. Tantalizingly, in view of my next chapter, de Gubernatis states that 'Dionysus after having been torn to pieces in the form of a bull was born again, according to those who were initiated in the Dionysian mysteries, in the form of a bee'. However, his source for this statement is unclear: de Gubernatis (1872) II 217; Cook (1895) 6 and n. 42.

XI

The Nile flood which forms the backdrop to *bugonia*, then, prefigures subsequent themes in the *Aristaeus*. The Nile introduces the notion of rebirth, and rebirth, specifically, of a paradoxical, counterintuitive nature. But contemplation of the nature of the Nile inundation tended to lead in two particular directions, and to two particular models of rebirth: that associated with cosmological speculation regarding the totality of the physical world, and that associated with the mysteries.

These two modes – physics and mystery – are difficult clearly to separate. Contemplation of the physical processes of the universe was habitually assimilated to the experience of the initiand at the mysteries – each activity imparted ultimate truths –, as indeed it is at *G.* 2.475–86.[129] Buffière points out the close association of (allegorical) Homeric myth and the mysteries in the text of Ps.-Heraclitus, and elsewhere.[130] Ps.-Heraclitus calls Homer 'the great hierophant of heaven and the gods who opened up for human souls the paths to heaven which were inaccessible and closed to them' (76.1): the hierophant was the high priest at Eleusis who, as his name implies, *showed* the sacred objects to the initiands,[131] including the ultimate revelation of the ear of grain.[132] In the context of the myth of Proteus (64.3), again, Ps.-Heraclitus talks of 'the Olympian τελεταί of Homer' which stand in need of a hierophant to elucidate them (εἰ μή τις ... ἱεροφαντήσειε).[133] Here Ps.-Heraclitus also imputes to *himself* the functions of the hierophant, relative to the *arcana* of the Homeric poems.[134] In fact the veiling devices of myth and mystery shared the

---

[129] Hardie (1986) 38–41.
[130] Buffière (1956) 36–9.
[131] Mylonas (1961) 298.
[132] Burkert (1987) 80–1.
[133] On the mystical associations of the term τελεταί see p. 188 n. 149 below.
[134] It is to the esoteric and revelatory aspect of myth also that Ps.-Heraclitus is looking when he interprets the Homeric description of Proteus as νημερτής, 'unerring, infallible', at *Od.* 4.384 (67.4). This is an appropriate epithet, Heraclitus says, for what is ἀληθουργέστερον, 'more true/real-acting', than the

function of limiting sublime knowledge to those suitable to receive it, creating an initiated elect.[135] In my discussions of the myth of Proteus I have overemphasized – necessarily, but nonetheless – the de-allegorized meanings of the myth. But to a great extent the allegory and obfuscation, and the mystery and religious awe thereby generated, are the point. Homer, like the mysteries, spoke δι᾽ αἰνιγμάτων καὶ μυθικῶν λόγων (Ps.-Plut. *De Vita et Poesi Homeri* B92) to restrict his sublime message to the worthy. Homeric myth could thus easily be considered analogous to mystery ritual: both because, like the mysteries, it conveyed information in this oblique fashion, and because the physical processes of the cosmos it was thought to convey were considered as mysterious as the information imparted to the initiand. Hence we find the Stoic Cleanthes, perhaps following Aristotle, comparing the universe to a huge mystery hall.[136] Porphyry (Euseb. *Praep. Evang.* 3.12) implies something similar when he tells us that in the Eleusinian mysteries the hierophant was got up in the likeness of the demiurge and the torch-bearer (δᾳδοῦχος) in the likeness of the sun. Myths and mysteries, as Buffière writes, were considered two complementary routes to an understanding of the divine, or, looked at another way, two complementary means employed by the divine to reveal itself to the pious: 'Les mythes apportent cette révélation enveloppée dans les drames légendaires, les mystères la présentent sous forme de tableaux vivants.'[137]

Hardie has discussed this assimilation of cosmological speculation to mystical experience with reference to the imagery of *G.* 2.475–86 and 490–2.[138] At 475–86, as we have

matter which Proteus represents and from which everything derives? The Protean ὕλη is ἀληθουργής, apparently, because it constitutes the underlying substance of everything, the *ultimate reality*, an ideal object of the mystical, natural-philosophical, revelatory project in which Heraclitus is engaged.

[135] Philo, *De Providentia* 2.40, a text only extant in an Armenian version translated into Latin by Aucher (1822), re-edited with chapter enumeration by Richter (1830).

[136] Festugière (1949) 235–8; Bywater (1877) 78, citing Cleanthes fr. theol. 4 Wachsmuth.

[137] Buffière (1956) 37.

[138] Hardie (1986) 38–41.

noted, Virgil presents himself as an initiand requesting elucidation from the Muses on the mystical questions of natural philosophy; and again at 490–2 Virgil combines an echo of Lucretius' rationalistic reection of religion (492, *subiecit pedibus*; *DRN* 1.78, *religio pedibus subiecta*) with the imagery of the mysteries: the mysteries, also, were a means of overcoming the fear of death. In so doing he is imitating, as Hardie has shown, the imagery of Lucretius, who ironically used the language of religious initiation to make an anti-religious, Epicurean point.[139] In *G.* 2 Virgil may appear to be following Lucretius' Epicurean rejection of religion: cultivation of the gods of the countryside and natural philosophy seem here antithetical.[140] Hardie writes of the contradiction, revealed in this passage, in Virgil's attitude to his great didactic predecessor:

attraction for the grandiose cosmic afflatus that pervades the *De Rerum Natura*, intellectual attraction to the resounding certainties of the Lucretian world-picture; but repulsion from the accompanying demand that the emotional ties to Rome and Italy, and perhaps to irrationality itself, must be cut once and for all.[141]

In *Georgic* 4, by contrast, I would like to suggest, part of Virgil's programme is the construction of a profoundly religious form of natural-philosophical didactic. Virgil's treatment of scientific themes is here framed as strongly religious. The connection between natural philosophy and mystery cult, which Lucretius sought ironically to undermine, is forcibly restated. In particular Virgil's emphasis on the miraculous, the *mirabile dictu*, runs pointedly counter to the central Lucretian imperative *mirari mitte* (6.1056).[142] In this context it is worth comparing Virgil's deliberate and programmatic emphasis on the paradoxicality of the Nile flood with Lucretius' rationalistic tabulation of its possible causes at *DRN* 6.712–37. And

---

[139] Hardie (1986) 40; see, for example, Lucr. *DRN* 3.1–30 and cf. Kenney (1971) ad 28–30.

[140] Hardie (1986) 43–4.

[141] Hardie (1986) 46.

[142] Schrijvers (1970) 262–6. Contrast the Stoic emphasis on the marvellous quality of natural phenomena – evidence for the providential organization of the universe – exemplified at Cic. *Nat. D.* 2.98–153.

there is perhaps a further respect in which Virgil marks his departure here from his Lucretian model.[143] Lucretius' poem ends with a plague, the ultimate test of our understanding and internalization of his Epicurean precepts: a reader with proper, rational understanding of the nature of the universe will appreciate – as Lucretius' Athenians do not – that there is nothing mysterious or terrible about the plague and nothing in it to fear.[144] This concluding plague – Schiesaro calls it Lucretius' 'final spiritual exercise' for the reader – originates in Egypt (6.1141). Virgil's pointedly religious, paradoxical *bugonia*, with which he concludes the *Georgics*, and which is itself very reminiscent of plague, also has its origin in Egypt.

Virgil and Lucretius are in one sense engaged in similar projects: religious initiation, like Epicureanism, claimed to impart an understanding of the underlying scheme of the world. In the case of mystery cult that understanding consisted in the revelation of a divine order wherein death is constructive. A funerary epigram of the Eleusinian hierophant Glaucus from the 2nd/3rd century AD (*IG* II² 3661.5–6) encapsulates this message of the Mysteries memorably: ἦ καλὸν ἐκ μακάρων μυστήριον, οὐ μόνον εἶναι | τὸν θάνατον θνητοῖς οὐ κακὸν ἀλλ' ἀγαθόν, 'Truly beautiful is the secret which comes from the blessed, that death is not only not an evil for mortals, but in fact a boon.' Virgil's emphasis on the miraculous, paradoxical processes of the physical universe, I would suggest, is part of an attempt to show 'that there is some wiser insight and plan in all that is going on'[145] which may make sense of the seeming arbitrariness of the processes of the cosmos as depicted hitherto in the poem. Such a reading might point the way to a broader interpretation of the *Aristaeus* as of a focally sacramental import, as a capping of the rationalistic Lucretian mode of didactic wisdom with a recourse to religious *gnosis* in

---

[143] The following was suggested to me by Don Fowler (*pers. comm.*).
[144] Schiesaro (1994) 102–3.
[145] Dio Chrys. 12.33, τὰ γιγνόμενα, ὡς μετὰ γνώμης καὶ παρασκευῆς πράττεται σοφωτέρας. The translation is that of Burkert (1987) 90. Dio is here drawing an analogy between the knowledge provided by mystery initiation and that vouchsafed by contemplation of the cosmos.

various forms, all of which share in common one particular feature: *paradoxicality*, a dynamic by which disaster appears constructive, an integral part of a providential scheme.

The Nile, then, prefigures the redemptive doctrines of the passage to come: it introduces the topic of *rerum natura*, the *miraculum* of physical creation, but also – potentially – that of religious mystery and providentiality. In my next chapter I shall further investigate the relevance of mystery cult, with particular reference to the story of Orpheus.

CHAPTER 4

POETA CREATUS

I

At the core of the *Aristaeus* lie two passages – the *Proteus* and the *Orpheus* – which advertise to an abnormal degree their generic allegiances. The *Proteus*, I have suggested, exemplifies what was expected of the Homeric-epic mode. Grand Epic was the mode in which it was proper to couch panegyric, praise-poetry: it was the poetry in which was celebrated the success of a military leader. The *Proteus* thus represents a poetry dealing in the themes of achievement, success, victory – indeed the ultimate achievement, the creation of the universe, which reflects the recent triumphs enjoyed by Octavian. The protagonist of the passage, Aristaeus, is thus the ideal epic figure: the heroic success-story.

But if Aristaeus is the characteristically successful epic hero, Proteus represents his antithesis. Aristaeus is the victor, Proteus his victim. Allegorically, I suggested, Proteus might be the passive principle of the universe (τὸ πάσχον), forcibly given structure by the active demiurge (τὸ ποιοῦν), and I have argued that the respective roles of Aristaeus and Proteus as the active and passive cosmic principles are reflected in Virgil's employment of words cognate (or considered by the ancients cognate) with *uis*.[1] Only by bringing *uis* (in the form of *uincula*) to bear on the recalcitrant sea god, Cyrene informs her son (396–400), will Aristaeus make him speak. The *uis*-terms pile up (396, 398, 399, 405, 412), until finally and emphatically Proteus is overcome, *uictus* (443), and 'at length, under the influence of great *uis*' (450), delivers his prophecy.[2]

---

[1] See pp. 89–90 above.
[2] At 450 an allusion is perhaps intended to the Varronian etymology *uates a ui mentis*: see Maltby (1991) s.v.

In the last instance it has seemed unclear to editors whether the compulsion under which Proteus labours is that applied by Aristaeus – the *uincula* – or the violence of inspiration.[3] But it can easily be both: his song is generated by a combination of Aristaeus' violence and Proteus' violent vatic possession.

Aristaeus is the controller of events, then, Proteus quite literally his, and their, victim. Now, I suggested that the *Proteus* might be read in terms of Lieberg's *poeta creator* motif, according to which the poet's own condition is reflected in the themes of his poetry. Thus Virgil's success – the emulation of Homer – consisted precisely in his oblique treatment of Octavian's victory.[4] I should now like to interpret Proteus' song in a similar light. Proteus' choice of theme, I believe, is intimately related to his status as the suffering victim. Proteus suffers, his song is a product of that suffering, and therefore suffering is the topic of his song.

It has been noted by Thomas that Proteus has much in common with the protagonist of the story he tells, Orpheus, rather as Virgil, the author of the primary narrative, has much in common with Aristaeus-Octavian. To begin with, the names Orpheus and Proteus are almost anagrams of each other. But perhaps more cogently, at 4.509 the two seem to coalesce even in respect of the telling of the story: Proteus describes Orpheus singing *haec*, that is, apparently, precisely the content of Proteus' story. Thomas writes, 'Orpheus is more than just a character in the action; Proteus suggests that he is responsible for the actual poem – *haec* refers to the entire song.'[5] We are perhaps reminded of the 'nesting' of singers at the end of *Ecl.* 6, where it is unclear whether the singer is the narrator of the poem, or Silenus,[6] or even Apollo. Here in the *Orpheus* the effect is to establish a degree of identity between Proteus and Orpheus. But I want to suggest another respect in which they are identical, a much more striking one.

My argument will presuppose something I seek to establish

---

[3] Thus Conington and Nettleship (1898) ad loc.
[4] See pp. 97–8 above.   [5] Thomas (1988) ad loc.
[6] Coleman (1977) ad *Ecl.* 6.74.

later on, namely that just as Aristaeus takes on much of the function and character of gods with whom he is associated – *viz.* Apollo and Jupiter – so Orpheus is to be understood partly as a reflection of another god to whom *he* is closely related: Dionysus.

After all his misfortunes Orpheus finally dies. His death is not the central event of the story, but can nonetheless be seen as its logical conclusion. Throughout the passage the death of Eurydice has seemed to imply Orpheus' death as well. His response to Eurydice's death is to enter the Underworld himself, and his existence after the second loss of his wife, wandering about the sterile Northern wastes, is another 'living death'.[7] When Eurydice is lost again to the Underworld, after Orpheus turns to look back at her, she implies that Orpheus' madness has killed not only her but himself as well (494–5): *illa 'quis et me' inquit 'miseram et te perdidit, Orpheu, | quis tantus furor?'*, 'She said, "what terrible madness has destroyed me in my misery and you, Orpheus?"' Eurydice's equation of her own and Orpheus' suffering smacks of the identification of lover and beloved conventional in Roman love poetry and discussed by Lilja.[8] This is the elegiac convention that life without the loved one is equivalent to death: the death of the lover is thus a natural extension of the death of the beloved. The elegists' lover is often (literally) their *uita* or their *lux*, as Burck says: 'Die Geliebte verkörpert für sie das Leben und das Licht, das ihr Dasein erhellt und ihm seinen Glanz gibt.'[9] In *Ecl.* 10, which, as Thomas has rightly insisted,[10] is a significant source for the depiction of Orpheus in *G.* 4, Gallus pines away from unhappy love (*peribat*, 10; cf. 33) in this same elegiac way.[11] In short, Orpheus' *actual* death can be seen as the logical extension and natural conclusion of all the suffering that he has previously endured.

---

[7] The cold sterility of the North, in particular, recalls the coldness associated with death, as at 506 (*illa … frigida*), 525 (*frigida lingua*); cf. 474 (*hibernus … imber*).

[8] Lilja (1978) 68–9, 196–7.

[9] Burck (1952) 167. See, for example, Prop. 2.28.42, Ov. *Am.* 2.13.15–16.

[10] Thomas (1988) I 15–16.

[11] As Papanghelis (1987) 41–5 points out, *amor* and *mori* might be thought etymologically (and thus metaphysically) related.

So how does Orpheus die? The form Orpheus' death takes is dismemberment, σπαραγμός.[12] Virgil gives us the precise context of his death. It occurs (521) during the mystery rites of Bacchus, or Dionysus: *inter sacra deum nocturnique orgia Bacchi*.[13] Servius *auctus* glosses *nocturni, quia sacra eius nocte celebrantur: ex quo Nyctelius est cognominatus,* 'because his rites are celebrated at night: hence he is named Nyctelius'. As Servius informs us, the god worshipped in these nocturnal Bacchic rites was (sometimes) called Νυκτέλιος, and the rites themselves τὰ Νυκτέλια. Elsewhere Plutarch states (*De E* 389a) that the god of these rites is known by four names: Dionysus, Nyctelius, Zagreus and Isodaetes. 'Dionysus Zagreus' is in fact the name we find most commonly in the sources. The general nature of these rites is explained (by Plutarch again) as follows (*De esu carn.* 996c):

τὰ γὰρ δὴ περὶ τὸν Διόνυσον μεμυθευμένα πάθη τοῦ διαμελισμοῦ καὶ τὰ Τιτάνων ἐπ' αὐτὸν τολμήματα, κολάσεις τε τούτων καὶ κεραυνώσεις γευσαμένων τοῦ φόνου, ἠνιγμένος ἐστί μῦθος εἰς τὴν παλιγγενεσίαν.

For the story told about the tribulations of dismemberment suffered by Dionysus and the Titans' abuses against him, and their punishments and blasting by thunderbolts when they had tasted his blood, in its inner meaning has to do with rebirth.

Mystery religions were always, by their very nature, arcane. What evidence there is that has come down to us is very sparse (though less so in this period than in the Classical era),[14] and definite conclusions of any kind are hard to come to. One element of Bacchic mystery-ritual, however, emerges clearly from Plutarch's comment in the *De esu carn.* just quoted. The divinities of ancient mystery cults, as a rule, tended to have one specific myth with which they were particularly associated.[15] A feature of many of the numerous varieties of Dionysiac ritual, including τὰ Νυκτέλια. was the

---

[12] As Thomas (1988) notes ad loc., *discerptum ... sparsere* (522) is practically a gloss on the term.
[13] The term *orgia* (ὄργια) 'is a word for ritual which is used especially for mysteries': Burkert (1977) 413.
[14] Seaford (1981) 252.
[15] Burkert (1987) 73.

myth of the dismemberment of Dionysus.[16] This myth was usefully summarized by Julian (*Gal.* 44b) as οἱ Διονύσου σπαραγμοὶ καὶ μελῶν κολλήσεις, but it has, in fact, a number of complicated variants, which are collated by Linforth.[17] In almost all cases Dionysus is dismembered by the Titans.[18] According to Σ Lycoph. 207 both Callimachus and Euphorion related how the Titans dismembered Dionysus, boiled the pieces and handed them over to Apollo, who buried them by his tripod at Delphi. Diodorus (3.62) and Arnobius (*Adv. Gent.* 5.19) say that his limbs were boiled, Clement of Alexandria (*Protr.* 2.18.1) boiled and roasted. Plutarch (*De esu carn.* 996c), Olympiodorus (*In Platonis Phaedonem* 61c) and Firmicus Maternus (*Err. Prof. Rel.* 6) have the Titans eat part or whole of the dead god. Sometimes the story continues with Athena rescuing Dionysus' heart and taking it to Zeus (Clem. Alex.; Firm. Mat.; Procl. *H.* 7.11–15; Σ Lycoph. 355).[19] The Callimachean and Euphorionic detail of his burial at Delphi by Apollo is picked up by Clement and Plutarch (*De Is. et Os.* 364f–365a). The myth culminates in the reunion of Dionysus' limbs and his restoration to life. The agent of his reassembly, however, is (predictably) in dispute. Euphorion (Phld. *Piet.* 44) and Cornutus (*Theol. Graec.* 30) make it Rhea, Diodorus Demeter; the Orphic versions read by the Neoplatonists made it Apollo (for example Olympiodorus, *In Phd.* 67c; Procl. *In T.* 35b). Plutarch seems to imply that the Dionysus buried at Delphi came to life again during the ceremony in which the Thyiades (Delphic Bacchants) awoke Dionysus Liknites. Macrobius (*In Somn.* 1.12.11) and *Myth. Vat.* 3.12.5 say no more than that the parts were buried and later emerged whole.[20]

---

[16] Burkert (1987) 5, 73, (1972) 249–50. Other authors also explicitly connect the myth with the mysteries: for example, Diod. 3.62, Harpocration s.v. λευκή, Σ Pind. *Isthm.* 7.3. For a fuller discussion see Burkert (1987) 155 n. 38.

[17] Linforth (1941) 307–64.

[18] The exception is Σ Clem. Alex. 92 P, which has Dionysus dismembered by Bacchanals: see below.

[19] This detail is 'frequently alluded to by the Neoplatonists': Linforth (1941) 313.

[20] *unus et integer emersisse*, Macrobius; *uiuum et integrum resurrexisse*, *Myth. Vat.* Justinus (*c. Tryph.* p. 295) and Origen (*contra Celsum* 4.17) – both of them, evi-

One authority – the Paris scholiast of Clement of Alexandria – has Dionysus himself suffer σπαραγμός by Maenads rather than by Titans. This was the fate of Orpheus, of course, but the fate also of the wild animals rent by Bacchants during the trieteric *oreibasia*. According to this scholiast, and also according to Photius and Firmicus Maternus,[21] the σπαραγμός and ὠμοφαγία (dismemberment and eating raw) of wild animals undertaken by the Bacchanals commemorated the archetypal dismemberment suffered by Dionysus at the hands of the Titans. As Dodds says, Dionysus' tendency to be envisioned as an animal – bull, snake or lion – makes it easy for us to recognize in these dismembered victims 'bestial incarnations of the god'.[22] Similarly, we are told by Plutarch at *Quaest Rom*. 291a of the use made of ivy in the rites of the Nyctelia and Agrionia (another Dionysiac festival): Bacchants rip it apart (σπαράττουσι) with their hands and their mouths. As Seaford says, 'the ivy is presumably in some sense the god'.[23]

Orpheus, then, in his death resembles the mystic Dionysus. We shall expand on this insight later. But an implication of my second chapter was that Virgilian myth is always likely to be allegorical. The capture of Proteus, in addition to any other reference, I argued, depicts the creative destruction of the universe. Orpheus' death is of a very specific kind. He dies by dismemberment during Dionysiac ritual, a death widely interpreted to commemorate the archetypal death by dismemberment of Dionysus himself. Considered this way there is a further similarity between Proteus and Orpheus: Proteus' capture and metamorphoses, and the Dionysiac death by dismemberment which Orpheus endures, are the only examples of which I am aware of myth allegorized to represent the

dently, christianizing versions – have Dionysus both rise from the dead and ascend to heaven. This account has closely followed Linforth (1941) 309–16.

[21] Σ Clem. Alex. 92 P, ὠμὰ γὰρ ἤσθιον κρέα οἱ μυούμενοι Διονύσῳ δεῖγμα τοῦτο τελούμενοι τοῦ σπαραγμοῦ ὃν ὑπέστη Διόνυσος πρὸς τῶν Μαινάδων; Photius s.v. νεβρίζειν, διασπᾶν νεβρούς κατὰ μίμησιν τοῦ περὶ τὸν Διόνυσον πάθους; Firmicus Maternus, *Err. prof. rel.* 6.5.

[22] Dodds (1944) xvi.

[23] Seaford (1981) 263 n. 96; cf. Bather (1894) 261.

creative destruction and differentiation (into the four elements) of the universe postulated by Stoic physics. The evidence is essentially twofold, deriving from a stray reference by Plutarch which has been fairly widely noted, and an extensive passage in the late Greek epicist Nonnus of which the academic mainstream is generally rather less aware.

Nonnus' *Dionysiaca* spends the first six of its forty-eight books describing the background to the birth of Dionysus.[24] Included in this section is an account of the birth of Zagreus, the first incarnation of Dionysus, which effectively runs from 5.565 to the end of Book 6. Dionysus Zagreus, as we now know, was the figure who is dismembered by the Titans and whose myth was one of the cardinal elements of Dionysiac mystery cult. Nonnus describes how Zeus mated with Persephone in the form of a snake; how she gave birth to Zagreus, the 'horned baby', who occupied the throne of the universe until the Titans, under the influence of Hera, dismembered him. I quote the translated passage *in extenso* (6.169–205),

But he did not hold the throne of Zeus for long. By the fierce resentment of implacable Hera, the Titans cunningly smeared their round faces with disguising chalk, and while he contemplated his changeling countenance reflected in a mirror they destroyed him with an infernal knife. There as his limbs were being rent[25] by the Titan steel, the end of his life was the beginning of a new life as Dionysos. He appeared in another shape, and changed into many forms: now young like crafty Cronides shaking the aegis-cape, now as ancient Cronos heavy-kneed, pouring rain. Sometimes he was a curiously formed baby, sometimes like a mad youth with the flower of the first down marking his rounded chin with black. Again, a mimic lion he uttered a horrible roar in furious rage from a wild snarling throat, as he lifted a neck shadowed by a thick mane, marking his body on both sides with the self-striking whip of a tail which flickered about over his hairy back. Next he left the shape of a lion's looks and let out a ringing

---

[24] For a succinct introduction to Nonnus see Hopkinson (1994a) 121–5.

[25] This is my translation of the present participle διχαζομένων (174), the only point at which I depart from the translation of Rouse (1940). The explanation of Chuvin (1992) ad loc. that the verb describes the 'doubling' of Dionysus' limbs through his reflection in the mirror is unconvincing. As I shall suggest below, the reasoning which leads Chuvin to this conclusion – the dismemberment happens later, after the metamorphoses, and so cannot be happening already here – is incorrect: the dismemberment is already happening (172), and the metamorphoses are taking place *during* the dismemberment.

neigh, now like an unbroken horse that lifts his neck on high to shake out the imperious tooth of the bit, and rubbing, whitened his cheek with hoary foam. Sometimes he poured out a whistling hiss from his mouth, a curling horned serpent covered with scales, darting out his tongue from his gaping throat, and leaping upon the grim head of some Titan encircled his neck in snaky spiral coils. Then he left the shape of the restless crawler and became a tiger with gay stripes on his body; or again like a bull emitting a counterfeit roar from his mouth he butted the Titans with sharp horn. So he fought for his life, until Hera with jealous throat bellowed harshly through the air – that heavy-resentful stepmother! and the gates of Olympos rattled in echo to her jealous throat from high heaven. Then the bold bull collapsed: the murderers each eager for his turn with the knife chopped piecemeal the bull-shaped Dionysos.

The sequence of events here seems to be as follows: the Titans set about dismembering Dionysus, but in the very moment of death Dionysus experiences new life (175) in the form of metamorphoses. At the end of his transformations his dismemberment – and killing – are completed. The metamorphoses of Zagreus take place, then, *during* his dismemberment. There is no parallel for this description of Dionysus–Zagreus metamorphosing at his death. Chuvin cites for comparison the Orphic hymns 29.8 and 39.5–10, the latter of which talks of Dionysus αἰολόμορφος and πολύμορφος.[26] But these references do not provide a parallel for the series of transformations which we find here. He also cites Plutarch, *De E* 388f–389a, which again is significantly different from this passage (though ultimately, as I shall argue later, derived from a similar source).

Zagreus transmogrifies into a young man, an old man, a baby and a youth: as Chuvin suggests,[27] the four ages of man, each, incidentally, associated with a god – the first with Zeus, the second with Cronos, while the third and fourth recall typical representations of Dionysus Zagreus, the infant, and Dionysus Bacchus, the crazed youth. There then follow transformations into five animals: the lion, horse, serpent, tiger and bull. Three of these animals – the lion, snake and bull – are commonly associated with the god (but are common else-

---

[26] Chuvin (1992) 152.   [27] Chuvin (1992) 29–30 and ad 176.

where as well).[28] The other two, however – horse and tiger – have no special connection with Dionysus. Chuvin is left rather at a loss. He does not feel that other metamorphoses by Dionysus in the poem (particularly at 36.291–353) can shine any light on these here, nor for that matter the metamorphosing god Proteus with whom the entire poem begins, and who as Hopkinson has shown can represent, all at once, the ποικιλία of the poem, of the poet and of the poem's protagonist, Dionysus.[29] What I wish to suggest is that the similarity between Dionysus Zagreus and Proteus in respect of metamorphosis, whatever other sources there may be for it, reflects similar allegorical interpretations of the two myths. The evidence here is from Plutarch. At *De E* 388e–389a Plutarch connects the myth of the dismembered Dionysus with physical theory:

ἐὰν οὖν ἔρηταί τις, τί ταῦτα πρὸς τὸν Ἀπόλλωνα, φήσομεν οὐχὶ μόνον ἀλλὰ καὶ πρὸς τὸν Διόνυσον, ᾧ τῶν Δελφῶν οὐδὲν ἧττον ἢ τῷ Ἀπόλλωνι μέτεστιν. ἀκούομεν οὖν τῶν θεολόγων τὰ μὲν ἐν ποιήμασι τὰ δ' ἄνευ μέτρου λεγόντων καὶ ὑμνούντων ὡς ἄφθαρτος ὁ θεὸς καὶ ἀίδιος πεφυκώς, ὑπὸ δή τινος εἱμαρμένης γνώμης καὶ λόγου μεταβολαῖς ἑαυτοῦ χρώμενος ἄλλοτε μὲν εἰς πῦρ ἀνῆψε τὴν φύσιν πάνθ' ὁμοιώσας πᾶσιν, ἄλλοτε δὲ παντοδαπὸς ἔν τε μορφαῖς καὶ ἐν πάθεσι καὶ δυνάμεσι διαφόροις γιγνόμενος, ὡς γίγνεται νῦν, κόσμος ὀνομάζεται τῷ γνωριμωτάτῳ τῶν ὀνομάτων. κρυπτόμενοι δὲ τοὺς πολλοὺς οἱ σοφώτεροι τὴν μὲν εἰς πῦρ μεταβολὴν Ἀπόλλωνά τε τῇ μονώσει Φοῖβόν τε τῷ καθαρῷ καὶ ἀμιάντῳ καλοῦσι, τῆς δ' εἰς πνεύματα καὶ ὕδωρ καὶ γῆν καὶ ἄστρα καὶ φυτῶν ζῴων τε γενέσεις τροπῆς αὐτοῦ καὶ διακοσμήσεως τὸ μὲν πάθημα καὶ τὴν μεταβολὴν διασπασμόν τινα καὶ διαμελισμὸν αἰνίττονται· Διόνυσον δὲ καὶ Ζαγρέα καὶ Νυκτέλιον καὶ Ἰσοδαίτην αὐτὸν ὀνομάζουσι καὶ φθορᾶς τινας καὶ ἀφανισμοὺς εἶτα δ' ἀναβιώσεις καὶ παλιγγενεσίας, οἰκεῖα ταῖς εἰρημέναις μεταβολαῖς αἰνίγματα καὶ μυθεύματα περαίνουσι.

If then someone should ask, 'What has this to do with Apollo?,' we shall say that it has to do not only with him but with Dionysus as well, whose share in Delphi is as great as Apollo's. We hear the theologians claiming, both in verse and prose, that the god is imperishable and eternal by nature, but that owing to some predestined plan and purpose he undergoes transformations of himself, at one time setting fire to his nature and making all things alike,

---

[28] Chuvin (1992) 153.

[29] Hopkinson (1994c) 10–11. I would obviously be tempted to suggest that Proteus' transformations at the beginning of the *Dionysiaca* also represent the creation of a poetic microcosm.

at another time becoming utterly diverse, with various forms, dispositions and powers, as is the case now, and he is called cosmos, the best known of his names. But the wiser people in their esoteric doctrines call his transformation into fire 'Apollo' because of his oneness [at this time] and Phoebus because of his purity and immaculacy. But in his change and differentiation into winds and water and earth and stars and the generations of plants and animals they describe this ordeal and transformation allegorically as a 'rending' and 'dismemberment'. They call him Dionysus, Zagreus, Nyctelius and Isodaetes, and they construct destructions and disappearances and then restorations to life and rebirths, riddles and myths in keeping with the aforesaid transformations.

This passage is as hard to interpret as to translate.[30] But for our purposes the important point is that Plutarch distinguishes two stages in the history of the divine universe, one during which he is fiery and uniform, and one when he is diverse, clearly the *ecpyrosis* and *diacosmesis* of Stoic physical theory. When he is uniform, Plutarch goes on, he is called Apollo (a relation is implied between Ἀπόλλων and ἄ-πολλα), and when differentiated Dionysus. This differentiation of the universe into its various components (Plutarch uses the technical term διακόσμησις) is described allegorically as the dismemberment of Dionysus, who is called Zagreus, Nyctelius and Isodaetes – names of the mystical Dionysus. On the evidence of this passage Jones convincingly postulated a Stoic allegory of Dionysus' dismemberment as a reflection of their theory of cosmogony: 'The rending of Zagreus by the Titans would naturally signify the *diacosmesis*, the breaking up of the unitary substance into the manifold entities of the κόσμος.'[31]

As an allegory of the differentiation of matter at Creation the dismemberment of Dionysus is clearly equivalent to the metamorphoses of Proteus. As it happens Chuvin specifically discounts the notion that the metamorphoses of Zagreus in Nonnus might represent the recreation of the universe. In

[30] My translation is indebted to those of Babbitt (1936) and Linforth (1941) 317–18.
[31] Jones (1980) 15. See also Linforth (1941) 317–18; Seaford (1981) 255. Compare Plut. *De def. or.* 415f, where we are told that the doctrine of *ecpyrosis* was read into Hesiod, Heraclitus – and Orpheus: Jones (1980) 15. There is a related (Neoplatonic) allegory of the dismemberment of Dionysus at Macrob. *In Somn.* 1.12.11–12: here Dionysus-Liber is the νοῦς ὑλικός from which the whole universe is constructed. The allegory is attributed by Macrobius to the Orphics.

that case, he argues, the metamorphoses would be into the different component realms of the differentiated universe – man, animals, vegetal, mineral and primordial elements, like Proteus' at Ov. *Met.* 8.732–7.[32] But we have seen how the Homeric metamorphoses of Proteus, in themselves far from representative of the physical world, came to be interpreted as representing the differentiated physical universe. That a similar interpretation is to be attached to the metamorphoses of Zagreus in Nonnus is confirmed, I think, by what follows in the text: namely, a long description of the destruction of the universe first by fire (206–23) and then, at greater length, by flood (224–370). The book concludes (371–88) with its regeneration, seemingly in a purified form.[33]

Now I would not wish to suggest that Nonnus' myth of Zagreus is a documentary account either of Dionysiac mystery myth or of any allegorical and philosophical reading of the myth there might have been. (For example, the fact that the destruction of the universe according to Nonnus is caused by both fire and flood is strictly contrary to Stoic theory, which seems to have talked – if not of *ecpyrosis* alone[34] – of an alternation in the total history of the world between dissolutions by flood, κατακλυσμός, and fire, ἐκπυρώσις.[35]) But I *would* argue that the passage is written against a backdrop of an (essentially Stoic) allegoresis of the Zagreus-myth.[36] According to this interpretation Dionysus Zagreus' dismemberment corresponds to the differentiation of the unitary substance of the universe at (re)creation.

Our conclusion, then, – if, as always, we feel entitled to interpret Virgilian myth allegorically – must be that the capture of Proteus and the death of Orpheus have the same allegorical meaning: they both depict the differentiation of the universe at

[32] Chuvin (1992) 30. It is unclear to me that these metamorphoses in Ovid in fact owe any more to the realities of the physical world than they do to the Homeric and Virgilian descriptions of Proteus' transformations.

[33] The phrase μείζονι τέχνῃ (383) is suggestive.

[34] Long and Sedley (1987) I 278.

[35] On the Stoic flood see Sen. *Q Nat.* 3.27–8; for the alternation of *ecpyrosis* and cataclysm, Ps.-Heracl., *Quaest. Hom.* 25.5.

[36] For evidence of Nonnus' familiarity with earlier Hellenistic culture (in this case specifically literary) see Hollis (1976) and (1994).

Creation. And I have already stated that these are the only two examples of such an allegory of which I am aware. Proteus and Orpheus, it transpires, have much more in common even than we thought. Not only are they both 'victims' but their tribulations symbolize the, as it were, original victim, the passive principle of the universe, that which must be violently acted upon by the active principle if the universe is to attain to existence in the first place. In short, once again we find the *poeta creator* motif: Proteus is what he sings. Inevitably, then, according to the logic of the motif, the *Orpheus*, narrated by the victimized Proteus, is a catalogue of disasters.

In this chapter, then, I shall argue that the *Orpheus* represents what we might call a poetry of the victim, just as the *Proteus* represented a poetry of the victor. Proteus, the 'author' of the passage, and Orpheus his hero each pointedly *suffer*, at the hands of Aristaeus and of events. Orpheus is in the first instance the victim of Aristaeus' actions, in broader terms the victim of love (as we shall see). But we have already noted the way Aristaeus seems to incorporate into himself the powers of the physical world, love in particular.[37]

The chapter will fall into two parts. The first will argue that the *Orpheus*, like the *Proteus*, is couched in a literary mode appropriate to its pathetic subject-matter: the Neoteric-elegiac. The second will seek to corroborate the implication of the allegorical resemblance I have identified between Proteus and Orpheus: Orpheus' suffering and death, like the tribulations of the *bugonia* ox or of Remus (or of Proteus), are to be understood as paradoxically necessary prerequisites of success.

A Orpheus *poeticus*

II

Proteus is presented, I have argued, as above all a Homeric figure, in fact as a representative of the entire Homeric (that

---

[37] See pp. 42–3 above.

is, epic) mode. But what this Homeric creation himself sings – his reply to Aristaeus, the story of Orpheus – is, *prima facie*, strikingly unexpected.[38] As has often been stated, the *Orpheus* is poetry on the model of the so-called 'epyllion', the characteristic production of the 'Neoterics' of the preceding half-century: Thomas, representatively, calls it 'in theme, style and emphasis absolutely typical of epyllion'.[39] Crabbe has displayed its indebtedness to Catullus 64,[40] and we would no doubt find many other echoes of Neoteric epyllion, as Thomas suggests, if others had survived in anything but an extremely fragmentary state. One of the respects in which Thomas finds the passage typical of Neoteric poetry, 'style', is notoriously hard to define, and Thomas makes little attempt to do so. Wiseman, however, finds 'the exquisite sophisticated erudition of Alexandrian literary taste' perfectly expressed in the term used by Parthenius in the Ἐρωτικὰ Παθήματα, *Love Romances* (*Narrationes Amatoriae*), a handbook of thirty-six abbreviated literary plots written for the use of the elegist Cornelius Gallus, to describe the characteristic quality of Gallus' verse: τὸ περιττόν, 'refinement' or 'elaboration'.[41] This Parthenius was a native of Nicaea in Bithynia, who according to the *Suda* (s.v.) was brought to Rome as a captive by 'Cinna' 'after the Romans defeated Mithridates'. Both the precise date of Parthenius' removal to Rome and the identity of the Cinna involved are unclear, but the latter may be the C. Helvius Cinna who composed the *Zmyrna* and was famously torn apart by the mob after Caesar's funeral, mistaken by it for an anti-Caesarian namesake;[42] and if not that Cinna it was probably his father. This possibility, and (more cogently) stylistic and thematic parallels between both the fragments of Parthenius

---

[38] As is suggested, for different reasons, by Wilkinson (1969) 115.
[39] Thomas (1988) ad 453–527. He means that it is a typically Neoteric production. However, see pp. 18–19 above for the confusion in Thomas' edition regarding the connotation of the term 'epyllion'.
[40] Crabbe (1977).
[41] Parth. *Narr. Am. praef.* 2; Wiseman (1979) 151–2.
[42] On Parthenius see, succinctly, Courtney (1993) 212–14. On the death of Cinna see Plut. *Brut.* 20.8–11, Ov. *Ibis* 539–40, and Morgan (1990). On Cinna in general see Wiseman (1974); Dahlmann (1977); Watson (1982); Courtney (1993) 212–14.

and the Ἐρωτικὰ Παθήματα and Neoteric poetry – especially Cinna, but also (apparently) Calvus and Catullus[43] – have led some scholars to see in Parthenius the medium by which the 'Alexandrian' poetics espoused by the Neoterics were transmitted to Rome.[44] Whatever the truth of that suggestion, Parthenius was unquestionably a prominent figure on the late-Republican literary scene. His influence on Cinna's *Zmyrna* is certain,[45] and his connection with Cornelius Gallus is clear from the preface to the Ἐρωτικὰ Παθήματα. According to Macrobius (*Sat.* 5.17.18) Parthenius was Virgil's tutor *in Graecis*; and some kind of mentor/pupil relationship is not implausible. At any rate – whether this be a sign of personal influence or his general visibility in the contemporary literary milieu – Parthenius is extremely prominent in Gellius' list (9.9.3) of Greek poets whose verse Virgil rendered. Only six are named: Homer, Hesiod, Apollonius, Parthenius, Callimachus, and Theocritus. Parthenius is thus in extremely elevated company.

At any rate, if Lyne's summary of the typically Neoteric 'emotionally expressive' devices of style manifested in the pseudo-Virgilian *Ciris* is compared to the *Orpheus* the kinship is clear.[46] Almost all of Lyne's categories find immediate echoes in Virgil's episode: Grecisms (particularly proper names),[47] epanalepsis and anaphora,[48] exclamation (notably the neoteric *a!*),[49] rhetorical questions, pronounced alliteration, and parenthesis. Metre perhaps constitutes even shakier ground for categorization than style, but Virgil's line 463,

---

[43] Courtney (1993) 208, 213, 220.

[44] See especially Clausen (1964); for a contrary view see Crowther (1980). Crowther points out instances of 'Alexandrian' myth in Latin verse (Laevius and Cicero) probably predating Parthenius' arrival in Rome. He concludes that there is no evidence for Parthenian influence on any of the Neoterics besides Cinna and Gallus. He is still himself willing to allow, however, that 'Parthenius was instrumental in introducing "epyllion" into Rome' (181). See also Crowther (1976).

[45] Courtney (1993) 220.

[46] Lyne (1978a) 28–31.

[47] With reference to the frequency of exotic geographical names in the *Orpheus*, compare the discussion of this by Watson (1982) 100–1 as a point of comparison between Cinna and Euphorion.

[48] 494–5; 525–7.

[49] Thomas (1988) ad 525–7.

atque Getae atque Hebrus et Actias Orithyia, is a σπονδειάζων, the rhythmical conceit Cicero (accurately, apparently) particularly associated with the Neoterics (*Att.* 7.2.1).[50]

Theme, nevertheless, is a more tangible commodity all round. Lyne talks of 'an alternative narrative, reacting to a convention of epic and orthodox heroes behaving heroically... The sex-lives of heroes were congenial.'[51] In a note he cites Parthenius' *Love Romances*, seeing it as representative of the subject matter of Neoteric epyllion. Wiseman summarizes the preoccupation of Parthenius' booklet as 'love doomed and tragic', and also likens it to the themes of contemporary *epyllia*.[52] Thomas, in the introduction to his edition,[53] compares 'Orpheus' tragic and unsuccessful love for Eurydice' with the themes of the Ἐρωτικὰ Παθήματα directly.

That the erotic – and in particular tragic love of the kind favoured as a topic by Parthenius – is the theme of the *Orpheus* is obvious, although the full ramifications of this theme have yet I think to be fully appreciated. Not only is Eurydice (all but) raped by Aristaeus: she is twice 'raped' (*rapta bis*, 504) by death, a turn of phrase which establishes (as Johnston points out)[54] an assimilation between Eurydice and perhaps the archetypal victim of rape, Proserpina, who appears at 487. Other such cameo appearances within the *Orpheus* seem to carry similar associations. For example, it can hardly be coincidental that Orithyia (463) was best known for being snatched away from beside the river Ilissus by Boreas and carried off to Thrace.[55] Her association in Virgil's text with Thracian locales, combined with her epithet *Actias*, 'Attic', points up the fact of her enforced removal from one location to the other. Ixion also, who stands metonymically for the

---

[50] See Lyne (1978a) 15–16. There are only four other σπονδειάζοντες in the entire *Georgics*. On the subject of σπονδειάζοντες and the Neoterics see also Crowther (1970) 322–3.
[51] Lyne (1978b) 182.
[52] Wiseman (1974) 55–6.
[53] Thomas (1988) 1 15 and n. 41.
[54] Johnston (1977) 169.
[55] Pl. *Phdr.* 229b–d; Ap. Rhod. *Argon.* 1.211–18; Stat. *Theb.* 12.630 (*rapta Orithyia*). In elegy, Prop. 3.7.13 (*rapta Orithyia*); Ov. *Am.* 1.6.53 (*rapta Orithyia*).

residents of Hades (484), earned the punishment of being strapped to a wheel for eternity by an attempted sexual assault on Hera.[56] Philomela (511), finally and famously, was raped by her brother-in-law Tereus, took her revenge by feeding him his son Itys, and was consequently turned into a nightingale or swallow.[57] Furthermore the death of Eurydice is related by verbal echo to another erotic tragedy delineated in the *Georgics*, the vignette describing Hero and Leander (though their names are suppressed) at 3.258–63. The phrase *moritura puella* used of Eurydice (4.458) picks up *moritura ... uirgo*, of Hero, at 3.263, another woman who died for love. It also, incidentally, anticipates Dido's death in *Aeneid* 4 (*moritura*, 415).

In the one Neoteric epyllion which survives in full, Catullus 64, the dimension of love and tragedy is visible enough, though if the scheme is less starkly present than in other Neoteric work this is perhaps because, as Wiseman says, Catullus' poetry is not typical of the movement: the focus of Neotericism lay elsewhere, with Cinna and Parthenius.[58] The *Ciris*, according to Lyne, is similarly of a type recognizably 'to the taste of later Alexandrian epyllion: heroine-centred, tragic, erotically motivated'.[59] Two, at least, of these criteria ring true of the *Orpheus*. Lyne compares the *Ciris* myth, once again, to a number of the Ἐρωτικὰ Παθήματα of Parthenius (whom he believes to be a discernible source of the *Ciris* poet).

At any rate, Cinna's epyllion, the *Zmyrna*, shares the preoccupations of the *Ciris* and of Parthenius. It told of Smyrna's incestuous love for her father Cinyras – the liaison from which sprang Adonis. Calvus, similarly, wrote an *Io*, recounting the wanderings which resulted from the rape of his protagonist by Zeus. Other participants in the Neoteric *milieu* seem to have been engaged on similar projects. Catullus 38 is addressed to a Cornificius who is probably the author of an epyllion *Glaucus* of which only one fragment survives.[60] Its subject may have

---

[56] Σ Eur. *Phoen.* 1185; Tib. 1.3.73–4; Serv. ad *Aen.* 6.601.
[57] For the variations in the myth see below, pp. 208–9.
[58] Wiseman (1974) 56.   [59] Lyne (1978a) 7.   [60] Courtney (1993) 225–7.

been the sea god Glaucus who fell in love (unrequitedly) with the nymph Scylla, a popular Hellenistic theme;[61] alternatively it may have concerned Glaucus of Potniae, killed by his horses, in the version gestured at by Virgil at *G.* 3.267–8, through the agency of Venus. Catullus 35 is addressed to Caecilius, the author of an unfinished *Magna Mater* or *Dindymi Domina.* Reading the poem, according to Catullus, makes Caecilius' girlfriend fall passionately, miserably in love: *nam quo tempore legit incohatam | Dindymi dominam, ex eo misellae | ignes interiorem edunt medullam,* 'For ever since she read the beginning of the *Mistress of Dindymus* fire has eaten away the poor girl's inner marrow'. Some kind of witty assimilation with the events related in the *Magna Mater* seems likely here. Perhaps Caecilius' poem told of Cybele's love for Attis.[62] Valerius Cato[63] wrote a *Diana* or *Dictynna.*[64] This poem, probably an epyllion, 'seems likely to have told of the aetiology of Diana's name Dictynna, i.e. the story of Britomartis who was pursued by Minos and leapt off a cliff'.[65] The author of the *Ciris* presumably used it in his treatment of the Britomartis myth.[66] As for Virgil and Gallus, if *Eclogue* 6 can be understood to reflect Neoteric thematics its leaning towards disastrous love stories (Hylas, Pasiphae, Scylla, Philomela) clearly confirms the tenor. The theme of the Grynean grove (72) which Virgil seems to encourage Gallus to undertake in this poem is very plausibly reconstructed by Lyne, following Servius *auctus ad* Aen. 4.345 (*Gryneus Apollo*). Servius records the tradition that Apollo was worshipped in the Grynean grove because (causality seems implied) it was there that he raped Gryne, an Amazon.[67] The theme may be Par-

---

[61] See Ov. *Met.* 13.898–14.74; Lyne (1978b) 173–4 and n. 24.

[62] As Wiseman (1974) 56 suggests. See Ovid's treatment of the myth at *Fast.* 4.221–46, where it is sited in the vicinity of Mt Dindymus (234). Fisher (1971) offers a slightly different interpretation: Catullus is criticizing Caecilius for allowing his composition of the epyllion *Magna Mater* to be interrupted by his writing of love poetry (represented by the *puella* who delays his journey to Verona).

[63] Courtney (1993) 189–91.

[64] The first name is given by Suet. *Gram.* 11.2, the second by Cinna fr. 14 Morel.

[65] Lyne (1978b) 173.

[66] See Lyne (1978a) ad 294–309.

[67] Lyne (1978b) 186.

thenius': Stephanus of Byzantium – s.v. Γρῦνοι (a geographical location) – informs us that in his elegiac poem *Delos* Parthenius employed the adjective Γρύνειος, a variant for the usual Γρυνεύς (feminine Γρυνηίς). Parthenius' full expression is the same as Virgil's at *Aen.* 4.345, Γρύνειος Ἀπόλλων. Did Parthenius then tell the story of Gryne's rape by Apollo?[68] This would undoubtedly be an extremely appropriate background for Virgil's re-employment of the expression during Aeneas' *Italiam non sponte sequor* speech to Dido. Aeneas has previously been compared to Apollo (4.143–50); Lyne summarizes the 'Amazonian' quality of Dido.[69] The implication that Aeneas is Dido's rapist would not be out of place.[70]

To summarize: the so-called Neoterics are a recognizably discrete group – if not actually in any sense a 'school' – in their sharing both of certain stylistic mannerisms and of a sense of what constituted a desirable theme. The latter seems to have tended to involve an erotic element, and appears to have foregrounded tragedy, suffering, violent emotion: in a word, I would suggest, victimhood.

It is hard at this juncture to separate epyllion too far from elegy. The preface of Parthenius' *Love Romances* enjoins Gallus' use of the book in either hexametrical or elegiac verse, implying that in all respects besides the metrical the epyllion and love elegy were closely related. In the *Orpheus* Thomas suggests a particular debt on Virgil's part to Gallus, a debt he deduces from parallels with *Ecl.* 6 and 10.[71] Now as Gallus certainly wrote elegiac poetry, and only possibly hexametrical,[72] this inevitably brings elegy into the equation. And indeed, according to Conte, 'Orpheus sings his "erotikon pathema" like an elegiac poet.'[73]

---

[68] Lyne (1978b) 186; Clausen (1964) 192; Courtney (1990) 105.

[69] Lyne (1987) 136 n. 57.

[70] This link was proposed to me by Philip Hardie.

[71] Thomas (1988) I 15–16.

[72] If he ever wrote on the Grynean Grove (*Ecl.* 6.72–3), that also would probably have been hexametrical epyllion (there is no evidence that he did, however): see Lyne (1978b) 185–6.

[73] Conte (1986) 137 n. 8. Thomas (1988) ad 4.514 finds the word *miserabile* particularly redolent of elegy. Cf. Nisbet and Hubbard (1970) ad Hor. *Carm.* 1.33.2 (Tibullus' *miserabiles elegos*).

In love elegy, as in epyllion, it would appear, the theme of suffering is paramount. Hollis, for example, has identified the central joke of Ovid's *Ars Amatoria* and *Remedia Amoris*:

All in all love, as presented by the elegists, might seem thoroughly unsuitable to be the subject of a didactic poem. How can one lay down rules for something so chaotic, over which the individual has so little control?[74]

In elegy, as Hollis says,

Love appears as an overwhelming force, even a disease or madness, which carries the poet by storm; he has little choice as to whom he falls in love with ... and little freedom of manoeuvre once he has succumbed. Often the painful rather than the pleasurable side of love is uppermost.[75]

Hollis illustrates his point from the very first poem of Propertius, remarking that Gallus' elegies probably 'possessed the same colouring in even greater degree'. In the opening line of Prop. 1.1, *Cynthia prima suis miserum me cepit ocellis*, 'Propertius himself is no more than a powerless victim'. In terms similar to Hollis' Lyne also remarks how Tibullus in his first elegy, in a manner characteristic of the elegiac ethos, 'sees himself as the *victim* of events'.[76] This 'Tibullan passivity' is particularly evident in the motif of *servitium amoris* common to all the elegists,[77] which, as Lyne writes

expressed ... the lover's state or sense of degradation. The love-poet who called himself or implied himself to be the slave of his beloved communicated thereby the humiliation and abasement to which as subject-lover of that person, he was or felt himself exposed.[78]

Miles quotes Allen on elegiac love to similar effect, seeing this as the ethos underlying the *Orpheus*:

Love is a violent passion, a fault that destroys the vision and perverts the will, but a power that the lover is helpless to control and from which there is no release. This kind of love is the subject matter of elegy.[79]

At the climax of his depiction of the elegist Gallus in *Ecl.* 10 Virgil has him give expression to what might summarize the ethos of Neoteric epyllion, of elegy and of the *Orpheus* (69):

---

[74] Hollis (1973) 95.   [75] Hollis (1973) 94.   [76] Lyne (1980) 157.
[77] Lyne (1980) 185; Hollis (1973) 94.
[78] Lyne (1979) 117–18; see also Lyne (1980) 80–1.
[79] Allen (1950) 264; Miles (1980) 276.

omnia uincit amor. This may well be the second half of a Gallan pentameter.[80]

Both Neoteric epyllion, then, and love elegy typically depict the condition of being a powerless victim. Watson talks of 'a highly charged or pathetic type of narrative, which was closely allied to ... cultivation of morbidly erotic themes'.[81] The Orpheus myth, as told by Virgil, is absolutely typical of this thematic, and Parthenius' term ἐρωτικὸν πάθημα, *suffering in love*,[82] captures the style exactly.[83]

Conte has suggested that Aristaeus and Orpheus represent a contrast between genres, Aristaeus fulfilling the role of the obedient learner of the didactic lesson, 'the ideal recipient of the *Georgics*', and Orpheus 'a character who chooses love, and the pain of love, as the one and only subject of his song'.[84] Clearly, then, the different genres entail different 'ways of life',[85] different ideologies. As Myers writes,

Because of the close link between Latin epic and nationalist ideology, it is always difficult at Rome to distinguish between aesthetic and Augustan politics. Callimachean anti-epic polemic can function ... as much as a rhetorical tool for the choice or avoidance of political themes as it does as a statement of a stylistic ideology.[86]

[80] Coleman (1977); Clausen (1994) ad loc.
[81] This is the restatement by Watson (1982) 106 of the standard view of Euphorion, who was supposed to have bequeathed this mode of poetry to the Neoterics. Watson disputes this view, suggesting that the emotional themes and treatment of Cinna's poetry were much more a feature of Parthenius' poetry than Euphorion's.
[82] The translation of Hubbard (1974) 11.
[83] Interestingly, perhaps, given the remainder of my argument in this chapter, there is one particular model of suffering which seems to have been to the taste of the Neoterics: mystery cult. Calvus fr. 14 Morel, *partus grauido portabat in aluo*, refers to Io's son Epaphus – identified with Apis – from whom the Isiac religion was supposed to derive: see Wiseman (1974) 56; Apollod. *Bibl.* 2.1.3; Ov. *Met.* 1.747–50. Calvus' expression recalls Cinna's line (fr. 7 Morel), *at scelus incesto Smyrnae crescebat in aluo*, which describes Smyrna's pregnancy with Adonis, whose festivals do not strictly count as mysteries but share many of their features – a suffering god, ritual lament and nocturnal rites: Burkert (1987) 75–6. The myth of Adonis seems related to that of Attis, and Lyne (1978b) 175 has pointed out the interesting shared preoccupation of Catullus (63) and Caecilius with Cybele: Caecilius' *Magna Mater* referred to by Catullus (35) was also, as we have seen, probably about Cybele and Attis. We have already noted (p. 194 above) the presence of the myth of Dionysus Zagreus in the work of Callimachus and Euphorion.
[84] Conte (1986) 135, 136.
[85] Conte (1986) 139.
[86] Myers (1994) 4.

The lifestyle represented for us both by Catullus and by the elegists in their poetry offered – both explicitly[87] and implicitly – a rejection of the fundamentally public-orientated Roman virtues. As Lyne explains, the mode of life presented in the poetry of Catullus, Propertius and Tibullus was essentially a rejection of the Roman social imperative of *negotium* in favour of the inglorious *otium* of love and love poetry.[88] I would seek to expand Conte's explanation of Aristaeus' actions: it is not only the didactic mode that he represents but the poetry of natural philosophy and of Grand Epic, the mode of action, control and success. Orpheus represents an opposite ethos of the general kind depicted in the pastoral idyll at the end of *G.* 2, an ethos which defined itself against the city, political engagement, *negotium* and so on, as well as against higher modes of poetry such as natural philosophy.

By total contrast to the dominant Aristaeus, Orpheus is a slave to *amor*. All his sufferings are engendered by the emotion. I have suggested that his status is above all that of a victim, like Proteus in the first instance through the agency of Aristaeus, but in the most memorable instance through the power of love. At the very centre of the *Orpheus* the protagonist commits his terrible error (490–1): *restitit Eurydicenque suam iam luce sub ipsa | immemor heu! uictusque animi respexit.* It is love which overcomes Orpheus here, and *amor* also which eventually causes his death at the hands of the spurned Thracian Bacchants. But we have seen how Aristaeus in his capture of Proteus seems to be assimilated to universal destructive powers such as, in particular, the power of love as depicted in *G.* 3.[89] Here the effects of love are equated with the effects of Aristaeus. Either way Orpheus, like Lyne's Tibullus, is the 'victim of events', the sufferer as opposed to the victor: *mutatis mutandis*, someone *elegis molles qui fleret amores.*[90]

---

[87] For Catullus see in particular his statement of political indifference in poem 93. See also Suet. *Jul.* 73 and Tac. *Ann.* 4.34 on Calvus' and Catullus' attacks on Julius Caesar.

[88] Lyne (1980) 67–78.

[89] Pp. 42–3 above.

[90] Domitius Marsus' description of Tibullus: fr. 7 Morel. It is quoted by Conte (1986) 137 n. 8, who states 'it could be applied to elegiac poetry in general', and –

III

What is odd about the juxtaposition of Homeric *epos* and Neoteric *epos* in the Proteus and Orpheus episodes is of course, as Otis noted some time ago,[91] that writing epic in the style of Homer and writing Neoteric epic were by convention ideologically incompatible activities. The contrast between the poetry of love and the poetry of martial valour or natural philosophy is a common *topos* in the elegists. Propertius 2.34 is a good example, presenting an opposition between love poetry and higher forms of composition, particularly tragedy and epic. 1.7.1–8 is similar.[92] Often much of the point of this opposition is metrical. The elegist will defend his erotic subject-matter on the grounds that it is appropriate to the elegiac metre (or to other non-hexametrical metres). But at Propertius 1.9.11, for example, *plus in amore ualet Mimnermi uersus Homero*, it is unclear whether the metre or the content of Mimnermus' love poetry is the issue; and the preface to Parthenius' Ἐρωτικὰ Παθήματα, as we have seen, presents itself as a source of material for Gallus whether he choose to write ἔπη or ἐλεγεῖαι. There is indeed plenty of evidence of a specifically intra-*epos* disagreement. The *Ciris* author employs comparable terminology to excuse his choice of the theme of Scylla, which he contrasts with a putative future undertaking of philosophical poetry *de rerum natura* (1–53). Catullus, in addition to his periodic tirades against Annalists,[93] in poem 95 famously praises Cinna's *Zmyrna*, a desirably highly

---

we might add – with the removal of *elegis* to Neoteric love poetry as well. Given the elegiac ethos of victimhood it is natural also that Propertius should compare his elegiac condition with that of the loser *par excellence* at this historical juncture, Mark Antony: see Griffin (1985) 32–47; Prop. 2.16.35–40; cf. 3.11.29–56.

[91] Otis (1963). See, for example, 197.

[92] Cf. 3.3.1–26, the contrast here being specifically with Ennius, and Ov. *Tr.* 2.421–70, which sets in opposition love poetry (including Catullus, Calvus, Cinna, Cornificius and Cato) and Ennius and Lucretius, and 259–62, which also presupposes a contradiction between the styles of the *Annals* and the *De Rerum Natura* on the one hand, and Ovid's own *Ars Amatoria* on the other: on the attitude of the elegists to Ennius see Miller (1983).

[93] See poems 14, 22, 36.

wrought composition by contrast with the *Annales* of Volusius
– both works were hexametrical.[94]

Cicero, at any rate, seems clearly to have considered what
we call Neoteric poetry and the Ennian tradition antithetical.
At *Tusc.* 3.45, datable to 45 BC, Cicero famously quotes
Ennius and exclaims, *O poetam egregium! quamquam ab his
cantoribus Euphorionis contemnitur*, 'Marvellous poet, though
he is despised by these chanters of Euphorion!' The expression 'chanters of Euphorion' obviously refers to the same
more or less discrete trend in poetry with which we are
concerned.[95] Courtney, following Watson, sees the primary
object of Cicero's remark as Cinna (rather than Gallus, for
whom it is a little early).[96] In his (perceived) scorn for Ennius,
as Courtney says,[97] Cinna would parallel Parthenius, who is
the likely referent of an epigram by Erycius which accuses
an elegiac poet named Parthenius of traducing the Homeric
poems (*AP* 7.377):

εἰ καὶ ὑπὸ χθονὶ κεῖται, ὅμως ἔτι καὶ κατὰ πίσσαν
  τοῦ μιαρογλώσσου χεύατε Παρθενίου,
οὕνεκα Πιερίδεσσιν ἐνήμεσε μυρία κεῖνα
  φλέγματα καὶ μυσαρῶν ἀπλυσίην ἐλέγων·
ἤλασε καὶ μανίης ἐπὶ δὴ τόσον ὥστ᾽ ἀγορεῦσαι

---

[94] If Munro (1878) 209–14 was right to emend *Hortensius* in line 3 to *Hatrianus*,
describing Volusius, probably a native of Atria, then the brevity of the *Zmyrna*
is being contrasted with Volusius' huge prolixity in the standard Callimachean
image: see Courtney (1993) 230–1. Similarly, at the beginning of Catullus 64 the
detailed verbal reminiscence of Ennius' *Medea* leads us to expect something sublime – a tragedy (or a conventional epic?) – on the subject of Jason and Medea,
but expectation is defeated when Catullus' poem turns into a love story: Bramble
(1970) 37; Kinsey (1965) 915–16. This may also figure Catullus' rejection of the
Annalist hexameter tradition. Similarly, in the last poem of Catullus' collection
(as we find it), 116, Skutsch suggests a parody in Catullus' *tu dabi' supplicium* of
Ennius' *dabi' sanguine poenas*: Skutsch (1985) ad *Ann.* 95. This is 'the only instance in Catullus of the suppression of the final -s after a short vowel before a
word beginning with a consonant': Fordyce (1961) ad loc. The dropping of final 's'
for metrical convenience was a regular practice in the poetry of Ennius, Lucilius
and Lucretius, but Cicero informs us (*Orat.* 161) that in the mid-forties BC it was
considered rather unurbane (*subrusticum*) and the modern poets (*poetae noui*)
avoided it. Catullus' parody, then, (if such it be) may well have a programmatic,
anti-Annalist connotation: Crowther (1970) 324–5.

[95] Lyne (1978b) 167, 174.

[96] Courtney (1990) 108; Watson (1982).

[97] Courtney (1993) 213.

πηλὸν Ὀδυσσείην καὶ πάτον Ἰλιάδα.
τοιγὰρ ὑπὸ ζοφίαισιν Ἐρινύσιν ἀμμέσον ἧπται
Κωκυτοῦ κλοιῷ λαιμὸν ἀπαγχόμενος.

Even though he lies under the earth, yet still pour pitch on foul-mouthed Parthenius for vomiting forth those myriad malignant humours upon the Muses and the filth of his loathsome elegies. He went so far in madness as to call the *Odyssey* mud and the *Iliad* dung; therefore in mid-Cocytus he is caught, in the power of the dark Furies, his throat choked by a collar.

This is a hard poem to interpret. Giangrande has probably confirmed the identification of Erycius' Parthenius by pointing out that the punishments which Erycius wishes meted out to Parthenius – liquid pitch and the application of the κλοιός – are forms habitually applied to slaves, 'an intentionally offensive allusion', Giangrande suggests, to Parthenius' erstwhile status as a slave, before his manumission διὰ τὴν παίδευσιν recorded by the *Suda*.[98] Nevertheless it is highly unlikely that Parthenius would have expressed the opinions which Erycius attributes to him. To criticize the Homeric poems is to contradict the core assumption of Callimacheanism. Homer was not to be imitated because Homer was *too good*. Grand Epic was to be shunned as a genre because it constituted hubristic emulation of the inimitable Homer, ἀπροτίμαστος Ὅμηρος, as an important model for the Neoterics and Parthenius, Euphorion,[99] called him (fr. 118 Powell).[100] Ennius, however, the self-proclaimed incarnation of Homer's genius *was* open to criticism on these grounds, and so – for that matter – would be the undertaking upon which I have suggested Virgil is engaged in the *Proteus*. Seth-Smith has attempted to resolve the dilemma by interpreting πηλός and πάτος as terms of literary criticism,[101] and his interpretation of πάτος as ambiguous, meaning both 'dung'[102] and 'well-trodden path', is attractive: Erycius is twisting Parthenius' words, presumably. But it

---

[98] Giangrande (1966).
[99] Watson (1982).
[100] The epigrammatist Pollianus seems to associate Parthenius with the standard Callimachean doctrine regarding Homer's inimitability at *AP* 11.130.
[101] Seth-Smith (1981).
[102] We might be reminded of the *sententia* attributed to Virgil that in his reading of Ennius *aurum in stercore quaero*, Cassiod. *Inst. Div.* 1.1.8.

remains difficult to see how πηλός, 'mud', could fail to be abusive (as Seth-Smith himself says, Callimacheans 'never faulted Homer himself'),[103] and what innocent remark of Parthenius might lie behind it. Even πάτος is sailing fairly close to the wind.[104]

Yet even if Erycius' epigram is overstated the background to his remarks is clear enough. The group of poets we are talking about (whom we call for convenience the Neoterics) defined their particular style of *epos* to a large extent by opposition to the values of the Annalist, martial, panegyrical or natural-philosophical tradition of *epos*, of which Homer was considered the archetypal exponent.

The text of Virgil offers further evidence of these Neoteric programmatics. *Eclogue* 6 is of course one of the most obscure passages in his oeuvre. But this much at least seems undeniable. A hexameter poem, *epos*, itself, it rejects the option of Grand Epic, depicted, conventionally, as a poetry of panegyric and war (6–7). The rejection is couched in the imagery of Callimachus' *Reply to the Telchines* (fr. 1 Pf.), and the message (bearing in mind the metrical difference between the *Aetia* and the *Eclogues*) is the same: extended poems of the kind demanded by Varus are unsatisfactory. The Callimachean alternative is preferred. The remainder of the poem, with what appears to be a catalogue of desirable poetic themes culminating in the *Dichterweihe* of Gallus into the tradition of Hesiod and Linus' exhortation of him to tell of the Grynean grove, seems to be closely allied to the self-defining imagery of the Neoterics, though the relevance of the natural-philosophical content of 31–42 remains a complication. Nevertheless, we can be clear that in *Ecl.* 6 Virgil assimilates his own poetic programme in his pastoral collection to that of Callimachus (at any rate, as his programme was

---

[103] Seth-Smith (1981) 64.

[104] Callimachus (*AP* 12.43) uses the image of the well-worn road of the cyclic poem, not of Homer, of whom it would be too critical, as Giangrande (1983) points out. But I find Giangrande's alternative interpretation – that Parthenius terms imply the 'insensitivity' of the Homeric poems – equally unsatisfactory, for similar reasons.

understood by the Neoterics), Gallus, and the Neoterics in general.

A related dichotomy is also to be found in *Georgic* 2. Now, however, the incompatibility of two poetic modes is presented by Virgil not as grounds to reject one and embrace the other, but as a personal dilemma: each, apparently, is equally laudable, and Virgil seems to express his readiness to do *both*, incompatible though they are. The two modes at issue in *G.* 2 cannot be understood simply as Grand Epic and Neoteric, but there is a similar wavering between modes conventionally considered 'high' and 'low'; here, according to Hardie, quite literally:

> The choices at the end of the second *Georgic* are presented largely in topographical terms, and point us towards the conventions of poetic geography; the *recusatio* may be interpreted in terms of the opposition between high and low places of poetry...[105]

At 458–74 Virgil praises the farmer's life. At 475–82 he expresses his desire to be initiated by the Muses into the Mysteries of natural philosophy. If, however, he should prove inadequate for the task (483–4), he will resort instead to the countryside (485–9). There follow the famous beatitudes (490–4),

> felix qui potuit rerum cognoscere causas,
> atque metus omnis et inexorabile fatum
> subiecit pedibus strepitumque Acherontis auari.
> fortunatus et ille deos qui nouit agrestis
> Panaque Siluanumque senem Nymphasque sorores.

Blessed the man who has been able to learn the causes of things, and has trampled beneath his feet all fear and relentless fate and the din of greedy Acheron! Happy, too, the man who knows the gods of the fields, Pan and old Silvanus and the sister Nymphs!

From here to the end of the book (495–542) the *laudatio* of the rustic life is resumed, partially effected by a complementary *vituperatio* of city life.

We have met this latter passage before. The section after the beatitudes depicts an idyll of non-violence such as that

[105] Hardie (1986) 47.

which obtained between *Remus et frater* (533), before the
human race took to feasting on slaughtered oxen (itself practically fratricidal): figuratively, before the Civil Wars. Subsequently the proem to Book 3 seems to offer a direct contradiction with the terms of the conclusion to Book 2. Now the
fratricide is the deified founder Quirinus and appears leading
the victorious Romans (27). The slaughter of oxen is now the
constructive institution of sacrifice. The collision between the
end of Book 2 and the beginning of Book 3 is an intimation of
the paradoxical scheme – destruction *constructs* – which I
have argued is central to Virgil's negotiation of the potential
of the Civil Wars for good in the *Aristaeus*.

But Virgil's internal debate in Book 2 clearly has a purely
literary dimension. Thomas claims at 475–94 that the 'passage
as a whole is best understood as applying to Virgil and his
career'. The choice lies between scientific poetry of the kind
undertaken by Aratus, Lucretius and (480–1 imply)[106]
Homer, and a less intellectual undertaking, related to the
countryside, which is inevitably to some extent coextensive
with the *Eclogues*.[107] Considered as Virgil's recognition of the
divergent literary options available to him within the didactic
mode, 475–542 corresponds pretty closely to the scheme we
have just been addressing. As Virgil expresses it, the option of
natural philosophy is desirable, but if he should prove inadequate to the task let him be satisfied with the 'inglorious' (486)
countryside, which is subsequently contrasted with the violence of the city. Each option has validity, as is clear from
490–4: 'the parataxis of *felix* ... *fortunatus* here refers to a
truly unresolved dichotomy'.[108]

The poetic dilemma of 2.475–542, I am suggesting, can be

---

[106] Nelis (1992a) 11–12 compares *Aen.* 1.742, 744 and 745 to material from Homer's
description of the shield of Achilles, a notable example of physical allegoresis: *Il.*
18.484, 486–7 and 489. See also Hardie (1986) 63 n. 72, and Servius ad *Aen.*
1.742, who notes the similarity between this line and *Il.* 18.484. Given that *G.*
2.481–2 are identical to *Aen.* 1.745–6 and *G.* 2.478 very similar to *Aen.* 1.742, the
natural-philosophical Homer of allegoresis would seem to be present in the
Georgics passage also. As is pointed out by Brown (1990) 184, *G.* 2.478 owes a
shared debt to *Il.* 18.484, Lucr. 5.751 and Ap. Rhod. *Argon.* 1.500.

[107] Thomas (1988) ad loc.

[108] Hardie (1986) 43.

analysed to yield the familiar antithesis of 'high' *epos* (natural-philosophical, as elsewhere martial-panegyrical: the *Proteus* combines the two) *versus* a lower mode closely associated with the peaceful existence of the countryside. And this generic dilemma is related to a 'real' dilemma, between country and city, peace and war, violence and non-violence, *otium* and *negotium*, marking the distance between the idyll of the countryside and the civil war of the city: between the pastoral existence of Romulus and Remus and the city of Rome.[109] Similarly in *Aen.* 7 the progression from peace to war provoked by Allecto can also be seen as a movement between genres, from pastoral to epic.[110] The 'real' dilemma and the literary dilemma in the *Georgics* interpenetrate, and in short at the end of Book 2 – with the apparent incompatibility both of civil war and idyllic peace and of high and low literary genres – we are playing with issues similar to those broached in the *Aristaeus.*

At the start of Book 3 Virgil seems firmly to reject the epyllion option, likely themes of which are listed (as trite) at 3.4–8.[111] But we have seen how ambiguous this passage is: it rejects Callimachus on Callimachean terms (*omnia uulgata, temptanda uia, deducam, lucos Molorchi*),[112] and forms a structural parallel with the *Aetia.* Similarly, as Hardie points out,[113] the temple representing his poem of martial epic has a strikingly pastoral location on the banks of the river Mincius (14–15), a description adapted from the *locus amoenus* of *Ecl.* 7.11–13: a place for pastoral song. (The Mincius itself is equivocal, being *ingens* but also fringing its banks *tenera ... harundine.*) Even in this confident prediction of the future Grand Epic Virgil remains torn between the Callimachean and Homeric modes.

---

[109] For the pastoral origins of Rome see Varro, *Rust.* 2.1.9 (a passage we have met before, p. 131 above).

[110] Putnam (1970) 418–19; Hardie (1992) 66.

[111] See Thomas (1988) ad loc.

[112] Thomas (1988) ad locc. The *Aonius uertex* of 11 takes in both Lucretius on Ennius (*DRN* 1.118) – Wilkinson (1969) 323 – and Callimachus on Hesiod: Thomas (1988) ad loc.

[113] Hardie (1986) 49–50.

At 2.475–542, then, Virgil aspires to writing natural philosophy, but then delineates an alternative, and antithetical, literary direction of apparently equal validity. Then, at the beginning of Book 3, he envisages writing a Grand Epic but in terms fundamentally indebted to Callimachean programmatics. Buchheit, similarly, points out how the addressees of Book 3.1–2, Pales, Apollo Nomios and Pan, may refer either to the nationalistic preoccupations of the planned Grand Epic or to the pastoral concerns of Book 3 (and 4, for that matter). This 'frustration of generic expectations', as Thomas has shown,[114] is a feature of the entire poem,[115] a work of didactic which encompasses both Callimacheanism and, ultimately, Homer in its didactic programme, a process investigated most thoroughly by Farrell.[116] Farrell suggests that the *Georgics* embodies a progressive literary programme extending from the structural and thematic imitation of Hesiod and Aratus in Book 1 (confirmed as 'a declaration of membership' in the Alexandrian/Neoteric tradition by the reference to the Callimachean Hymn to Apollo at 1.509, and most memorably expressed in the *Acraeum cano . . . carmen* claim of 2.176)[117] to the Homeric affiliations of the *Aristaeus*.[118] In Farrell's view 'Virgil's allusive program' possesses an 'integrative function', 'linking poetic traditions that might normally be regarded as discrete'.[119]

Virgil fully exploits the implications of the intermediary position of the poem, its 'transitional tension', as Thomas calls it.[120] At 2.39–45, for example, Virgil appears to commit

---

[114] Thomas (1985). The expression is from p. 62.

[115] Thus, for example, Virgil seems to exploit the fact that Aratus, the second major model for Book 1, was – according to his scholia – a poet whose literary affiliations were disputed. Callimachus famously claimed that the *Phaenomena* were Hesiodic, thus also Callimachean (*Ep.* 27.1): 'Ἡσιόδου τό τ' ἄεισμα καὶ ὁ τρόπος. But this claim seems to have been a contribution to a debate: the scholia record the contrary opinion that Aratus was a ζηλωτής . . . τοῦ Ὁμηρικοῦ χαρακτῆρος, 'emulator of the Homeric style': *Isagoga bis excerpta* 2.4–5 (Maass (1898) 324); Farrell (1991) 217. Aratus – like the *Georgics* – hovers between the two traditions.

[116] Farrell (1991).

[117] Farrell (1991) 165.

[118] For a summary of Farrell's detailed argument see Farrell (1991) 157 and 159.

[119] Farrell (1991) 216.

[120] Thomas (1985) 70.

himself to the 'open sea' of Grand Epic. But he draws back
and indicates instead a wish to skirt the shore (44). Line 42,
non ego cuncta meis amplecti uersibus opto, a reference to the
'totalizing' claims of Grand Epic,[121] is somewhat reminiscent
of Catullus' description of Ocean (64.30). But Virgil is here
rejecting the Homeric / Ennian mode: Virgil's subsequent lines
(43–4), *non, mihi si linguae centum sint oraque centum, | ferrea
uox*, are a development of passages in Homer, Ennius, Hostius, and possibly Lucretius.[122] Hostius is the closest parallel,
in his *Bellum Histricum*, probably a panegyric of C. Sempro-
nius Tuditanus, who waged a *bellum Histricum* in 129 BC.[123]
Virgil thus seems to combine rejection of martial *epos*
(Homer, Ennius, Hostius), panegyrical *epos* (Hostius) and the
epos of natural philosophy (Lucretius). The passage embodies
a contradiction, a simultaneous leaning towards higher and
lower literary genres, which is true of the whole poem: an epic
motif (the 'hundred mouths') is used to reject the epic mode, a
clear parallel to the Callimachean rejection of Callimachean
themes in the prologue to Book 3. The passage is thus an early
statement of the generic dilemma of the poem. Thomas cites
the similarly mixed imagery of 3.289–95 and 4.3–7, and we
could add the passage at 3.40–5 where Virgil describes the
lower form of poetry (of the countryside) to which – in the
interim before writing the promised epic – he is returning. The
terms he uses to describe his undertaking, *intactos, haud mollia iussa* (41), *altum* (42), all seem designed to locate it halfway between pastoral and Grand Epic.

Hinds has written of the 'generic paradox' of Ovid's *Metamorphoses*: 'How can the *Metamorphoses* aspire to the grand
epic tradition of the *perpetuum carmen*, if it also seeks to align
itself with the opposing, unepic *deductum carmen*?'[124] The
same question seems to be begged by the *Georgics*: in a similar

---

[121] See Hardie (1993) 3, and pp. 63–4 above. The alternative to this epic undertaking
would seem to be the humble agricultural content of the *Georgics*, to which *in
manibus terrae* (45) looks like a subtle allusion. Cf. n. 126 below.
[122] *Il.* 2.488–90; *Ann.* 469–70 Sk.; Serv. ad loc.
[123] Courtney (1993) 52; Macrob. *Sat.* 6.3.6.
[124] Hinds (1987) 132.

way the literary affiliations of the *Georgics* are always an issue throughout its length. The basic issue is the same: how can these modes of expression – rendered mutually exclusive by years of poetic self-definition – be reconciled?

Homer, on Farrell's account, is the climax of the 'allusive programme' of the poem – as I would put it, he constitutes the final resolution of the poem's central literary dilemma. This is a poem – and a poet – torn between two traditions in poetry, the 'low' (Hesiodic / Callimachean / Neoteric) and the 'high' (Homeric / annalistic / natural-philosophic). I now wish to suggest how the relation between the *Proteus* and the *Orpheus* might seek to offer a resolution of this dilemma.

Hardie remarks how at 2.483–9 'the rural alternative to scientific poetry seems deliberately to eschew the Muses'.[125] Whilst the writing of scientific poetry is closely bound to the figures of the Muses – it is from them as from a hierophant that Virgil hopes for enlightenment on the subject (and this is perhaps significantly the first mention of the Muses in the poem)[126] – Hardie suggests that for the alternative, rustic option Virgil seems to substitute the Nymphs (*Nymphasque sorores*, 494) for the Muses as sources of inspiration. Subsequently, when Virgil turns back to his current, pastoral undertaking at 3.40 after imagining the epic to come, again 'it is to the company of Nymphs that he resorts, just as at 2.494'.[127] The definition of genre by reference to the Nymphs as its patron deities recalls pastoral poetry and the standard conflation therein, mentioned by Coleman, of the Νύμφαι and the βουκολικαὶ Μοῦσαι.[128]

The expression *Nymphasque sorores*, specifically, is repeated

---

[125] Hardie (1986) 45–6.

[126] The invocation – or not – of the Muses was perhaps made an issue for Virgil at least partially by Varro, to whom Virgil was indebted for his twelve-god invocation at the beginning of Book 1. Varro advertised his difference in this respect from epic poets (*Rust.* 1.1.4): *nec ut Homerus et Ennius Musas sed duodecim Deos Consentis.* When the Muses do appear it may be no coincidence that they do so in the context of a dilemma between the life of the farmer and some form of high poetic genre.

[127] Hardie (1986) 49.

[128] Coleman (1977) ad *Ecl.* 7.21 (*Nymphae ... Libethrides*), 2.46, 4.1, 10.9; Theoc. *Id.* 7.92, 9.28.

at the by now much-discussed *G.* 4.382, *Oceanumque patrem rerum Nymphasque sorores*, where Thomas finds it difficult: nymphs are 'somewhat odd as objects of the libation, since the nymphs, Cyrene's sisters ... are *participants* in the libation'. But one explanation of the presence of the phrase might be that it deliberately recalls the rustic literary option from the dilemma at the end of Book 2, possibly with a view to resolving the dilemma there presented. For at 4.382 the implications of the phrase are potentially rather interesting. There the Nymphs seem to represent the daughters of Ocean, a notion (his paternity)[129] already broached, I have suggested, in the preceding description of the cave (apparently belonging to Ocean) containing the nymphs and rivers of the world, who according to Hesiod, *Theog.* 337–70 were the daughters and sons of Ocean and Tethys. Ocean is the father, then, the origin, of the Nymphs. Could this gesture at some sort of source-tributary relationship between Homer and that humble poetry of the countryside which in Book 2 seemed straightforwardly incompatible with the more lofty poetry of science?

This, at any rate, is how Farrell interprets the relationship of the *Orpheus* to its context. His own analysis of the passage displays how much of it is constructed from, of all things, *Homeric* material.[130] At 471–80 Virgil describes the souls in the Underworld:

> at cantu commotae Erebi de sedibus imis
> umbrae ibant tenues ...
> matres atque uiri defunctaque corpora uita
> magnanimum heroum, pueri innuptaeque puellae,
> impositique rogis iuuenes ante ora parentum,
> quos circum limus niger et deformis harundo
> Cocyti tardaque palus inamabilis unda
> alligat...

But roused by his song came insubstantial shades from the lowest haunts of Erebus ... mothers and men and bodies of noble heroes now done with life, boys and unwedded girls, young men placed on pyres before their parents' eyes. Around them the black mud and unsightly reeds of Cocytus and the hateful swamp bound them with its sluggish water.

---

[129] Cat. 88.6; Ap. Rhod. *Argon.* 4.1414.   [130] Farrell (1991) 320–4.

The chief model here, as Farrell points out, is Homer's *Nekyia*
(*Od.* 11.36–43):

αἱ δ' ἀγέροντο
ψυχαὶ ὑπὲξ 'Ερέβευς νεκύων κατατεθνηώτων.
νύμφαι τ' ἠΐθεοί τε πολύτλητοί τε γέροντες
παρθενικαί τ' ἀταλαὶ νεοπενθέα θυμὸν ἔχουσαι·
πολλοὶ δ' οὐτάμενοι χαλκήρεσιν ἐγχείῃσιν
ἄνδρες ἀρηΐφατοι, βεβροτωμένα τεύχε' ἔχοντες·
οἳ πολλοὶ περὶ βόθρον ἐφοίτων ἄλλοθεν ἄλλος
θεσπεσίῃ ἰαχῇ.

There gathered from out of Erebus the souls of the dead: brides and un-
married youths, toil-worn old men, tender virgins with hearts inexperienced
in sorrow, many men killed in war, wounded with bronze-tipped spears,
wearing blood-stained armour. These wandered in great numbers around
the trench from all sides with an amazing cry.

Similarly, when Eurydice disappears like a puff of smoke (*ceu
fumus in auras*, 499) after Orpheus turns round to look at her
there is a reminiscence of Odysseus' attempt to embrace the
shade of his mother, which flies away 'like a shadow or a
dream' (*Od.* 11.204–8). The shade of Patroclus, also, evades
Achilles' embrace and returns underground ἠΰτε καπνός (*Il.*
23.100).

Towards the end of the story Orpheus, now conclusively
widowed, is compared in his grief to a nightingale, or, strictly,
to Philomela.[131] Here two Homeric passages are conflated:
first the simile at *Od.* 19.518–23, which talks of the daughter
of Pandareus mourning for her son; and secondly *Od.* 16.216–
18, where the emotions of Odysseus and his son on their
meeting are compared to those of birds whose offspring – as in
the Virgilian passage – have been taken away by farmers.

A final reference is not to Homer but to Ennius, Homer's
Latin *alter ego* and – until the composition of the *Aeneid* – the
leading representative of Grand Epic in Roman literature.
Orpheus is dismembered by Bacchanals and his severed head
flows down to the sea. His head is described (523) as *caput a*

---

[131] See pp. 208–9 below.

ceruice reuulsum, a direct quotation from Ennius (*Ann.* 483 Sk.):[132] the context of the phrase in Ennius is sadly unclear.

The fact that this pastiche of Neoteric poetry is spoken by that most Homeric of figures, Proteus, that it is associated with the *Nymphae sorores*, daughters of Ocean, and that, finally, it is periodically signposted as derived from Homeric poetry, suggests that Virgil's point here is to argue that even Neoteric poetry – conventionally so alien to the Grand Epic ethos – is part of the epic scheme as defined by Homer: the universal Homeric mode also includes the pathos of Neotericism. We have seen one aspect of the notion of Homer as the 'comprehensive' poet, the poet of limitless scope: all knowledge was thought to be present in his poetry, and ultimate forms of knowledge, particularly concerning the underlying physical processes of the universe, to be conveyed by it. Epic poetry, *qua* Homeric poetry, talked about the whole universe, and I suggested it was no coincidence that what I interpreted as the emulation of Homer – Virgil's Proteus episode – addressed the creation of the universe. But there is another dimension to the 'totalizing' or 'maximizing' impulse – Hardie's terms[133] – of Grand Epic, which we have also encountered: a desire for a more straightforwardly *literary* comprehensiveness. The ethos has been well expressed by Quint with reference to Tasso and Renaissance Epic, but the same very much applies to Virgil, as Hardie has shown. Quint writes,[134]

the Epic is imperialistic – its usual subject is, not coincidentally, empire – and all-inclusive ... Epic swallows up other genres into its own: in order to comprehend the entire range of human experience, the epic poet exploits all literary forms ... Epic plenitude ... implicitly equates the epic fiction to the multiplicity of the phenomenal world ... Epic wants to say it all, once and for all.

---

[132] The evidence comes from Serv. ad *Aen.* 10.396, where he states that the Ennian context was copied not only by Virgil at this point in *Aen.* 10 but also by Varro of Atax.

[133] Hardie (1993) 3.

[134] Quint (1983) 44–5.

Epic wants to say everything, and this impulse leads in two directions, the urge to universalize, to talk about the totality of existence, the whole universe (as we saw in the *Proteus*), and the urge to comprise within the epic programme *every manner of speech*, every literary mode. Cairns has discerned this process in the *Aeneid*, with particular reference to the depictions of Dido and Lavinia.[135] He writes,

Ancient scholarship believed that Homer had invented and generated all the literary forms. In an attempt at inverse emulation of Homer ... Virgil was trying to reabsorb into his epic all the diverse forms of literature which had originated from the homeric epics.

In a footnote at this point Cairns, naturally enough, cites the image of Homer as Ocean. And this, I suggest, is what Virgil is implying by following his emulation of Homer with the Neotericism of the *Orpheus*: Homeric poetry is not only the poetry of victory and of success, as it appears in the *Proteus* – a standard view of epic *qua* martial, panegyrical poetry – but the poetry of absolutely everything. Within the Homeric mode which Virgil here undertakes is included even (the conventionally anti-Grand Epic) Neotericism: emulating Homer thus resolves Virgil's poetic dilemma. This, at any rate, is how Farrell interprets the presence of the myth of Orpheus in the *Aristaeus*. He writes,[136] 'In *Georgics* 4, even Orpheus is subsumed under the penumbra of the quintessential poet of science, as of all else, Homer.'

B   Orpheus *mysticus*

IV

In Virgil's *Orpheus* the protagonist suffers and ultimately dies. It has seemed hard to many to subsume such a passage into any scheme that might be termed propagandistic. However,

[135] Cairns (1989) 150; cf. Hinds (1987) 133–4 on the non-epic affiliations of the Dido episode.
[136] Farrell (1991) 324.

the argument of my last chapter was essentially that one aim of the *Georgics* would seem to be precisely to argue the paradoxical *efficacy* of violence and death. The fact that something is a disaster, in other words, does not preclude its being constructive. We need to be clear about this. Virgil's point does not seem to be that the sufferings of, say, the *bugonia* cow are in any way mitigated by their productive outcome. On the contrary, it rather seems that the more appalling the tribulations, the more constructive they will be. It took fratricide to found Rome. It takes killing man's best friend, the ox, to appease the gods and bring about the rebirth of a bee-swarm. The sufferings of Orpheus are perhaps the most thoroughgoing described in the poem. But again I shall argue in this chapter that they are another instance of constructive suffering, suffering that is part of the necessary scheme of things. My core argument will be that the tragic myth of Orpheus related by Virgil is profoundly coloured by the rituals of mystery cult, perhaps the most salient ancient source of the notion which in my last chapter I sought to place at the core of the *Georgics'* propagandistic scheme: the paradox that death leads to life, destruction to creation.

V

Motifs in the Virgilian myth of Orpheus derived from mystery cult have been noted by a number of critics. Johnston, for example, has shown how the fate of Eurydice at the end of the poem forms a doublet with the reference to Proserpina at the beginning.[137] Thus 4.487, of Eurydice, *pone sequens (namque hanc dederat Proserpina legem)*, recalls 1.39, *nec repetita sequi curet Proserpina matrem*. In particular Johnston displays how the description of Eurydice's 'deaths' – she is termed *rapta* three times (456, 504, 519), though she is never actually 'raped', only figuratively 'carried off' by death – 'suggests that she has been ravished'[138] and assimilates her to Proserpina, the victim of *rapina* by Hades/Death (as, of course, in a sense

---

[137] Johnston (1977).   [138] Johnston (1977) 169.

Eurydice is as well) and perhaps the mystical figure *par excellence*. The objection could be made that there is one significant difference between the fate of Eurydice and that of Proserpina, as the latter is most familiar: whereas Eurydice stays dead, in the Homeric *Hymn to Demeter*, and most other accounts, Proserpina-Persephone was restored to the Upper World at Demeter's insistence and divided her time between there and Hades. This is not, however, how it stands in the *Georgics*. At 1.39 (quoted above) Proserpina is apparently depicted as permanently resident in the Underworld: she does not follow her mother back to the Upper World. Zuntz, discussing the Locrian *pinakes*, votive tablets associated with a temple of Persephone which recount her myth, finds parallels for Virgil's version in Lucan, Columella and the *Brevis Expositio*, as well as the *pinakes*.[139] The conclusion Johnston draws from this Proserpina–Eurydice doublet is not dissimilar to my own paradoxical scheme: 'some benefits can be derived from past disasters'.[140] As a consequence of the abduction of Proserpina, Johnston suggests, the art of cultivating grain was discovered: Proserpina must die for grain to be discovered. Similarly, as a result of the 'rape' of Eurydice, according to Johnston, another agricultural art, *bugonia*, was discovered. This is as may be, but the assimilation of Proserpina and Eurydice is striking, and a strong indication of the kind of themes Virgil is here concerned with. It cannot be coincidental that the fate of Eurydice's close analogue in the *Aeneid*, Aeneas' wife Creusa (elsewhere known as Eur-

---

[139] Zuntz (1971) 165, 400–2; Columella 10.268–74, Luc. 6.699–700, 739–42 (see also *Comm.* ad 740). As Zuntz says, both Probus and Servius ad loc. imply that this version was Virgil's invention (Probus calls it *contra historiam*). The *Brevis Expositio* ad loc., however, describes how Ceres-Demeter went after Proserpina to the Underworld, but Proserpina refused to return with her. This question is related to the vexed issue of whether Virgil was the first to make Orpheus' quest after Eurydice fruitless, i.e. to make Eurydice remain dead the way Proserpina does. I tend, with Anderson (1982) 27 and 48 n. 2, to follow K. Ziegler (*RE*, s.v. 'Orpheus') in believing that Virgil was not innovating. For a contrary view, see Heurgon (1932); and for a powerful recent reassertion of the position that Orpheus had always before Virgil failed to restore Eurydice to life see Heath (1994).

[140] Johnston (1977) 172.

ydice),[141] also carries strong suggestions of mystery cult. Her statement to Aeneas when she appears to him as a ghost (2.788), *sed me magna deum genetrix his detinet oris*, is rather obscure, but it involves another form of mystery cult, that of Magna Mater.[142]

VI

As we have seen, Orpheus' death occurs in the context of mystery cult.[143] The dismemberment suffered by Orpheus was originally the fate of the mystic Dionysus. Indeed the term 'Orphic' tends to crop up often in connection with the myth of Dionysus' dismemberment, and this is no coincidence. The myth of the dismembered Dionysus has been considered – in both ancient and modern times – central to the highly diffuse religious movement known as Orphism. Nilsson talks of 'the cardinal myth of Orphism, the dismemberment of Dionysus–Zagreus'.[144] This is primarily because the myth was told in the mystic poems traditionally attributed to Orpheus. The myth, however, as was clear from my list of sources,[145] had a life quite independent of the doctrines of the Orphic sect (if anything quite so discrete ever existed): but even when their versions differ from any strictly 'Orphic' version ancient authors who allude to the dismemberment myth continue to associate it above all with the name of Orpheus.[146] Conventionally, then, the myth of Dionysus' dismemberment was

---

[141] See Skutsch (1985) ad *Ann.* 36. There is extensive verbal parallelism between the depictions of Eurydice in *G.* 4 and Creusa in *Aen.* 2: see Austin (1964) ad *Aen.* 2.795.

[142] On which see Burkert (1987) 5–6.

[143] See p. 153 above.

[144] Nilsson (1935) 202. See also Rohde (1894) 117: 'der Zielpunkt, auf den die orphischen Lehrdichtungen ausliefen'; and Guthrie (1935) 107: 'for a worshipper the central point of Orphic story'. The citations are from Linforth (1941) 307.

[145] See p. 154 above.

[146] Diodorus, for example, at 3.62.3–8 relates a version according to which the reconstitution of Dionysus is effected by Demeter, a non-Orphic version. Nonetheless Diodorus still claims that his account is in agreement with the Orphic poems and mystic rites.

primarily Orpheus' story. Thus at 5.75.4 Diodorus, in a summary of the functions of the Olympian gods, states of Dionysus, τοῦτον δὲ τὸν θεὸν γεγονέναι φασὶν ἐκ Διὸς καὶ Φερσεφόνης κατὰ τὴν Κρήτην, ὃν Ὀρφεὺς κατὰ τὰς τελετὰς παρέδωκε διασπώμενον ὑπὸ τῶν Τιτάνων, 'It is said that this god was born of Zeus and Persephone in Crete; Orpheus has handed down the tradition in the initiatory rites that he was torn to pieces by the Titans.'[147]

So the dismemberment of Dionysus (with all its variations) is strongly associated with Dionysiac mystery-ritual, and is widely considered the creation of Orpheus. As Burkert writes, 'we get a complex of "Orpheus," secret mysteries, and Dionysus myth'.[148] The link consists in what is perhaps the achievement most commonly attributed by the ancients to Orpheus. It is Wender's suggestion that the Orpheus of *Georgic* 4 is to be understood as the culture hero who invented τελεταί, the εὑρετής of mystery-religion.[149] Orpheus was always considered, as Linforth states, a poet-musician first and foremost.[150] But from his musical or poetic ability flowed further achievements, chief amongst which was the establishment of mystery-cults. This role as, simultaneously, poet and founder of mysteries is very widely attested (always given the paucity of evidence concerning mystery religion). Orpheus (and Orphism) is primarily associated with Dionysiac mystery cult, and this is naturally enough the form of mystery he is most often accorded the status of having founded.[151] But in addition we often find Orpheus associated with the establish-

---

[147] Other texts which name Orpheus in the context of Dionysus' dismemberment – excluding the Neoplatonists – are Diod. 1.96.4–5 and 3.62.8; Phld. *Piet.* 44 (citing Euphorion); Clem. Alex. *Protr.* 2.17 (15P) and *Strom.* 6.2.26.1 (751P); Arn. *Adv. Nat.* 5.19; Serv. ad *G.* 1.166; Macrob. *In Somn.* 1.12.11; *Myth. Vat.* 3.12.5.

[148] Burkert (1987) 155 n. 38.

[149] Wender (1969) 434. Τελεταί, like *orgia*, is a word which can be used of religious celebrations generally, but is very often applied to mystery-ritual in particular: Burkert (1987) 9.

[150] Linforth (1941) 165.

[151] For a detailed discussion of the references see Linforth (1941) 206–32; cf. West (1983) 26.

ment of the Eleusinian mysteries,[152] or else credited with the invention of mystical τελεταί in general.[153]

Orpheus, then, was intimately connected with the mysteries, whether as their founder or their poet or merely as a figure particularly skilled in their practice. In particular Orpheus is credited with the establishment of the mysteries of Dionysus, the rites in which his death occurs in the *Georgics*. The myth commonly associated with these mysteries, and associated also with the ritual-poetic productions of Orpheus, was the σπαραγμός of Dionysus. Thus Orpheus not only related the central mystery of Dionysiac religion – the god's death and rebirth – but also suffered a similar death himself. Proclus draws an explicit connection between Orpheus' role as instigator of the Dionysiac mysteries and his death during them. He writes (*In R.* 1.174–5),

ἀλλ' Ὀρφεὺς μὲν ἅτε τῶν Διονύσου τελετῶν ἡγεμὼν γενόμενος τὰ ὅμοια παθεῖν ὑπὸ τῶν μύθων εἴρηται τῷ σφετέρῳ θεῷ (καὶ γὰρ ὁ σπαραγμὸς τῶν Διονυσιακῶν ἕν ἐστιν συνθημάτων)

Orpheus, inasmuch as he was the pioneer of the rites of Dionysus, is said to have suffered the same fate as his own god (for dismemberment is one of the Dionysiac doctrines)

Lactantius also draws a connection between Orpheus' institution of Dionysiac cult and his ritualistic death during it.[154] It is similarities like these which have led scholars such as Ferguson and Kerényi to see in Orpheus often almost an aspect of his god, Dionysus. For Ferguson he is 'a kind of double of Dionysus', for Kerényi, more boldly, he was 'torn to pieces by women like a second Dionysus'. Martin lists the biographical similarities between Dionysus and Orpheus: they have a common origin in Thrace; they both go on sea-journeys and also extensive wanderings on dry land; they both undertake

---

[152] Linforth (1941) 189–97.
[153] See Linforth (1941) 232–59. He states (244–5), in the context of Plutarch's discussion of the rites of the Bona Dea (*Caesar* 9), that for Greek authors Ὀρφικά and 'Greek mysteries' were often interchangeable terms.
[154] *Div. Inst.* 1.22.16: *ea sacra etiamnunc Orphica nominantur, in quibus ipse postea dilaceratus et carptus est.*

καταβάσεις to the Underworld (Dionysus to rescue Semele, Orpheus to rescue Eurydice); both of them die by dismemberment; both are particularly associated with oracles.[155]

Thus Orpheus' life displays many similarities to the life of Dionysus; but in his death, as we recall, the resemblance is particularly salient since whoever, or whatever, is ripped apart in Dionysiac ritual was considered in some sense to represent Dionysus himself.[156]

The suggestion that the aspect of Orpheus in play in the *Georgics* is that of the mystic Orpheus also seems to follow from the description of Orpheus' κατάβασις which constitutes the body of the passage. Orpheus' κατάβασις, like Orpheus' σπαραγμός, cannot be separated from his role as *Mysterienstifter*. For Harrison Orpheus' κατάβασις, like his death for Kerényi, is 'a piece of theology taken over from Dionysos';[157] and this view, like the interpretation of his death, has a parallel in antiquity. At 4.25.2–4 Diodorus takes the opportunity to offer a brisk biography of Orpheus – his origins in Thrace, exceptional poetic ability, journey to Egypt and transferral from there to Greece of ritual knowledge, his time as an Argonaut – and his descent to Hades:

συνεστρατεύσατο δὲ καὶ τοῖς Ἀργοναύταις, καὶ διὰ τὸν ἔρωτα τὸν πρὸς τὴν γυναῖκα καταβῆναι μὲν εἰς ᾅδου παραδόξως ἐτόλμησε, τὴν δὲ Φερσεφόνην διὰ τῆς εὐμελείας ψυχαγωγήσας ἔπεισε συνεργῆσαι ταῖς ἐπιθυμίαις καὶ συγχωρῆσαι τὴν γυναῖκα αὐτοῦ τετελευτηκυῖαν ἀναγαγεῖν ἐξ ᾅδου παραπλησίως τῷ Διονύσῳ· καὶ γὰρ ἐκεῖνον μυθολογοῦσιν ἀναγαγεῖν τὴν μητέρα Σεμέλην ἐξ ᾅδου, καὶ μεταδόντα τῆς ἀθανασίας Θυώνην μετονομάσαι.

he took part in the expedition of the Argonauts and because of his love for his wife dared the remarkable deed of descending to Hades; and charming Persephone with his melodiousness he prevailed upon her to assist his desires and allow him to bring up his dead wife from Hades, in rather similar fashion to Dionysus. For the story goes that *he* brought up his mother

---

[155] Ferguson (1970) 102; Kerényi (1976) 267; Martin (1987) 99. For similarities between the two see also Lobeck (1829) 294; Guépin (1968) 227.

[156] Compare Cairns (1992) 20 on Theocritus, *Id.* 26: 'The idyll may point to a re-enactment of the death of Pentheus, who was at times identified with Dionysus; and the tearing and eating of Pentheus could refer to an initiation rite in which a sacrificial victim representing Pentheus/Dionysus was, in some sense, consumed.'

[157] Harrison (1903b) 603.

Semele from Hades, and sharing his immortality with her changed her name to Thyone.

In respect of his κατάβασις, then, as in respect of his death by dismemberment, Orpheus resembles Dionysus: Dionysus, like Orpheus, descended to Hades to rescue a close female relative.[158] Orpheus' descent was also closely associated with his status as an imparter of mystic knowledge. A poem attributed at a very early stage to Orpheus, the Ἐις Ἅιδου κατάβασις, probably told, in autobiographical form, of his descent in search of his wife, and of all that he saw in the Underworld.[159] There is what appears to be a summary of the content of the poem in the Orphic *Argonautica*, a late (at least fourth century AD, West thinks)[160] text at the beginning of which (8–46) 'Orpheus' reminds Apollo of his previous poetry. Lines 40–2 describe the Ἐις Ἅιδου κατάβασις:

> ἄλλα δέ σοι κατέλεξ᾿, ἅπερ εἴσιδον ἠδ᾿ ἐνόησα,
> Ταίναρον[161] ἡνίκ᾿ ἔβην σκοτίην ὁδὸν Ἄιδος εἴσω
> ἡμετέρῃ πίσυνος κιθάρῃ, δι᾿ ἔρωτ᾿ ἀλόχοιο.

And I told you of the other things which I saw and perceived when I went the dark way to Taenarus into the Underworld, trusting in my lyre, out of love for my wife.

The *Descent* was thus a mystic document, Orpheus' κατάβασις an action of Orpheus *qua* hierophant: Orpheus' description of what he saw in Hades imparted religious knowledge of an eschatological nature.[162] The suggestion that he himself visited the Underworld in person was a kind of guarantee of the truthfulness of his teaching. Another figure with much to say on the nature of death, Pythagoras, was also, in a similar fashion, said to have seen Hades at first hand.[163] Diodorus, again, states that Orpheus introduced *both* his mystic rites *and*

---

[158] Cf. Hor. *Carm.* 2.19.29–32; Paus. 2.31.2, 2.37.5; Apollod. *Bibl.* 3.5.3; Plut. *De sera* 566a; Clem. Alex. *Protr.* 2.34 (29–30P.); Arn. *Adv. nat.* 5.28.
[159] West (1983) 12.
[160] West (1983) 37.
[161] Norden (1916) ad *Aen.* 6.120 compares this expression to *G.* 4.467–9: *Taenarias etiam fauces, alta ostia Ditis | et caligantem nigra formidine lucum | ingressus ...*
[162] West (1983) 12.
[163] West (1983) 12.

his description (μυθοποία) of his descent to Hades from Egypt, the latter apparently in imitation of Egyptian funeral custom (1.96.4–6). For Diodorus also, then, Orpheus' κατάβασις was a kind of mythologization of his role as teacher of the mysteries.[164]

Much of the detail of Virgil's story of Orpheus – his death and his descent to Hades in particular – would thus seem to relate to Orpheus in his aspect as mystic and founder of mystical τελεταί. And there is also another line of approach which yields a similar conclusion. Dionysiac ritual involves an identification of god and worshipper unparalleled elsewhere in Greek religion. Both initiate and god are called βάκχος, for example.[165] Another example is the cardinal motif of the Dionysiac mysteries whereby the initiand underwent a ritual death and rebirth. This process was apparently dramatized during the initiation ritual through some kind of κατάβασις in the course of which the initiands experienced and overcame their terror of death and gained knowledge of the joy which would come to them after death.[166] Lada has recently argued that the κατάβασις of Dionysus which forms the framework of Aristophanes' *Frogs* is to be interpreted in terms of initiation-ritual.[167] In fact Lada suggests that the descent of Dionysus constituted the prototype of the descents undertaken during initiation ceremonies. As in Dionysiac rites, so also at Eleusis the initiation may have taken the form of a kind of descent to Hades, if it only consisted in the darkness of the Telesterion.[168] Lucian (*Cat.* 22) compares a descent to the Lower World with the experience of the Eleusinian mys-

---

[164] See also Bowra (1952) 122–3: 'we may deduce [from the reference at the start of the Orphic *Argonautica*] that [Orpheus'] descent was connected with the Orphic mysteries and that the recovery of his wife did not necessarily have pride of place in it'.

[165] Burkert (1977) 252.

[166] Seaford (1981) 261.

[167] Lada (1993) 99: 'the very sequence of descent/ascent upon which the structure of the play is built ... should be seen as operative in the context of both a Dionysiac and an Eleusinian initiation-rite'.

[168] Seaford (1981) 261; Burkert (1972) 308–9.

teries. At any rate, as Lada points out, following Mylonas,[169] the descent and ascent of Persephone seems to have been enacted by the priests of the Eleusinian cult.

Luck, following Bishop Warburton's *Divine Legation of Moses Demonstrated on the Principles of a Religious Deist*, has argued for the profound influence of mystery cult on Virgil's depiction of Aeneas' κατάβασις in *Aeneid* 6.[170] The Sibyl's role, he suggests, is strongly suggestive of the role of a μυσταγωγός to the μύστης Aeneas. Similarly, after the Sibyl's exclusion of the uninitiated (258), *procul o procul este, profani*, 'any ancient reader would immediately think of the ἑκὰς ἑκὰς ἔστε, βέβηλοι of the Mysteries'.[171] Also redolent of mystical practice are Virgil's request for permission to reveal what he has heard of the Underworld (264–7), as if they are unspeakable secrets, the darkness and terror of Aeneas' first entry into the Underworld and its supersession by the bliss of Elysium, where he is made a party to a kind of ἱερὸς λόγος, culminating revelation, by Anchises.[172] Luck's interpretation is convincing. It has been widely noted that Aeneas emerges from the Underworld a new man, confident of his role in the scheme of things,[173] precisely the effect of mystical revelation. But his 'death' and 'rebirth' also figure the birth of Rome through the death of Troy, which in its many variations is the subject of the *Aeneid*. If nothing else, Luck establishes the intimate proximity of the scheme of κατάβασις and the doctrines of mystery cult. When at 119–23 Aeneas offers precedents for his descent – Orpheus, Castor and Pollux, Theseus and Hercules – Luck suggests that perhaps all these heroes 'had some con-

---

[169] Lada (1993) 100–1; Mylonas (1961) 147–8, speculating on the function of an elliptical opening leading from a chamber in the cave containing the temple of Pluto at Eleusis.

[170] Warburton (1738–41); Luck (1973).

[171] Luck (1973) 159.

[172] Cf. Solmsen (1972) 40: Anchises is a 'hierophant' whose words constitute an initiation of his son into cosmic secrets.

[173] See, for example, Boyle (1972) 113–14: 'In Book VI however Aeneas experiences what might be construed as a spiritual regeneration ... [he] returns to his task as the conscious, unfaltering bearer of the imperial destiny of Rome.'

nection with Mystery Religions'.[174] Scazzoso is thus surely
right to read this initiatory scheme into Orpheus' κατάβασις
in the *Georgics*: 'infine la discesa d' Orfeo agli Inferi è il
simbolo della morte fittizia a cui ogni iniziato era sottoposto
ritualmente'.[175]

A very similar account might be given of σπαραγμός. The
manner of death suffered by the mystic Dionysus, and by the
figure commonly considered his high priest, Orpheus, was
considered by Harrison a reflection of 'primitive rites of tribal
initiation'.[176] More recently West has argued substantially the
same.[177] Dionysus' death by dismemberment, West suggests,
reflects two forms of initiation for which there is a large
quantity of comparative data: that into adult society or a
secret community, or that which makes of the initiate a
shaman. Each commonly involves the initiand's ritual death
by dismemberment. As Dionysus' κατάβασις was the prototype of the descent-motif of Dionysiac ritual, then, so also
in his death, as Lada puts it, 'the god [takes] the role of an
archetypal initiand who has to *die* so that he can be *reborn*'.[178]
This detail of the mystery rites seems also to crop up (in dis-
torted form) in Livy's account of the Bacchanalia of 186 BC.
The historian talks of 'secret murders' committed amid all the
racket of drums and cymbals which accompanied the rites
(39.8.8),[179] and at 39.10.7–8, in Hispala's account to Aebu-
tius, a similar scene is drawn:

ut quisque introductus sit, uelut uictimam tradi sacerdotibus. eos deducere
in locum, qui circumsonet ululatibus cantuque symphoniae et cymbalorum
et tympanorum pulsu, ne uox quiritantis, cum per uim stuprum inferatur,
exaudiri possit.

As each person was introduced he became a kind of sacrificial victim for the
priests. They would lead him, she said, into a place which would resonate
with howls and the song of a choir and the beating of cymbals and drums,

---

[174] Luck (1973) 152. Hercules – see Mylonas (1961) 205–8 – and Orpheus were certainly associated with them. For the Dioscuri see Luck (1973) 157.
[175] Scazzoso (1956) 27. Cf. Wilkinson (1969) 117–18, 326.
[176] Harrison (1912) 16.
[177] West (1983) 143–50. Cf. Seaford (1981) 265–6.
[178] Lada (1993) 104.
[179] Seaford (1981) 262 and n. 88.

in order that his voice might not be heard crying out in protest as he was forcibly raped.

Livy makes of the rite an assault on the initiand's virtue. But it is easy to perceive behind this travesty the initiand's *ritual* pseudo-death by dismemberment. The same is also true of Hispala's stated fear that if she reveals the secrets of the rites to the (uninitiated) authorities she will be torn limb from limb (39.13.5–6).

In summary, then: both Orpheus' descent to the Underworld and his death by σπαραγμός amidst the Bacchic *orgia* strongly suggest that the aspect of Orpheus in play in Virgil's passage is that which placed him in proximity to mystery religion, the mysteries of Dionysus in particular but also those of Demeter and Persephone-Proserpina at Eleusis. Perhaps Orpheus' most commonly noted achievement in the ancient world was his establishment of (or composition of the poetry for) mystery cults. The motifs of κατάβασις and σπαραγμός, in particular, assimilate the sufferings of Orpheus both to the very similar ones attributed to the Dionysus of mystery cult – with whom in some sense all victims of Bacchic ritual were identified – and to the initiands of mystery cult, who also, apparently, underwent the pretend deaths of κατάβασις and σπαραγμός in *imitation* of the sufferings of the god. Descent to Hades and dismemberment are above all *mystic* motifs.

But assuming there is such a schema in operation, what can it signify? The answer must be that at the core of the phenomenon of the Mysteries were the very same notions as I have identified elsewhere in the *Aristaeus*: death and rebirth, rebirth *through* death. 'The fate of the initiate,' Burkert puts it (of mysteries in general), 'is modelled on the fate of the god as represented in myth and ritual, following the peripety from catastrophe to salvation.'[180]

In the Dionysiac Mysteries, to concentrate on the most germane variety, initiands, following the model of the mythological experiences of their god, gained blessedness (tending,

---

[180] Burkert (1987) 75.

as in Christianity, to be somewhat vaguely defined) through πάθος, suffering. Through a ritual experience which anticipated their deaths they gained knowledge and certainty of their lot after death. The desirability of the latter is indicated by scattered references in Plutarch and elsewhere, and perhaps most strikingly in the gold leaves found in tombs in Italy, Thessaly and Crete containing directions for the initiate dead in their journey through the other world.[181] The most extensive of the gold-leaf texts is that from Hipponion-Vibo Valentia. It describes μύσται ('initiates') and βάκχοι, amongst them the dead person to whom the instructions of the text are directed, on the 'sacred way' to a blissful existence in Elysium. The knowledge possessed by the initiate thus, apparently, guaranteed a blessed existence after death, a rebirth into idyllic conditions. The aspiration is starkly expressed in one of the bone tablets – associated with a Dionysiac cult – discovered at the site of the Mytilenean colony of Olbia, on the northern coast of the Black Sea. The inscription on it begins ΒΙΟΣ ΘΑΝΑΤΟΣ ΒΙΟΣ. It continues with a zigzag symbol of obscure significance (a snake perhaps, or lightning), the word ΑΛΗ-ΘΕΙΑ, a large A, ΔΙΟ (an abbreviation of the name of Dionysus) and ΟΡΦΙΚ-.[182] Whatever is precisely meant by these terms, the 'Orphics' or 'Bacchics' of Olbia clearly had some conception of life after death. The gold leaves discovered in 1985 on the site of ancient Pellina, in Thessaly, express a similar sense of life after death. Their texts begin, νῦν ἔθανες καὶ νῦν ἐγένου, τρισόλβιε, ἄματι τῷδε.[183] Death, for this initiate, is just a new birth. Whether or not Dionysiac belief embraced a concept of reincarnation – rebirth into *this* life – is unknown.[184] But West cites fifth-century texts which offer an equally likely interpretation of the 'life' after death. For ini-

---

[181] Burkert (1977) 436–40; Pind. fr. 131a Maehler; Plut. *Non posse* 1105b; Ar. *Ran.* 312–459. For the Hipponion gold tablet, in particular, see Foti and Pugliese Carratelli (1974).
[182] West (1982) 18–22.
[183] Lada (1993) 106; Tsantsanoglou and Parássoglou (1987) 11: 'the meaning is rather clear: death for the initiate does not mean complete annihilation but a change, via (re)birth, into another condition'.
[184] Burkert (1977) 437.

tiates, of Eleusis at least, there is a real 'life' in Hades, but for the uninitiated only misery, only death.[185]

So the dismemberment of an animal or a mythological figure (or an initiand) which occurs – as the dismemberment of Orpheus in the *Georgics* does – in the context of *nocturni orgia Bacchi* is not the last word. Bacchic *orgia* entail (some kind of) rebirth: at the least the ritual dismemberment is a token of the power to redeem possessed by the god Dionysus, whose own death by dismemberment – from which he was reborn – it seems to commemorate. Orpheus, then, dies the same death as the god himself once died, as wild animals died in the *oreibasia*, as initiands died during initiation: a death which was a prerequisite of joyful rebirth, a paradoxically *constructive* death.

If this reading is convincing, then the reference to mystery cult would seem to be a topical one. According to Dio, Augustus was twice in attendance at the Eleusinian mysteries, in 31 and 19 BC.[186] It is unclear why he returned in 19, but the time of his arrival in Greece in 31 – late September – suggests that he witnessed the Greater Mysteries in that year.[187]

VII

As we saw at the beginning of this chapter, the death of Dionysus/Orpheus might carry cosmogonical associations. But the capture and metamorphoses of Proteus, as we may recall, were interpreted in another way besides as a figure for the Creation. According to the scholia ad *Od.* 4.384 Proteus can represent the dead earth of winter transformed into the diverse vegetation of spring: his metamorphoses figure the proliferation of new life in springtime.[188] I compared this interpretation with Virgil's description of the onset of spring at 4.306, itself figured by the dissemination of the bee-swarm

---

[185] West (1982) 26: Soph. fr. 837 (τοῖσδε γὰρ μόνοις ἐκεῖ | ζῆν ἔστι); Ar. *Ran.* 454–9 (μόνοις γὰρ ἡμῖν ἥλιος); Pind. fr. 129–31 Maehler; Pl. *Resp.* 363c–e.

[186] Dio 51.4.1, 54.9.10; Bernhardt (1975).

[187] Bernhardt (1975) 234.

[188] See pp. 77–8 above.

from an ox-carcase. In effect Proteus' metamorphoses represent a fairly abstract notion of creation which might be applied to specific cases such as Creation or spring, two phenomena easily conflated (as at *G.* 2.336–42). Similarly *bugonia* might reflect the events of spring or the re-foundation of Rome. So also there is considerable evidence that Dionysiac mystery cult could be interpreted by Virgil's contemporaries as an agrarian rite of spring as well as a figure for the Creation; and it is in fact this interpretation, I shall now suggest, which is the more dominant in Virgil's description of the death of Orpheus.

Wender suggests that the dismemberment of Orpheus is a fertility ritual. The fragments of Orpheus' dismembered body are scattered over the fields (520–2). Wender notes Sir James Frazer's conclusion (largely based on this passage) that Orpheus' death, along with those of Pentheus and Lycurgus, was a reminiscence of a time when priest-kings, impersonating and representing the god Dionysus, were sacrificed as a means of fertilizing the land.[189] Whatever the current status of Frazer's broader anthropological theory, he – and Wender – seem to have a point here. The description of Orpheus' σπαραγμός at 522, *discerptum latos iuuenem sparsere per agros*, does sound very much like a fertility rite, almost as if Orpheus' limbs were *seed*. Miles, coming to a similar interpretation, suggests that by calling the Bacchanals who dismember Orpheus *matres* Virgil points up 'their role as agents of life and fertility'. 'Their murder of Orpheus', he goes on, 'incorporates his death and that of Eurydice into the regenerative processes of nature.'[190] Lyne has established the special resonance of *agri* in this poem: 'they are after all the ground of the World of the *Georgics*'.[191] *Agri* in the *Georgics* are above all the arena for *agricultura*. Is the death of Orpheus the death of a kind of Corn God, then, a means of ensuring the vital power of the land? Wender certainly thinks so. She writes that the Bacchanals 'work "inter sacra deum nocturnique

---

[189] Wender (1969) 434; Frazer (1906) 271.
[190] Miles (1980) 280. [191] Lyne (1974) 54.

orgia Bacchi", and they scatter his body "per agros"; thus it is clear that they are performing a fertility rite'.[192] If my confidence on this matter falls slightly short of Wender's, it is mainly because she places a lot of faith in the now rather discredited theories of Frazer. Nevertheless it can, I think, be established that Virgil's contemporaries would have interpreted the death of Orpheus as an agrarian rite, though I relegate my complex discussion of this point to Appendix III.[193]

However, if Orpheus is to be interpreted in his death as 'a victim of the inexorable processes of nature',[194] there would be a parallel earlier in Virgil's own text. At 511–15, just prior to his death, Orpheus is compared to the victim of the arator, the nightingale whose unfledged young are removed by the ploughman. The passage looks back to G. 2.207–11, where land is commended for ploughing from which the 'angry arator' has stripped the verdure, birds and all, for the purposes of agriculture. The vignette is designed to suggest, presumably, like the arma imagery, the violence and destruction which is a necessary element of farming.[195]

This, I would argue, is the intended implication of the suffering, death and dismemberment of Orpheus. It is another instance of constructive death, derived from perhaps the most important ancient source for doctrines of the miraculous and paradoxical: mystery cult, wherein was presented the death and rebirth (in some form) of the god or of an initiate-figure mimicking the god. I further believe that for the generation after Varro and perhaps contemporary with Diodorus the general notion of redemption promised by the mysteries of Dionysus would have been grounded in the processes of

---

[192] Wender (1969) 434.
[193] The agricultural dimension of the killing would appear to be foregrounded in Ovid's account. Pursuing Orpheus, the Maenads come across peasants tilling their land with a plough and various types of hoe (sarcula, rastri, ligones). Snatching up these arma operis sui – with an eye on G. 1.160–75 it is tempting to take opus in its literary sense – they use them to kill Orpheus (Met. 11.30–43). Ovid seems to be drawing out the implication in Virgil's account that the death of Orpheus is part of the agricultural process.
[194] Miles (1980) 281.
[195] Miles (1980) 279.

agriculture (see Appendix III): the death of Orpheus stands for the violence which is a prerequisite of that agricultural life which is the topic of the whole poem.

VIII

But whether or not this suggestion of a specifically seasonal connotation for Orpheus' death is ultimately convincing, the basic point stands: the sufferings of Orpheus, in so far as they reflect doctrines of the mysteries, though utter, miraculously serve a purpose.

There is a parallel for the death of Orpheus earlier in the poem; and by this stage it should hardly surprise us that the earlier event to which Orpheus' death bears such a similarity is a terrible event: civil war, in fact. At 1.489–92 the two battles of Philippi are depicted, either the two engagements at Philippi in 42 BC or (with poetic licence) the battle of Philippi and the earlier battle of Pharsalus (48):

> ergo inter sese paribus concurrere telis
> Romanas acies iterum uidere Philippi;
> nec fuit indignum superis, bis sanguine nostro
> Emathiam et latos Haemi pinguescere campos.

Therefore once again Philippi saw Roman armies clash with matching weapons, and it was not monstrous in the gods' eyes that twice Emathia and the wide plains of Haemus should grow rich with our blood.

Dead bodies fertilizing broad fields,[196] and in a similar geographical location. Lyne has written an eloquent criticism of the end of Book 1,[197] a 'peroration on civil war and the chaos of the present world'[198] which in a manner now familiar to us generalizes the particular phenomena of the Roman Civil Wars into an apocalyptic vision of cosmic disorder and dissolution redolent of Gigantomachy.[199] In addition the notion of primeval sin occurs again. The battle of Philippi is assimi-

[196] See Lyne (1974) 56 on the similar resonance within the Georgics of agri and campi (see p. 198 above).
[197] Lyne (1974).
[198] Lyne (1974) 51.
[199] Lyne (1974) 53–4.

lated to the dishonest dealings of Laomedon, king of Troy, with the gods who built the city's walls. This, like the fratricide of Remus, could be seen to have engendered or prefigured subsequent tribulations endured by the Trojan or Roman race.[200] Similarly the *impia saecula* of 468 foreshadow the *impia gens* which commits the catastrophic, epochal slaughter of cattle at the end of Book 2 (537). The Civil Wars, then, are the nadir. The *saeculum* is *euersum* (500), and correspondingly *fas uersum atque nefas*. Lyne talks of the mood of the latter part of the passage: 'bewilderment at a seemingly unending tragic process of crime begetting crime', 'bafflement', Virgil depicts 'a vast, inexplicable chaos', 'Virgil does not really know *what* [the gods] are doing'.[201] I need hardly labour the point that the movement from chaos in this passage to order in the (religiously sanctioned) death of Orpheus, from bafflement to understanding, exactly parallels my interpretation of Virgil's 'slaughtered cattle' imagery, and is also typical of the dynamics of mystery cult. The progression from terror to revelation in mystery cult is memorably expressed in a fragment of Plutarch relating the experience of initiation to the experience of death (fr. 178.7–12 Sandbach):

πλάναι τὰ πρῶτα καὶ περιδρομαὶ κοπώδεις καὶ διὰ σκότους τινὲς ὕποπτοι πορεῖαι καὶ ἀτέλεστοι, εἶτα πρὸ τοῦ τέλους αὐτοῦ τὰ δεινὰ πάντα, φρίκη καὶ τρόμος καὶ ἱδρὼς καὶ θάμβος· ἐκ δὲ τούτου φῶς τι θαυμάσιον ἀπήντησεν καὶ τόποι καθαροὶ καὶ λειμῶνες ἐδέξαντο...

Wanderings astray in the beginning, tiresome walkings in circles, some frightening paths in darkness that lead nowhere; then immediately before the end all the terrible things, panic and shivering and sweat, and amazement. And then some wonderful light comes to meet you, pure regions and meadows are there to greet you...[202]

What appears in Book 1 as an appalling perversion of the processes of agriculture,[203] similar to the slaughter of plough-oxen, the enriching of the fields with human blood, becomes in Book 4 an event which is not a perversion but a prerequisite

---

[200] Compare 491 and 501, Hor. *Carm.* 3.3.18–24; and see Thomas (1988) ad 501–2.
[201] Lyne (1974) 58, 64, 62.
[202] Translated by Burkert (1987) 91.
[203] Lyne (1974) 58.

of agriculture.[204] The paradoxes proliferate: sand that fertilizes, *ecpyrosis*, pious cattle-slaughter, foundational fratricide,
creative conflict between heat and water; now killing which
mysteriously underpins agriculture.

Conclusion

IX

I interpreted the Proteus episode as representing Virgil's undertaking of the Grand Epic mode of literature, of which the
archetype was Homer. The episode exemplifies much of what
was expected of epic at this time. It is at some level concerned
with natural philosophy, for example, as Homeric epic was
supposed to be, and it is *panegyrical*: it depicts success. I have
drawn attention to the emphasis in the passage on the *uis*
which Aristaeus employs. I related this to the physical imagery which I argued underlay the narrative: Aristaeus reflects
the fiery, demiurgic, active principle (*illa uis*, Cic., *Acad. post.*
28) which creates by acting upon the wet, material passive reflected by Proteus. I now want to follow up my suggestion
that the Orpheus episode represents the precise opposite of
this panegyrical, natural-philosophical *Siegeslied*.

A description commonly applied to the gods of mystery
cult, and Dionysus in particular, is that of the 'suffering
god'.[205] As Otto puts it, 'Dionysus, himself, is a suffering,
dying god who must succumb to the violence of terrible enemies in the midst of the glory of his youthful greatness.'[206]
The death is a precursor of rebirth, of course, and the suffering of joy: this is the 'peripety from catastrophe to salvation'
that Burkert considers typical of mystery cult (and which I
believe is focal to the scheme of the *Georgics*). Fagles and

---

[204] The relation between these two passages was originally suggested to me by Philip
Hardie.
[205] Burkert (1987) 74–5 and 156 n. 46.
[206] Otto (1965) 103.

Stanford talk of 'the god whose death releases vital energies'.[207] But suffering comes first. Both the experiences of the initiand and the archetypal experiences of the god which these seem to reflect are typically described in terms of, we might say, *passivity*. The words πάθος and πάθημα figure prominently. Thus Aristotle (Synesius, *Dio* 10.48a) defined the effect of the mysteries on those taking part as not *learning* but *experiencing/suffering*: καθάπερ Ἀριστοτέλης ἀξιοῖ τοὺς τελουμένους οὐ μαθεῖν τι δεῖν ἀλλὰ παθεῖν καὶ διατεθῆναι, δηλονότι γενομένους ἐπιτηδείους, 'as Aristotle claims that those who are being initiated into the mysteries are to be expected not to *learn* anything but to *experience/endure* something, to be put into a certain condition, i.e. to become fitted for some purpose'. Similarly on the Bacchic Thurian gold leaf A4 (3–4) the mystery initiate is greeted with the phrase, χαῖρε παθὼν τὸ πάθημα τὸ δ' οὔπω πρόσθε ἐπεπόνθεις· | θεὸς ἐγένου ἐξ ἀνθρώπου, 'Greetings, you who have experienced an experience such as you had never experienced before: you became a god from a man.'[208]

πάσχω, πάθος and πάθημα are broad in sense, obviously. πάθος is 'suffering' or merely 'being the object of'. But in Dionysiac cult the πάθος of the initiand or of the god certainly ranks at the intense end of the range of experience. The πάθημα of the Thurian initiate has been plausibly interpreted as his or her death;[209] and the (*per se*) extremely unpleasant ordeal of the Dionysiac initiand – the terror which preceded the revelation – is also perhaps given visual expression in the image of the flagellation in the Villa of the Mysteries.[210] We thus have good grounds for translating it as 'suffering'. Certainly when the terms πάθος and πάθημα are applied to the 'experiences' of the mystical Dionysus – as they very frequently are – we are talking about very violent suffering: πάθη or παθήματα are the standard descriptions of Dionysus' tribulations at the hands of the Titans. Thus Diodorus talks of ἡ περὶ τὰ πάθη τῶν θεῶν ἱστορία (1.97.4), amongst which

---

[207] In the introductory essay to Fagles (1976) 19.   [208] Zuntz (1971) 329.
[209] Seaford (1981) 262.   [210] Seaford (1978) 64–6.

is the myth of Dionysus' dismemberment. Dionysius, more narrowly, speaks of τὰ Διονύσου πάθη (*Ant. Rom.* 2.19.2). Pausanias attributes to Onomacritus the authorship of doctrines normally attributed to Orpheus, Ὀνομάκριτος ... τοὺς Τιτᾶνας τῷ Διονύσῳ τῶν παθημάτων ἐποίησεν αὐτουργούς (8.37.5), and Plutarch repeats the description: τὰ ... περὶ τὸν Διόνυσον μεμυθευμένα πάθη τοῦ διαμελισμοῦ καὶ τὰ Τιτάνων ἐπ' αὐτὸν τολμήματα (*De esu carn.* 996c). Herodotus (2.171) and Plutarch (*De Is. et Os.* 360d) use the same terms of the dismemberment of Osiris (which they identify with that of Dionysus), and we may recall how according to Proclus (*In R.* 1.174.30) it was said that Orpheus 'suffered the same', τὰ ὅμοια παθεῖν, as Dionysus. Livy's distortion of the ritual, which makes the initiand *uelut uictima*, 'a kind of victim', of the priests (39.10.7), also contains a grain of truth: mystery initiation was a frightening and unsettling experience – akin to death – out of which alone could come revelation. At *De E* 388e–389a, as we have seen,[211] Plutarch connects the 'suffering' (πάθημα) of the dismembered Dionysus with physical theory, which assimilates Dionysus-Orpheus to the role of the passive principle of the universe which I attributed to Proteus. Proteus represented τὸ πάσχον, the passive principle of the universe on which the divine active principle forcibly imposed structure and order.

If the *Proteus* constitutes a poetry of the victor, then, the *Orpheus* is a poetry of the victim, appropriate – I have suggested – to its singer.[212] Aristaeus' capture of Proteus is a model of success, the story of Orpheus a catalogue of suffering. If one is a *Siegeslied*, the other is a *Niederlagelied*. And each is couched in a poetic style appropriate to its subject. The capture of Proteus was told in Homeric mode, the proper mode for panegyric. The myth of Orpheus is told in the style

---

[211] Pp. 158–9 above.

[212] The *Orpheus*, whether considered the song of Proteus or the song of Orpheus, is generated by the suffering of its author(s). Proteus will only sing once captured (*sine ui non ulla dabit praecepta*, 398). Orpheus' song, similarly, is a lament, an outcrop of his tribulations: even after his death his *frigida lingua* continues to sing it. This is appropriate: to a large degree his death *is* his song.

of a Neoteric epyllion, the preoccupations of which – victim-hood, I suggested earlier – are exemplified in Parthenius' collection of plot-summaries aptly entitled Ἐρωτικὰ Παθήματα, *Amorous Sufferings*.[213]

X

... the incomprehensible currents of violence for order which are at the heart of the poem and its empire.[214]

In summary, Quint has talked of 'epic's promise of an ultimate coherence in history',[215] and it is this epic promise, I suggest, that Virgil is seeking to exploit in the *Aristaeus*. Some of the implications of the 'universality' attributed to Homer have emerged as this book has gone on: Homeric epic deals with the totality of existence, and Homeric epic speaks in every poetic form. Here these two notions seem to dovetail: the Homeric mode is presented by Virgil as containing both the poetry of success – panegyrical poetry, the traditional scope of Grand Epic – and also its antithesis, the poetry of disaster and suffering, the song of the victimized Proteus. Crucially, however, both success and disaster are *constructive*: disaster and death are presented by Virgil as constituent parts of the greater, providential scheme. There is clearly a close parallelism between a mystical-religious scheme which presents destruction as constructive, such as I discussed in Chapter 3, and a universal poetic scheme which encompasses – and again presents as a necessary, functional, explicable component of the larger scheme – a poetry (the Neoteric-elegiac) which foregrounds suffering and destruction. Virgil's emulation of Homer introduces a universal poetic scheme – implying, as we have seen, a universal scheme *simpliciter* – containing modes

---

[213] Cf. Segal (1966) 322: 'And just as Vergil in the Fourth *Georgic* has separated what is later to be fused with greater complexity into a single figure, so his style is divided: the heroic, "objective" style of success, Homeric achievement and impact on the world for Aristaeus; the subjective, "empathetic" style for the private tragedy and aloneness of Orpheus.'

[214] Feeney (1991) 150 on the *Aeneid*.

[215] Quint (1993) 61.

of poetry conventionally thought antithetical, and also containing the two poles of experience: victory and defeat, success and disaster, (at its starkest) action and suffering. When Cicero (in the persona of the Stoic Balbus) talks of the perfection of the total universe, *mundus quoniam omnia complexus est neque est quicquam quod non insit in eo, perfectus undique est* (*Nat. D.* 2.38), we can compare with his statement the descriptions of the universality of (Homeric) epic such as that at *G.* 2.42, *non ego cuncta meis amplecti uersibus opto*, or Silius' description of Homer (13.788), *carmine complexus terram, mare, sidera, manes*. Homer, like a demiurge, contains and embodies a total providential scheme within which all events are explicable.

Dio Chrysostom (*Or.* 36.50) offers an illuminating parallel when he gives a profoundly Stoic account, which he attributes to the Magi, of the periodic catastrophes visited upon the world, and the role of these *prima facie* unmitigated disasters in the total scheme of things:

ταῦτα δὲ σπανίως ξυμβαίνοντα δοκεῖν μὲν ἀνθρώποις διὰ τὸν αὑτῶν ὄλεθρον γίγνεσθαι μὴ κατὰ λόγον μηδὲ μετέχειν τῆς τοῦ παντὸς τάξεως, λανθάνειν δὲ αὐτοὺς ὀρθῶς γιγνόμενα καὶ κατὰ γνώμην τοῦ σῴζοντος καὶ κυβερνῶντος τὸ πᾶν.

These rare occurrences [the Magi say] seem to humans to be designed for their destruction and not to happen in accordance with reason or to be a part of the organization of the universe, but they are unaware that they occur properly and in accordance with the plan of the preserver and governor of the universe.[216]

The cosmos, when viewed as a whole, is good. It is providentially governed. All events that occur subserve the greater plan. Seneca, in similar vein to Dio, suggests the appropriate mental defence against ill fortune (*Ep.* 74.20):

Quod sit hoc instrumentum, scire desideras? nihil indignetur sibi accidere sciatque illa ipsa, quibus laedi uidetur, ad conseruationem uniuersi pertinere et ex iis esse quae cursum mundi officiumque consummant.

---

[216] See Russell (1992) 231–3 for a discussion of the difficulties of this 'myth of the Magi', and in particular of the question of how these *partial* catastrophes relate to the total destruction, by *ecpyrosis*, which Dio goes on to describe.

Do you wish to know what this weapon of defence is? It is the ability to refrain from chafing over whatever happens to one, of knowing that the very agencies which seem to bring harm are working for the preservation of the world and are part of the scheme for bringing to fulfilment the order of the universe and its functions.[217]

The death of Orpheus, like those of the Civil Wars which it reflects, is sanitized in the Virgilian scheme as a *sine qua non* of this eventual coming-right *sub specie aeternitatis*: Orpheus represents the figure who *must* die, in the scheme of things, and can be presented as dying (purposefully) in a poetry the ultimate purpose of which is to depict a coherent, ordered totality where even death has its place. Epic, the *Weltdichtung*, offers an insight into this ultimate organization.

In the *Aristaeus*, then, we are party to a revelation in the light of which dilemmas elaborated in the poem which had seemed irresoluble – at the core of which always lies the (seemingly) arbitrary catastrophe of the Civil Wars – find resolution. A transcendent scheme is adumbrated in which death and disaster, which had seemed simply antithetical to success, are unveiled as – miraculously – *integral* to it: at its simplest, death is a prerequisite of life. To the bewilderment generated by images of utter disaster – civil war, plague and so on – succeeds a sense of an ultimate rationale underlying such events, built upon this understanding of the constructive power of destruction.

XI

The episode of Philomela will help to elucidate how I think the *Orpheus* is to be read: the 'double focus' which will allow us to interpret unmitigated catastrophe as constructive. The plight of Philomela (4.511) reflects Orpheus' in a number of

---

[217] The translation is that of Gummere (1970). We might compare the words of the Stoic Cleanthes in his *Hymn to Zeus* on Zeus' capacity to turn all events to the good (20–2): ὧδε γὰρ εἰς ἓν πάντα συνήρμοκας ἐσθλὰ κακοῖσιν | ὥσθ' ἓν γίγνεσ-θαι πάντων λόγον αἰὲν ἐόντα, 'For you have joined together all good and bad things into one, in such a way as to create one eternal reason belonging to all things'. On this poem see Hopkinson (1988) 131–6.

ways: she has lost loved ones; she is proverbially a peerless
singer (if understood as a nightingale: see below);[218] the song
she sings is an elegiac *miserabile carmen* (but she is at the same
time a Homeric figure); she is also, I would add, a victim of
the farming-process. But what *precisely* is she? She might be
either a nightingale or a swallow. Philomela was a daughter of
Pandarus who was raped by her brother-in-law Tereus, husband of her sister Procne. Tereus cut out her tongue to pre-
vent her telling her sister, but she managed to convey the truth
by weaving the story into a robe. In punishment of Tereus the
two sisters served up the son of Tereus and Procne, Itys, to
Tereus for him to eat. The three were transformed into birds,
and the tradition is agreed that the bird Tereus turned into
was a hoopoe. However the tradition regarding Philomela and
Procne is complicated. Greek writers, on the one hand, make
Procne, the mother of Itys, the nightingale who plaintively
sings out her son's name, Ἴτυν, Ἴτυν (Soph. *El.* 148), and the
mute Philomela the less-tuneful swallow. Thus Apollodorus
(*Bibl.* 3.14.8): Πρόκνη μὲν γίνεται ἀηδών, Φιλομήλα δὲ χελιδών.
By the time of the Roman mythographers, however, (for example Hyg. *Fab.* 45) the sisters have been switched round,
perhaps influenced by etymology of Philomela's name: Procne
is still the mother of Itys, but turns into the swallow, whilst
Philomela turns into the melodious nightingale.[219] In the
Augustan period the issue seems still to be in a state of
flux. Ovid in the *Metamorphoses* is non-committal: one of the
sisters became a swallow and one a nightingale, but he does
not name either (*Met.* 6.668–9). In the *Fasti* Procne is the
swallow (2.853). However, according to an etymology of
Varro Procne is still the nightingale (*Ling.* 5.76): *lusci⟨ni⟩ola,
quod luctuose canere existimatur atque esse ex Attica Progne in*

---

[218] The nightingale very often represents the poet (see the *TGL* s.v. ἀηδών) and
nightingales were particularly associated with the figure of Orpheus: Antig. Car.
Hist. Mir. 5 states that the nightingales on Orpheus' tomb sang even more
sweetly than those elsewhere.

[219] I am assuming a perceived etymological connection between -μηλ- and -μελ-.
Differences in vowel quantity are often of little concern to ancient etymologists.
Cf. O'Hara (1996) 61–2: 'The Greeks and Romans ... clearly thought that words
with different vowel quantities could be related etymologically.'

luctu facta auis, 'the nightingale [sc. is so called] because it is thought to sing sorrowfully and to be the Athenian Procne made a bird in grief'. In the *Eclogues* Virgil perhaps implies that there was some scholarly dispute on the matter (6.78–81): *narrauerit... | ... Philomela... | ... quibus... | infelix sua tecta super uolitauerit alis.* At *G.* 4.15 *Procne* is unambiguously a swallow; but at 4.511 *Philomela* cannot help but be assimilated to the mythological Procne to some degree because, like her, she mourns her own offspring. So when we ask, what *is* Philomela?, Servius *auctus* is clearly (in a sense) right to say, 'the nightingale': Philomela must be either a nightingale or a swallow, and of the two this sedentary bird with a mournful song must be a nightingale. But all in all the metonymy *Philomela* for 'nightingale' – something, I think, unparalleled – serves to relate it to Procne the swallow at 4.15 who appears again at 4.307. At 4.15 Procne is associated with the beginnings of the bee-community in spring; at 307 the arrival of the swallow actually stands for the onset of spring. There are many parallels: Simonides, typically, addresses the ἄγγελε ... ἔαρος ... χελιδοῖ (46 Diehl).[220]

In respect of being a harbinger of spring the swallow is very similar to the nightingale. Thus Sappho (121 Diehl): ἦρος ἄγγελος ἱμερόφωνος ἀήδων.[221] Aristotle tells us, in a work which was a major influence on the *Georgics*, ἡ δ' ἀηδὼν ᾄδει μὲν συνεχῶς ἡμέρας καὶ νύκτας δεκαπέντε ὅταν τὸ ὄρος ἤδη δασύνηται· μετὰ δὲ ταῦτα ᾄδει μέν, συνεχῶς δ' οὐκέτι, 'The nightingale sings for fifteen days and nights continuously when the mountain vegetation is already getting thick. After that it sings, but no longer continuously' (*Hist. an.* 632b21–3).[222] Pliny the Elder repeats the fact, which was clearly standard lore: *luscinis diebus ac noctibus continuis XV garrulus sine intermissu cantus densante se frondium germine,*

---

[220] Cf. Ov. *Fast.* 2.853; Varro, *Sat. Men.* 579a; Hor. *Epist.* 1.7.13; Arist. *Eth. Nic.* 1098a18–19 (μία γὰρ χελιδὼν ἔαρ οὐ ποιεῖ).

[221] Cf. Soph. *El.* 149 and the scholiast ad loc.; Jebb (1886) xii–xiii and n. 1. For post-Classical treatment of the theme see Chandler (1934–5) 82–4.

[222] For the influence of the *Historia animalium* on the *Georgics* see Mynors (1990) 330–3.

'Nightingales pour out a ceaseless gush of song for fifteen days and nights on end when the buds of the leaves are swelling' (*HN* 10.81). The terms of Virgil's simile make it clear that it is to this continuous song by the nightingale at the start of spring that he is referring. The term *integrat* (515), 'resume', must imply repetition: Servius *auctus* glosses it *renouat*. The phrase *flet noctem*, again, carries similar suggestions. The *Scholia Bernensia* glosses the words FLET NOCTEM *iugi nocte, continuo fletu*, and Servius similarly (*iugi nocte, continua*). It is a ploughman who causes the nightingale her grief, of course, and springtime is the season of ploughing *par excellence*.[223] Ploughing, furthermore, is the archetypal image of farming in the *Georgics*. Here, towards the very end of the poem, we seem to return to its beginning – spring again – a form of ring-composition imaging a passage through death to the rebirth of the countryside. This, then, is the continuous song of the nightingale in spring, as indeed it is – perhaps most significantly of all – in Virgil's main source at this point, *Od.* 19.518–19: ὡς δ' ὅτε Πανδαρέου κούρη, χλωρηῗς[224] ἀηδών, | καλὸν ἀείδησιν ἔαρος νέον ἱσταμένοιο, 'as when the daughter of Pandarus, the nightingale of the woodland, sings beautifully when spring has newly arrived'.[225]

We might conclude with a poem from the *Anthologia Palatina* depicting the onset of springtime, *AP* 9.363, attrib-

[223] Thus 1.43–6.
[224] The word χλωρηῗς is a *hapax* of doubtful meaning; see Russo, Fernandez-Galiano and Heubeck (1992) ad loc. Eustathius glosses the word, χλωρηῗς δὲ ἀηδὼν ἢ ὡς ἐν χλωροῖς, φασί, διατρίβουσα, ἢ ὡς ἅμα τοῖς χλωροῖς φαινομένη· ἔαρος γὰρ φαίνεται, ἢ διὰ τὸ χρῶμα ... 'the nightingale is termed *chloreis* either because its habitat is verdure or because it appears at the same time as verdure – for it appears in spring – or because of its colouring ...'
[225] Another indication of the proximity of nightingale and swallow is Hesiod's treatment of the swallow at *Op.* 568–9. She also is the daughter of Pandion/ Pandareus and she arrives in spring: the onset of spring is described in the same expression as Homer used of the nightingale, ἔαρος νέον ἱσταμένοιο (569). The choice of the poplar as the tree in which Virgil's nightingale sits may be equally suggestive. As Coleman (1860) 105 writes, the Black Poplar is also a harbinger of spring: 'Early in spring, when the branches of the Black Poplar are yet leafless, they are loaded with such a profusion of deep red catkins, or pendulous flower-spikes, that the tree, especially when lit up by the sun, presents an exceedingly rich and striking appearance, the more remarkable from the general absence of any lively tint in nature at this period.'

uted by the manuscripts to Meleager. Stadtmüller disputes this attribution, and concludes (on the basis of its location in *AP*) that it was probably not included in Meleager's *Garland* either. His opinion is that it is the work of Nicander, the author of another *Georgica* whose *floruit* was probably around 130 BC.[226] Spring is heralded in this poem, predictably, by the growth of flowers (3–6, 19), the birth of animals (7–8), the West Wind (9–10), but also – grist to my mill – Dionysiac rites (11–12, 21), the activities of 'ox-born bees' (13–15, 22), and the singing of birds (16–18), including swallows and the nightingale (ὑπ' ἄλσος ἀηδών).

In short, there is a disjunction between the meaning of Philomela's song and what it connotes: though it commemorates a tragedy, the appalling murder by a woman of her own son, it heralds the arrival of spring, the joyful time of creation and rebirth: and this in the midst of the barren, wintry landscape occupied by Orpheus after the second loss of Eurydice. From Philomela's point of view, we might say, this is an utter tragedy; but the tragedy itself, paradoxically, is good news. There is thus a further parallelism with the story of Orpheus, as I have interpreted it. Each, though definitively tragic, is a source of hope for better things. The catastrophe itself bodes well.

[226] Stadtmüller (1906) ad loc.

POSTSCRIPT: *SPHRAGIS*

The aspirations of Virgil as presented or implied in the *Proteus* and the *Orpheus* are, I have argued, quite enormous. Virgil depicts himself as a poet capable of aspiring to a universal mode of poetry, a universality manifested both in its unlimited content – literally the whole universe – and its incorporation of all modes of speech. And yet after all the hyperbole of these episodes there is the second Euphrates-parallel. The *Georgics* ends in a *sphragis*, a personal 'seal', or signature, 'a vehicle for discussion of the poet's literary achievement':[1]

> Haec super aruorum cultu pecorumque canebam
> et super arboribus, Caesar dum magnus ad altum   560
> fulminat Euphraten bello uictorque uolentis
> per populos dat iura uiamque adfectat Olympo.
> illo Vergilium me tempore dulcis alebat
> Parthenope studiis florentem ignobilis oti,
> carmina qui lusi pastorum audaxque iuuenta,   565
> Tityre, te patulae cecini sub tegmine fagi.

I sang this song on the care of fields and herds and on trees whilst great Caesar lightened at the deep Euphrates and in victory bestowed justice throughout the willing peoples, and embarked on the path to Olympus. In that time I, Virgil, was nourished by sweet Parthenope, flourishing in the pursuits of inglorious leisure, I who toyed with the songs of shepherds and in the boldness of youth sang of you, Tityrus, beneath the shelter of a broad beech-tree.

This passage, though, seems mainly designed to *dissemble* Virgil's literary achievement. Here, at the end of the poem, Virgil depicts himself not as a poetic analogue of his ruler but very firmly as Octavian's subordinate: any aspiration to be *poeta creator* is abandoned.

---

[1] Thomas (1988) ad 559–66.

The *sphragis* is thus an exercise in self-diminution. The ignobleness of Virgil's poetic vocation (564) contrasts implicitly with Octavian's military success. Virgil's *otium* in the same place recalls the pejorative *uacuae mentes* of 3.3 whose taste in literature Virgil there dismissed and the 'inglorious' literary option of 2.486, and in direct contradiction of the clear political content of the preceding 300 lines defines him precisely as *not* politically engaged.[2] The term *lusi* in 565, similarly, implies a triviality which is representative of Alexandrian programmatics.[3] And the *audax* of *audax iuuenta* (565), a term which at *G.* 1.40 served to assimilate Virgil's and Octavian's activities,[4] here ironically points up the divergence between them: whilst Virgil spent his youth writing pastoral verse, Octavian spent it conquering the world.

Of course Virgil in the *sphragis* protests too much. By insisting that the poem is *not* politically motivated, is not (by the same token) in any way related to the epic mode and its preoccupations, he only draws attention to the political (and epic) quality of what has preceded. This is particularly the case given that the passage is such a blatant misrepresentation of the poem it purports to epitomize. According to the *sphragis* the *Georgics* is just a poem about agriculture. This would be a simplistic interpretation even of Books 1 to 3, but in fact, as Wormell writes, 'when Virgil summarises his achievement in the concluding *sphragis* ... the theme of the fourth Georgic goes unnoticed'.[5]

Virgil's belittlement of himself in the *sphragis* serves above all to magnify Octavian. *Magnus* and warlike, Octavian hurls lightning like the Gigantomachic Zeus.[6] The expression *uiamque adfectat Olympo* looks back to the beginning of *G.* 1 (24–42), where Octavian seemed to substitute for Jupiter, and confirms the implication.[7] But while his ruler acts like the

---

[2] On the quietist associations of the term *otium* see, succinctly, Woodman (1983) 239–44.
[3] See, for example, Virg. *Ecl.* 1.10, and Clausen (1994) ad loc.
[4] For the epic and martial associations of poetic *audacia* see also Ov. *Am.* 2.1.11.
[5] Wormell (1971) 430.
[6] Compare Ov. *Am.* 2.1.11–20; and see Innes (1979); Thomas (1988) ad loc.
[7] Thomas (1988) ad locc.

archetypal subject of epic, Virgil, here, is emphatically not writing it. Octavian's fulminations in fact illustrate the *counter*-epic Callimachean motto (fr. 1.20 Pf.), βροντᾶν οὐκ ἐμόν, ἀλλὰ Διός, and they are directed at Eastern enemies represented by the Euphrates, six lines from the end, another structural reference to the *Hymn to Apollo*. The broad format of the conclusion reinforces the Callimachean tone: the four-book *Aetia* also ended in a *sphragis*.[8] Furthermore the closing reference to the *Eclogues*, as Fowler puts it,[9] 'retrospectively fashions [the *Eclogues* and the *Georgics*] into an oeuvre'. Virgil's summary of the *Georgics* – the tending of fields, herds and trees – pointedly omits any reference to the rather more elevated preoccupations of the *Proteus* so as to suggest an affiliation between the two superficially agricultural poems.[10] The description *carmina pastorum*, which might refer to the *Georgics* as well as the *Eclogues*, wittily conspires to include the whole *Aristaeus* in the same category as the *Eclogues*, the humble category of pastoral poetry: both Aristaeus (317) and Proteus (395) are after all, strictly, *pastores*. We have also noted the programmatic implications of *lusi* (565). In short, if during the Proteus episode we were in a kind of *Odyssey*, with this *sphragis* we are back in an *Aetia*.

Since the introduction to Book 3, as I have already argued,[11] the generic affiliations of the *Georgics* have in fact been constantly in doubt. That introduction emulated the equivalent section of the *Aetia*, implying a correlation between the two poems. Its rejection of Callimachean themes might count against this. But it entirely depends on what one concludes Virgil's prediction in this prologue refers to: the

---

[8] See Thomas (1988) ad 559–66; Call. fr. 112 Pf.; Knox (1985a). On an apparent contrast between Callimachus' future undertaking – the *Iambi*, probably, lower down the genre-hierarchy – and Virgil's (a step *up*), see Fowler (1989) 83–4.

[9] Fowler (1989) 83.

[10] Thomas (1988) ad 559–60 detects an ironic ambiguity in *super*, which (he suggests) could mean 'on' (i.e. 'concerning') as it is generally interpreted to, or 'over and above' (i.e. 'in addition to'), in which case *haec* refers to the contents of Book 4 and *super* marks out the difference between these and the contents of Books 1–3. However, *super* with the ablative meaning 'besides' is a thinly attested usage.

[11] See pp. 53–5 above.

current poem or some later project? Buckets of ink have been expended arguing for one or the other option. But the ambiguity, I suggested, was in fact quite deliberate, precisely designed to promote uncertainty as to the genre of the *Georgics*: what appears in Book 3 to copy the *Aetia* seems in Book 4 to imitate the *Telemachy*, and certain parallels seem to confirm that the *Aristaeus* does indeed fit the terms of the prediction in Book 3. Furthermore, the coordination of *Proteus* and *Orpheus* seems designed to efface any epic/Neoteric antithesis: all is contained under the Homeric penumbra. But then again in the *sphragis* to Book 4 Virgil's poem comes to imitate Callimachean contexts once more, a reassertion of the dilemma. Are we in a Roman *Aetia*, or is it really the start of a Roman *Odyssey*?

This is a clever play, and the Callimacheanism of the *sphragis* is in a sense fundamentally true to the poem: a work of the size and themes of the *Georgics* cannot realistically lay claim to the status of Grand Epic (though its metre, dactylic hexameters rather than the elegiacs of the *Aetia*, may tend to pull it in that direction). But there is also a rationale to raising the issue of epic identity *outside* a real epic. The generic joke, by placing the issue in doubt in this way, defuses some of the anxiety necessarily associated with the claim to be *alter Homerus*. There is always the possibility that Virgil's grandiose pretensions are not for real.

I have already spoken about the enormous hyperbole which attended the figure of Homer at this period. Seeking to emulate this figure would engender enough anxiety in itself. But Virgil perhaps faced a somewhat different problem as well. His own aspirations to match Ocean, *pater rerum*, a cosmogonical figure, bear a close (and deliberate) similarity – I have suggested – to the claims he makes on behalf of Aristaeus (whom I have interpreted as reflecting Octavian). Aristaeus also figuratively creates the universe, by subduing Proteus, and seems largely identical in function to the demiurgic Jupiter. Zeus-Jupiter and Ocean are not dissimilar figures. Sextus Empiricus, for example, was able to exploit their similarity in his sceptical programme. At *Pyr.* 1.150 he describes how Sceptics expose the inadequacies of traditional mythical belief

ὅταν ὅπου μὲν ⟨λέγωμεν⟩ τὸν Δία μυθεύεσθαι πατέρα ἀνδρῶν τε θεῶν τε
ὅπου δὲ τὸν Ὠκεανόν, λέγοντες
    Ὠκεανόν τε θεῶν γένεσιν καὶ μητέρα Τηθύν

when we say that in one legend Zeus is said to be the father of men and gods and in another Ocean, quoting
    Ocean the origin of gods and Tethys their mother

The statements that Zeus is the father of gods and men and that Ocean is the origin of gods, Sextus suggests, are mutually exclusive. The Homeric quotation is, of course, the much-quoted *Il.* 14.201 and 302, and the contradiction Sextus presents is in fact within the Homeric text itself: the description of Zeus as πατὴρ ἀνδρῶν τε θεῶν τε is a Homeric formula, as at, for example, *Od.* 1.28 and *Il.* 1.544. Furthermore Virgil has already implied a form of identification of himself with Jupiter. When Virgil presents himself as a *triumphator* in the prologue to Book 3 he is of course associating himself with one of the very central features of Octavianic self-definition,[12] a theme founded above all in the massive triple triumph of 29 BC, the precise context, seemingly, of the publication of the *Georgics*.[13] The triumph was the greatest honour available to a Roman (Livy 30.15.12). Furthermore, 'in no other Roman ceremony do god and man approach each other as closely as they do in the triumph'.[14] A reasonable interpretation of the triumphal ritual is that the *triumphator* was Jupiter for the day:[15] he wore Jupiter's dress (the purple cloak,[16] *toga picta* and *toga palmata*), taken from the temple of Jupiter Optimus Maximus on the Capitoline, he carried Jupiter's attributes (a sceptre and a golden crown), and his face was painted red like

---

[12] See Gruen (1990) 411.
[13] *Vita Donati* 27; and pp. 4–5 above.
[14] Versnel (1970) 1. The slave's apotropaeic admonition to the *triumphator, hominem te esse memento*, was presumably necessary because all appearances were to the contrary: cf. Levi (1938) 109 n. 40.
[15] See Weinstock (1971) 60–79, esp. 67–8.
[16] Cf. *G.* 3.17, *uictor ego et Tyrio conspectus in ostro*.

the statue of Capitoline Jupiter. The chariot of the *triumpha-tor* also implied his divinity, since generally mortals were for-bidden to use them in Rome. Thus as Weinstock says, 'on the day of his triumph, [the *triumphator*] represented Iuppiter'.[17] When Virgil depicts himself as the *triumphator* at the begin-ning of Book 3, then, a passage which I have suggested else-where prefigures his emulation of Homer,[18] he is also, by implication, impersonating a Jupiter-like figure. Virgil's refer-ence to the *Aetia* in this *sphragis* would appear to carry similar implications. One figure inevitably evoked by the thundering Zeus of Callimachus' aphorism βροντᾶν οὐκ ἐμόν is, as Bulloch points out, Homer, the Zeus-like *Überdichter* of Archelaus' relief.[19] Virgil's belated *recusatio* in the *sphragis* is thus beau-tifully succinct: his reference to the *Aetia* prologue simulta-neously negates any assimilation of himself and Zeus and promotes Octavian's right to the association, driving a wedge – at the very end – between the poet and the statesman hith-erto almost completely assimilated.

Between a Zeus-like-Aristaeus-like Octavian, we might say, and an Ocean-like- (or Zeus-like-) Homer-like Virgil there is not a lot of daylight. We have a superfluity of Jupiters, or if not Jupiters, at least supreme, creative fathers; and Virgil is in danger of, so to speak, stealing Octavian's thunder. Hence perhaps another reason for Virgil to withdraw, in the end, from the boldness and paradox of the claim to be a second Homer. In conclusion Virgil retreats to the more deferential Callimachean mode in which the respective realms of action of poet and ruler were that much more rigidly demarcated. All the poet's pretensions to comparability with his ruler fall away, leaving Octavian the emphatically singular *Weltherr-scher* the *Georgics* has argued he must be.

---

[17] Weinstock (1971) 302.   [18] See pp. 57–60 above.
[19] A. W. Bulloch, in *CHCL* I 559.

APPENDIX I PROTEUS AND Πρωτεύς[1]

Georgics 4:	*Odyssey 4:*
388,	384,
caeruleus	ἅλιος
396–7,	388–9,
hic tibi, nate, prius uinclis capiendus, ut . . .	τόν γ᾽, εἴ πως σὺ δύναιο λοχησάμενος λελαβέσθαι,
expediat . . .	ὅς κέν τοι εἴπῃσιν . . . .
401,	400,
ipsa ego te, medios cum sol accenderit aestus	ἦμος δ᾽ ἠέλιος μέσον οὐρανὸν ἀμφιβεβήκῃ
	407,
	ἔνθα σ᾽ ἐγών
	401,
403–4,	τῆμος ἄρ᾽ ἐξ ἁλὸς εἶσι γέρων ἅλιος νημερτὴς
in secreta senis ducam, quo fessus ab undis	403,
se recipit, facile ut somno adgrediare iacentem	ἐκ δ᾽ ἐλθὼν κοιμᾶται ὑπὸ σπέεσι γλαφυροῖσιν
	407,
	ἀγαγοῦσα
	414.
	τὸν μὲν ἐπὴν δὴ πρῶτα κατευνηθέντα ἴδησθε
405,	454–5.
manibus uinclisque tenebis	ἀμφὶ δὲ χεῖρας
	βάλλομεν

[1] The most useful editions for this *Quellenforschung* were Thomas (1988) and Jahn (1973).

Georgics 4:	Odyssey 4:
407–8, fiet enim subito sus horridus atraque tigris squamosusque draco et fulua ceruice leaena	456–7, ἀλλ' ἦ τοι πρώτιστα λέων γένετ' ἠυγένειος αὐτὰρ ἔπειτα δράκων καὶ πάρδαλις ἠδὲ μέγας σῦς
410, aut in aquas tenuis dilapsus abibit	458, γίγνετο δ' ὑγρὸν ὕδωρ
412, tam tu, nate, magis contende tenacia uincla	419, ὑμεῖς δ' ἀστεμφέως ἐχέμεν μᾶλλόν τε πιέζειν
413–4, donec talis erit mutato corpore qualem uideris incepto tegeret cum lumina somno	421, τοῖος ἔων οἷόν κε κατευνηθέντα ἴδησθε
415, haec ait et liquidum ambrosiae defundit odorem	445, ἀμβροσίην ὑπὸ ῥῖνα ἑκάστῳ θῆκε φέρουσα
426–7, et medium sol igneus orbem hauserat	400, ἦμος δ' ἠέλιος μέσον οὐρανὸν ἀμφιβεβήκη
429, cum Proteus consueta petens e fluctibus antra ibat	401, τῆμος ἄρ' ἐξ ἁλὸς εἶσι γέρων ἅλιος νημερτής 403, ἐκ δ' ἐλθὼν κοιμᾶται ὑπὸ σπέεσσι γλαφυροῖσιν

430, eum uasti circum gens umida ponti	404, ἀμφὶ δέ μιν φῶκαι νέποδες καλῆς ἁλοσύδνης
431, exsultans rorem late dispergit amarum	406, πικρὸν ἀποπνείουσαι ἁλὸς πολυβενθέος ὀδμήν
432, sternunt se somno diuersae in litore focae	448, φῶκαι 448–9, αἱ μὲν ἔπειτα ἑξῆς εὐνάζοντο παρὰ ῥηγμῖνι θαλάσσης
433, ipse, uelut stabuli custos in montibus olim	413, νομεὺς ὣς πώεσι μήλων
436, consedit scopulo medius, numerumque recenset	413, λέξεται ἐν μέσῃσι 451, λέκτο δ' ἀριθμόν
439–40, cum clamore ruit magno, manicisque iacentem occupat. ille suae contra non immemor artis[2]	454–5, ἡμεῖς δὲ ἰάχοντες ἐπεσσύμεθ', ἀμφὶ δὲ χεῖρας βάλλομεν· οὐδ' ὁ γέρων δολίης ἐπελήθετο τέχνης

[2] Here the match is particularly close. Thomas (1988) ad loc. points out that *occupat* (440) 'responds precisely in position and scansion to the Homeric βάλλομεν' and calls *ille ... artis* 'a translation of *Od.* 4.455'. Cf. Mynors (1990) ad 437–40; Thomas (1988) ad 445 (*nam quis te* = τίς νύ τοι) and 447.

Georgics 4:	*Odyssey 4:*
	417–18,
441–2,	πάντα δὲ γιγνόμενος πειρήσεται, ὅσσ' ἐπὶ γαῖαν
omnia transformat sese in miracula rerum	ἑρπετὰ γίγνονται, καὶ ὕδωρ καὶ θεσπιδαὲς πῦρ
ignemque horribilemque feram fluuiumque	
liquentem	
	460,
443,	ἀλλ' ὅτε δή ῥ' ἀνίαζ' ὁ γέρων ὀλοφώϊα εἰδώς
uerum ubi nulla fugam reperit fallacia	
	462–3,
445–6,	τίς νύ τοι, Ἀτρέος υἱέ, θεῶν συμφράσσατο βουλάς,
nam quis te, iuuenum confidentissime, nostras	ὄφρα μ' ἕλοις ἀέκοντα λοχησάμενος; τέο σε χρή;
iussit adire domos? quidue hinc petis?	
	465,
447,	οἶσθα, γέρον, τί με ταῦτα παρατροπέων ἐρεείνεις;
scis, Proteu, scis ipse, neque est te fallere	
quicquam	
	468,
448,	ἀλλὰ σύ πέρ μοι εἰπέ
sed tu desine uelle	
	471,
450,	ὣς ἐφάμην
tantum effatus	
	570,
528–9,	ὣς εἰπὼν ὑπὸ πόντον ἐδύσετο κυμαίνοντα
haec Proteus, et se iactu dedit aequor in altum,	
quaque dedit, spumantem undam sub uertice torsit	

4.400

My suggested parallel at *Od.* and *G.* 4.400 raises two main difficulties, which I shall deal with in order. The first involves the visibility of any parallel and in particular how prevalent 'current stichometry' seems to have been in texts contemporary with the *Georgics*. The second and ultimately more intractable issue is the question of the state of the Homeric text in Virgil's time.

I

Running, current, partial or marginal stichometry is a way of describing the practice of numbering the lines of a text by ascending letters of the alphabet, often between two horizontal bars, or else by a series of dots,[1] normally every hundred lines or the prose equivalent.[2] The convention of numbering texts every hundred lines in all probability had its origin as a method of calculating how much the scribe who copied a text was owed for his work. The *Edictum Diocletiani*, though belonging to a period when running stichometry was in decline (see below), gives some idea of its rationale, recording the fees due to scribes for copies of different quality *per hundred lines*: for top-quality script twenty-five denarii, for second-best twenty, and so on.[3] This leads Turner to suggest that stichometrical marks may identify a text as a 'professional copy', the (higher quality) product of a commercial copying establishment.[4] As Turner allows, however, it is impossible to say to what extent such markings transcended their role in the manufacturing process and actually came to be considered an integral part of the paradosis, to be copied from a model along with the text.[5] The fact that running stichometry dies out in the Byzantine period certainly indicates, as Turner

---

[1] Cavallo (1983) 22. The evidence is entirely Greek: as far as I can discover, there are no such marks in the very few surviving Latin papyri.
[2] Cavallo (1983) 21: in prose texts stichometric marks are placed where they would be if the lines of prose were as long as an average line of poetry. In practice they are shorter, and thus from one mark to the next there are normally between 180 and 200 lines of prose.
[3] Lauffer (1971) 7.39–41.
[4] Turner (1968) 95, (1971) 19.
[5] Turner (1971) ibid.

argues, that the marks were never fully integrated into the tradition; but it also suggests that the note of the final total of lines with which the Byzantine copyists were content was sufficient for all the practical requirements of copying including, presumably, the calculation of payment. Running stichometry thus perhaps developed the further function of facilitating reference. As a practice, running stichometry falls out of fashion at the same time as the book-roll was yielding its place to the codex as the dominant form of text,[6] and it is tempting to associate these two developments: the page-numbering of codices has also often been interpreted as an aid to reference, and its introduction may help to account for the increasing rarity of marginal stichometry.[7] As to the frequency of these symbols, the evidence is necessarily sparse: single letters every hundred lines are easily lost, and only in a very few cases is there a sufficient number of surviving texts of a work of literature (of which the line-numbering is known to us) for their frequency to be gauged. Where we can best gauge it is, of course, in texts of the Homeric poems.

The texts of the *Odyssey* would seem an appropriate place to try. I have counted eighteen ancient texts of the *Odyssey* which cover a hundredth line and for which there is information available (where they are published) that the left margin is intact at the requisite point. Of these eight disqualify themselves from consideration by date: we know that the practice of running stichometry was rare in the Byzantine era (conventionally dated by papyrologists from the reign of Diocletian).[8] We are left with ten texts of the third century or earlier, of which no fewer than eight carry stichometrical

---

[6] For the change in textual format see the statistics of Roberts and Skeat (1983) 37, which place the moment when codices begin to predominate at about AD 300; for the decline of running stichometry in this same period see below (main text).

[7] Reynolds and Wilson (1991) 30. See, however, Roberts and Skeat (1983) 50–1, who deny that either marginal stichometry in rolls or page-numbering in codices can have had any use as aids to reference; in which case there would be no clear reason to connect the decline of running stichometry with the rise to prominence of the codex. References by στίχοι are certainly not common in the ancient world (Ohly (1928) 109–18 cites them). But McCormick (1985), a review of Roberts and Skeat (1983), envisages (156) a type of private reference to the Scriptures by Christians in which such aspects of the codex as pagination might have been a useful aid: a 'rather frequent consultation, i.e. opening the book and hunting through it for the particular passage in question', for example to discover the correct wording of a Biblical passage. We might imagine that a similar type of private orientation within a well-cited text (for example Homer) would be provided by marginal stichometry: not all forms of reference can have been done by memory alone.

[8] Turner (1971) 19. These late texts are *P Amh* II. 23, *P Ryl.* 53 (3/4C AD), *P Leipz.* III (4C AD), *P Antinoop.* 168, *P Oxy.* 954 (4/5C AD), *P Antinoop.* 173 (5C AD), *P Oxy.* 1820, *PSI* 1299 (6/7C AD). Collart (1939) 306 states that there is a stichometrical mark in *P Leipz.* III, but I can find no reference to this in the original publication of the text by Blass (1904) 211–12. All of these texts are papyrus or parchment codices.

markings, an overwhelming majority, always bearing in mind the smallness of the sample.[9]

If these Egyptian texts strongly suggest that running stichometry was the norm, at any rate in Homeric texts, then the papyri uncovered at Herculaneum only confirm the picture. These texts, preserved carbonized in the so-called Villa dei Papiri (or dei Pisoni), are valuable witnesses to the format of literary texts in Virgil's time, since, though buried over a century after the composition of the *Georgics*, it is generally agreed that they comprise the library which had once belonged to the Epicurean philosopher Philodemus of Gadara, who died about 35 BC.[10] They thus originate in the same period, geographical vicinity and, we might say, social milieu as the *Georgics*. In these texts stichometry of every kind and combination – *Totalstichometrie* (the total of lines at the conclusion of a work), running stichometry, and a running total of columns, in various combinations – is extremely common.[11] And as Bassi says the state of the papyri – which is notoriously poor – allows us to assume that they were more common even than the surviving markings indicate.[12]

The prevalence of stichometrical notation at Herculaneum is potentially very significant since, as Grenfell and Hunt point out, running stichometry is in general less frequent in papyri of prose works than poetic.[13] The vast majority of papyri at Herculaneum are prose. The extensive use of running stichometry in these texts, then, implies a strong contemporary commitment to the practice which we must imagine would have made its use considerably more prevalent in comparable poetic texts.[14]

The difference between Egyptian and Herculanean papyri is the difference between Oxyrhynchus or Tebtunis and Naples. As Cavallo writes, the papyri from Herculaneum reflect the conventions of book-production in the great centres of Hellenistic culture, as opposed to the remote χώρα of provincial Egypt.[15] Any divergence between the two groups in the use of stichometry either reflects the greater proportion of commercially produced copies in the library at Herculaneum, or else, if we are right to understand stichometry as

---

[9] Those that carry markings are *P Sorbonne Inv.* 2254A (3C BC), *P Rainer* 26746 & 26754–60 (IC AD), *PSI inv. CNR* 69 (end IC AD), *PSI inv. CNR* 66 & 67, *P Univ. Govern. Milano* 431 (I/2C AD), *P Teb.* 432, *P Oxy.* 1819 (2C AD), *P Oxy.* 448 (3C AD); *P Merton* I (2C BC) possibly has *decimal* stichometry at *Od.* 6.242 and 252: Bell and Roberts (1948) 1–2. The two that seem not to carry markings are *P Fay.* 310 (I/2C AD) and *P Oxy.* 565 (2/3C AD). All the texts that carry markings are rolls (with the possible exception of *P Leipz.* III; see previous note).

[10] Gallo (1986) 37.

[11] Ohly (1924) 190 ('besonders zahlreich').

[12] Bassi (1909) 325.

[13] Grenfell and Hunt (1915) 103 (1364.188), with the qualifications of Ohly (1928) 56.

[14] On stichometry in the Herculaneum papyri see also now Obbink (1996) 62–73.

[15] Cavallo (1983) 49–50.

more than merely evidence of a professional copy, the greater sophistication of texts produced for the urbane readership of Campania. Either way, it seems clear that the privileged public of Virgil would in all probability have possessed numbered texts of both the *Georgics* and the *Odyssey*. And since the numbers only fell every 100 lines, if a poet wanted to construct a visible stichometrical parallel with another text at any distance from the beginning or end of a book it perhaps in fact *had* to be done at a multiple of one hundred lines.[16] We may thus be entitled to imagine an exemplary reader of the *Georgics* having for comparison side by side with his Latin text a roll of the *Odyssey*, and noting the remarkable similarity of the lines marked in each manuscript by the symbol

$$\overline{\delta}$$

(or an equivalent) in the left-hand margin.[17]

II

A more intractable problem involves the Homeric text of Virgil's time. Clearly, for there to be a correspondence between *Georgics* and *Odyssey* at 4.400 the text of the *Odyssey* in 30 BC would need to have been identical (in the number of lines it contained, at least) to that of modern editions. Was our *Odyssey* 4.400 also Virgil's?

The Homeric text underwent a revolution in the second century BC. Up until about 150 BC the papyri of Homer discovered are 'wild', that is, their texts differ markedly from our own. After this date texts have substantially the same form – as each other, and as modern texts. Grenfell and Hunt attribute the phenomenon to the scholarly activity of the Alexandrian Library, and in particular Aristarchus, who died in 145,[18] and this seems undeniable.

---

[16] Asconius' commentary on the speeches of Cicero refers to lines in the text in multiples of *ten* as well as one hundred, though M. D. Reeve raises the possibility that these references were added by a later reader: Reynolds (1983) 55.

[17] There are, however, other proposed line-number parallels of this kind which are apparently completely sundered from any possible textual marking. Thus *Met.* and *Aen.* 10.475, pointed out by Smith (1990) an article brought to my attention by Don Fowler. From the same source came another example suggested by Joseph Farrell, who noted a similarity between *G.* and *Aen.* 1.105. A somewhat similar case (to which Dr Fowler also alerted me) has been suggested by Wills (1996) 159 n. 82, discussing a possible reference to Gallus at Prop. 2.7.17–18. Propertius here mentions the Borysthenes. Wills suggests that Gallus may have mentioned the Borysthenes in the same poem as his pentameter on the Hypanis, which until the papyrus fragment was all that remained of him. The only other poetic mention of the Borysthenes surviving is at Ov. *Pont.* 4.10.53 in the catalogue of Black Sea rivers, a passage which parallels the catalogue of poets in *Tr.* 4.10. The precise parallel, *Tr.* 4.10.53, runs *successor fuit hic tibi, Galle, Propertius illi.*

[18] Grenfell and Hunt (1906) 68–75.

Some critics have further suggested that if Aristarchus brought about the substantial homogeneity in Homeric texts which obtains after 150 BC a special significance must attach to those lines for which the MS testimony is (relatively) weak: lines which are omitted from some MSS, Bolling argues, can only be later interpolations into the Aristarchean text.[19] There may be some truth in this view, but care is needed. Quite how significant divergences in the MSS are depends on how rigid the putative 'Aristarchean text' was. West, for one, doubts the existence of a monolithic 'Aristarchean text' at all. In her view Aristarchus' scholarly work was certainly responsible for the disappearance of 'wild' papyri, but the nature of his influence was more subtle than is supposed by Bolling. Rather than following a text produced by Aristarchus, later texts merely took into account his critical readings, and produced texts generally in accordance with them.[20] Familiarly now, 'there was no Alexandrian University Press', and quite probably no Aristarchean text forming the archetype of the entire later tradition, only influential critical readings. There is in fact, as West says, 'considerable diversity within the post-aristarchean tradition',[21] more than Bolling takes account of.

It seems probable that a number of lines in our *Od.* 4 prior to line 400 were unknown, or unacceptable, to Aristarchus. This, at any rate, might explain the less than unanimous attestation given by the MSS to in all five lines of the first half of the book: 57–8, 273, 303 and 399. But at what stage *were* these lines widespread? Evidence regarding the first two lines is forthcoming from Athenaeus.[22] In a garbled passage in the *Deipnosophistae* Athenaeus states (193b), διαμαρτάνουσι δὲ πολλοὶ παρὰ τῷ ποιητῇ ἐφεξῆς τιθέντες τούτους τοὺς στίχους, 'many make the mistake of placing the following lines in sequence in the poet's text'. He then quotes three lines which occur twice in our text of the *Odyssey*, at 1.139–41 and at 4.55–7, criticizes (confusedly) the third line of each, and concludes that 'the [first] two verses are sufficient'. Since 1.141–2 have the complete support of our MSS, whilst 'a very substantial minority'[23] omit 4.57–8, Athenaeus (or rather the source he is in all probability using) is fairly clearly criticizing the lines as they stand in Book 4. It is also pretty clear that Athenaeus means to condemn the line that follows on from 57, since 58 shares the relatively weak MS attestation of 57.

The question is how widely 4.57–8 would have been found in the Homeric text. Athenaeus was probably writing around the end of the second century, his source perhaps considerably earlier. The reading Athenaeus condemns is widespread (πολλοί). Apthorp concludes that since the lines are omitted by

---

[19] Bolling (1925) 3–15; see also Apthorp (1980).
[20] See West (1967) 16–17. West's conclusions follow Collart (1933) 52–4.
[21] West (1967) 16. Cf. Haslam (1997) 63.
[22] Apthorp (1980) 20–1.
[23] Apthorp (1980) 21.

so many MSS – including L[8], the second oldest minuscule – it is undoubt-edly a post-Aristarchean interpolation. He also concludes, however, that its presence in a majority of MSS establishes the 'interpolation' as of an early date: even if Apthorp's assumptions are correct, then, 'it may well have been made fairly soon after the time of Aristarchus'.

We may be fortunate enough to have confirmation of their presence in Roman texts from Virgil himself. Thomas points out how the main imita-tion of *Od.* 4 in *G.* 4 – the Proteus episode – is anticipated earlier in *G.* 4 by rather more brief references to the same Homeric book. At 363 and 376–9 Virgil imitates details of Telemachus' arrival and welcome at Sparta, from *Od.* 4.43–4 and 47–58 respectively.[24] Virgil's second passage, 376–9, seems to follow the order of the *unexpurgated* Homeric lines: Telemachus and Pisistratus wash (52–4), a table is brought (54), they are served food by a housewife and a carver (54–7), and they are served wine (58). The serving of wine, we note, is only specified in one of the questionable lines. In Virgil's passage Aristaeus and Cyrene wash, napkins are brought, and they are served food and *wine*. Virgil's *plena reponunt | pocula* (378–9) surely recalls *Od.* 4.58, παρὰ δέ σφι τίθει χρύσεια κύπελλα, one of the lines condemned, in which case the lines were at any rate present in the text consulted by Virgil.[25]

The other two 'interpolations', 303 and 399, are considerably better attested than 57–8. Both have the overwhelming support of the MSS, but are missing from the oldest minuscule, L[4], and the only papyri which cover them, the second century *P Gr. Vindob.* 39834, which omits 303, and *P Oxy.* 775 (of the third century), which omits 399. Clearly the testimony of L[4] and the papyri indicates a divergence at some stage of the tradition; but by Bolling's own general principle, 'the sooner an interpolation gets its start the farther it goes',[26] these lines were also widespread in the tradition very early. The evidence of the papyri is only disconcerting if we believe in Bolling's single Aristarchean archetype which is progressively contaminated by in-terpolations. This will lead us to understand omission from a papyrus as a *terminus post quem* for entry into the tradition. In fact omission from papyri may well reflect disagreement between *contemporary* texts of a work, some of which may have contained a given line and some not. The strong, if not unanimous, testimony in favour of these lines forthcoming from our MSS would certainly suggest that they were current at a time before the date of the papyri which omit them: in which case even at the time of their pro-duction the papyri were only reproducing *one* version of the *Odyssey* text of

[24] Thomas (1988) ad locc.

[25] At *Aen.* 1.701–6 Virgil imitates his own scene here in the *Georgics*. The reference to the Homeric description of wine-serving is even clearer (*pocula ponant*, 706), though cross-reference to the lines as they appear in *Od.* 1 cannot, of course, be totally ruled out.

[26] Bolling (1925) 8.

the time. The same considerations will apply to line 273, about which there is MS disagreement of the same order as 303 and 399, but which is not covered by any papyrus.

It is thus highly plausible that Virgil's text of the *Odyssey* would have contained these lines, and would have had line 400 at the same point as modern editions. Unfortunately certainty in such matters is not attainable, and the correlation between *Od.* and *G.* 4.400 may always just be a remarkable coincidence. I repeat, however, that a general parallel comparable to that between the beginnings of *Aetia* 3 and *Georgic* 3 is indisputable.

SPARSERE PER AGROS

Evidence to suggest that an agrarian interpretation of the death of Orpheus during Dionysiac rites – we might call it the Frazerian view –[1] would have been a natural one for Virgil's ancient readership is diffuse but nonetheless, I think, ultimately cogent. One of Frazer's own examples is striking: in Apollodorus' account of the death of Lycurgus at Dionysus' instigation Lycurgus, having unwisely expelled Dionysus from the kingdom of the Edonians, is dismembered by horses. The effect of this dismemberment is to restore fertility to the land (Apollod. *Bibl.* 3.5.1).[2] There is evidence that the myths of Dionysus' descent to and ascent from the Underworld were interpreted similarly. Pindar, in particular, strongly associates the figure of

---

[1] For this view see Frazer (1906) 268–75 (on Orpheus, and in particular Ovid's Orpheus, 271 n. 1); Harrison (1903b) 426; Farnell (1896–1909) v 163; Nilsson (1940) 62–3. Nilsson, however, subsequently altered his emphasis somewhat, mainly on the basis of the timing of the Bacchic *orgia*, which tended to occur every two years and in winter: he concludes that 'the biennial period is contradictory to the yearly awakening of vegetation', and therefore that the agrarian element must be less fundamental to Dionysiac cult than he had previously thought: Nilsson (1957) 40. This is cogent, but it is nonetheless absolutely clear that elements of 'vegetation magic' did adhere to Dionysiac ritual. Thus Griffiths, whilst accepting Nilsson's argument, nevertheless insists that the vegetation and fruit which used to appear with the phallus in Hellenistic representations of the Dionysiac *liknon* (winnowing-fan) – perhaps the most prominent Dionysiac emblem – must in some sense relate Dionysus' life-giving power (symbolized by the phallus) to the notion of fertility in nature: Griffiths (1970) 435. Originally, at any rate, the *liknon* was an agricultural tool: see Harrison (1903a). Though particularly associated with Dionysiac cult it is also found in representations of Eleusinian ritual, e.g. the Lovatelli Urn – Kerényi (1967) 54–7 – and Virgil includes the *mystica uannus Iacchi*, along with other items related to Eleusis, amongst the tools essential to the sowing and harvesting of grain (*G.* 1.160–75). Virgil, then, is clear about its agricultural function. For further elements of fertility ritual in Bacchic cult see Thomson (1941) 130–50, and Seaford (1981) 263 on patterns of ritual in the myth of Pentheus and their resemblance to the 'Carrying out Death' and 'Bringing in the Summer' customs analysed by Mannhardt and Frazer. Modern scholars, at any rate, remain willing to read an agrarian dimension into Dionysiac cult. Bianchi (1976) 14 emphasizes the role in Dionysiac cult of the *liknon* containing the phallus, stating that it is 'obviously a fertility emblem', and talks of 'representations which frequently include the *genre* scene, an idyllic countryside, quite in keeping with the remote but still perceptible agrarian origin of the rite', overlaid but not erased by symbolism relating to happiness for the initiated beyond the grave.

[2] Frazer (1906) 271.

APPENDIX III: *SPARSERE PER AGROS*

Semele and the joys of spring, presumably in the context of her *anodos* with Dionysus.[3] Certainly given the extensive syncretism between Dionysiac cult and other mystery cults – the Eleusinian[4] and Isiac[5] – with strong agrarian associations[6] such an interpretation would have come fairly easily; and indeed a number of references in Diodorus (and elsewhere) significantly associate the Dionysus of the mysteries, Osiris-like, with the innovation of agriculture.[7]

[3] Pind. fr. 75 Maehler. Similarly one of the Hope Vases depicts the *anodos* of Dionysus with an 'abundance of foliage'. Tillyard interprets the scene as 'Dionysus, as the embodiment of the spirit of growth' rising again in the spring, citing a parallel, involving the *anodos* of an 'earth-goddess', in Berlin: Tillyard (1923) 97–9 (no. 163): cf. Metzger (1944/5) 296–313. More parallels are provided, from Attic black-figure vases, by Elia (1961) with special reference to a bust which she interprets to be of Dionysus, god of reborn vegetation and agrarian fertility, discovered at Pompeii. For a photograph and full bibliography on this bust see Conticello et al. (1990) 136–7 (no. 3). It emerges from a stellar base as if from the earth. On his head the figure carries a *kalathos* and *kiste* – two forms of basket particularly associated with mystery cult – containing symbols of fertility.

[4] On the prevalence of syncretism in mystery cult see Angus (1925) 187–95; and in Hellenistic religion generally Martin (1987) 10–11, Cairns (1979) 41 and n. 25. On syncretism between Dionysiac cult and Eleusis see Seaford (1981) 253 and n. 10. In particular the two were assimilated through the Eleusinian figure of Iacchus, considered the same as Dionysus: Burkert (1972) 308 and n. 23; *Ecl.* 6.15 and Clausen (1994) ad loc.; Ov. *Met.* 4.15; Cat. 64.251 (note the paraphernalia of *Dionysiac* mysteries, 256–64). The main similarity between them would seem to be that Dionysus Zagreus and Iacchus were both generally described as sons of Zeus and Persephone: O. Kern, in *R.E.* 9.621.51–7; the *Suda* s.v. *Zagreus*; Σ Pind. *Isthm.* 7.3. Lucian, *Salt.* 39 even talks of the ʼ Ἰάκχου σπαραγμός.

[5] Dionysus was equated with Osiris by Herodotus (2.144) and by Plutarch half a millennium later (*De Is. et Os.* 364d–365b). See also Hdt. 2.42, 81; Diod. 1.11, 13, 25.2, 4.1.6; Orphica fr. 237 Kern. Both Plutarch and Herodotus imply that the similarity between Dionysus and Osiris mainly lies in the sufferings of the two gods, and in particular in each god's dismemberment: Burkert (1987) 160 n. 119, (1972) 249 n. 43. A good example of the close association of the two is the temple of Isis at Pompeii, which had in a niche at the rear of the *cella* a statuette of Bacchus with a panther: Malaise (1972) 197; illustration in Overbeck (1875) 478. In the propaganda exchanges of the 30s Antony had styled himself the νέος Διόνυσος. The Dionysus to whom Antony assimilated himself was a syncretistic Dionysus-Osiris: Antony was the Διόνυσος νέος to Cleopatra's νέα Ἶσις (Plut. *Ant.* 941c, 944a; Dio 50.25.4). At a similar historical juncture Tibullus was also able to exploit the proximity of the two gods. At 1.7.29–48, according to the interpretation of Koenen (1976) 142–53, Tibullus presents an 'aretalogy' of Osiris, a list of his achievements. Osiris is presented as the εὑρετής of agriculture, including the vine. At 39–42 he seems to coalesce with the figure of *Bacchus*.

[6] Eleusis: Martin (1987) 68–9. For a contemporary view see Varro *apud* August. *De civ. D.* 7.20, pp. 298–9. Isis: Martin (1987) 75; Diod. 1.14, 21; Witt (1971) 127–8.

[7] Diodorus attributes to Dionysus agricultural functions of varying degrees of broadness. At 3.62.6–10 he records an interpretation of the *pathe* of the mystical Dionysus as an allegory of the wine-harvest. See also Cornutus, *ND* 30. At 5.75.4 Diodorus tells us that the dismembered Dionysus, the son of Zeus and Persephone, discovered wine and also the storing and use of πολλοὺς τῶν ἐκ τῆς ὀπώρας

231

The rituals of the city of Rome itself may have provided their own impetus in this syncretistic direction. Initially Liber, 'an old Italian god of fertility and especially (though perhaps not originally) of the vine',[8] became identified with Dionysus. He and his female counterpart Libera had a festival, the Liberalia, on 17 March. However this festival seems to have been a rather low-key and rustic affair. Liber 'is not known to have had a temple in Rome in Republican times'.[9] The Liberalia was eclipsed by the worship of Liber in combination with Ceres and Libera at the Cerealia of 19 April. Ovid tells us that in his day, although there had been games in honour of Liber on 17 March, he now shared games with Ceres on 19 April (*Fast.* 3.785–6; cf. Cic. *Verr.* 2.5.36). Hence, apparently, the coupling of Ceres and Liber in the invocations by Varro and Virgil (*G.* 1.7; Varro, *Rust.* 1.1.5): this, at any rate, is the interpretation of Servius *auctus* ad loc.: *uel ideo simul Liberum et Cererem posuit, quia et templa eis simul posita sunt et ludi simul eduntur*, 'or else he placed Liber and Ceres together because their temples were established together and their games were held together'. The temple of Ceres – in combination with Liber and Libera – was on the Aventine. These three deities corresponded to the Eleusinian triad Demeter, Core and Iacchus. The legend of the foundation of this cult in 493 BC is told by Dionysius of Halicarnassus. A campaign against the Latins was in danger of being compromised by failure of the harvest. The Sibylline books were consulted and they advised that Ceres, Liber and Libera (in Dionysius' Greek Demeter, Dionysus and Core) be propitiated. The dictator A. Postumius vowed a temple, fertility was restored, and a temple (Dionysius talks of temples in the plural, but there was only one) was duly constructed (*Ant. Rom.* 6.17.2–4).[10] This Liber, then, is closely associated with fertility.

καρπῶν. Elsewhere Diodorus' description of Dionysus' functions is broader still. At both 3.64.1–2 and 4.4.1–2 the 'second Dionysus' (of, in all, three) is said to be this same son of Zeus and Persephone (or according to some Demeter). This Dionysus was an agricultural pioneer like Osiris. He was the first to yoke oxen to the plough and thus to sow seed, and he also invented other agricultural equipment. As a consequence, according to Diodorus, this Dionysus was represented with horns (often a special feature of the mystical Dionysus), in commemoration of his invention of ox-ploughing. This last detail is repeated by Plutarch at *Quaest. Graec.* 299b. To the question why the women of Elis address a hymn to Dionysus 'with his foot of a bull', i.e. in the form of a bull, Plutarch's third answer is, ἢ ὅτι καὶ ἀρότου καὶ σπόρου πολλοὶ τὸν θεὸν ἀρχηγὸν γεγονέναι νομίζουσι;, 'or is it because many believe that the god was the pioneer both of ploughing and sowing?' Cf. Ps.-Arist. *Mir. Ausc.* 122.

8 Scullard (1981) 91. Cf. Bruhl (1953) 5, 'dieu de la végétation renaissante'.
9 Scullard (1981) 91.
10 It was a celebrated temple, described by Vitruvius (*Arch.* 3.3.5), Pliny (*HN* 35.155, citing Varro) and Cicero, who called it *pulcherrimum et magnificentissimum* (*Verr.* 2.4.108). According to Tacitus (*Ann.* 2.49.1) it was one of the ancient temples Augustus set about restoring, perhaps some time before 27 BC – Pliny cites Varro (who died in 27) discussing its restoration. For a discussion of the dating of the Augustan restoration see Le Bonniec (1958) 264–6.

Further evidence is forthcoming from Varro of Reate's *Antiquitates*, an encyclopaedic work which must have dominated Roman perception of religion in the years following its appearance.[11] It was a work of forty-one books divided into two parts, *Rerum humanarum libri XXV* and *Rerum divinarum libri XVI*,[12] our knowledge of which mainly derives from Augustine's *City of God*. Augustine treats Varro's work as representative of the whole edifice of pagan Roman religion which is the target of his Christian attack. In the process of this attack he reveals much about Varro's views on Liber-Dionysus. Varro's programme was explanatory – he aimed by elucidating the sphere of activity proper to each deity to promote a revival of old-fashioned religious practice[13] – and his methodology was much influenced by Stoicism. Each deity, according to Varro, operated in the physical world: the true gods, in this scheme, are *anima mundi ac partes eius*, 'the soul of the world and its constituent parts' (August. *De civ. D.* 7.9, p. 286). So deities correspond to constituent parts of the world. Liber – generally paired by Varro with Libera, reflecting Roman cult – '[the pagans] put in charge of moist seeds', Augustine says (though the view he cites is strictly Varro's), namely the juice of fruits (wine in particular) and also the seeds of animals (7.21, p. 299). This repeats an attribution to Liber – seed – also recorded at *De civ. D.* 4.11, p. 160, 6.9, p. 263, 7.2, p. 274, 7.3, p. 275, 276, and 7.16, p. 294, which will serve to summarize their contents: *Liberum et Cererem praeponunt seminibus, uel illum masculinis, illam femininis; uel illum liquori, illam uero ariditati seminum*, 'They put Liber and Ceres in charge of seeds, either him in charge of male seeds and her of female, or him in charge of the liquid part, her of the dry element, of seeds.'

Augustine proceeds to condemn the woeful depravity of Liber's rituals. He singles out rites celebrated at the crossroads of Italy – the *compitalia* – involving the display of a phallus: *sic uidelicet Liber deus placandus fuerat pro euentibus seminum, sic ab agris fascinatio repellenda*, 'In this way the god Liber had to be appeased to ensure the success of the seeds, in this way evil influences had to be averted from the fields.' Clearly the ritual to which Varro here had given such a straightforwardly fertility-orientated meaning is a strictly Italian one. But as Meuli explains, Varro identified the Italian festival of the *compitalia* with the Rural Dionysia in Attica; and indeed Virgil follows Varro's syncretistic lead at *G.* 2.380–96, where he also amalgamates *compitalia* and Dionysia, foregrounding their function as rituals of fertility (390–2).[14] Virgil also (not, I think, coincidentally) frames the account with references to the sacrifice of a goat (380–1, 395–6). The final image of 'juicy' entrails roasted on spits (*pinguia ... torrebimus exta*) par-

---

[11] It is referred to by Cicero (*Acad. post.* 8), apparently as a recent work, in 45, and is generally dated to 47: see Cardauns (1976) I 132–3.
[12] August., *De civ. D.* 6.3, p. 248; Hagendahl (1967) 601.
[13] August., *De civ. D.* 6.2, p. 248; Hagendahl (1967) 602.
[14] Meuli (1955); Wilkinson (1969) 149.

allels the creative collision of heat and moisture embodied, as Ross argues,[15] in the *pinguis arista* and represented also, as I have suggested, in *bugonia* and Aristaeus' capture of Proteus. Here in *G.* 2, then, we have Dionysiac ritual credited with influence over the processes of agriculture, and also centred upon an act of killing.

Varro also mentions the Greek Bacchanalia in the same context as an earlier reference to Liber's control of seed and to the role of the phallus in his cult (6.9, p. 263); and it seems clear that Varro will have either stated explicitly or at least implied that the explanation of these rites was the same as that of the *compitalia*: his radically positivistic understanding of the gods as components of the universe, common to all, in fact entails as much. In Varro's Stoic-influenced theorizing, which locates gods in the physical universe, a deity's *power over* a segment of the universe is closely allied to an *identification* of the deity with the natural phenomenon he or she controls. Thus Neptune has dominion over the sea and is *identical* with the sea:[16] there are parallels in the *Aeneid* considered by Feeney,[17] and I have suggested something similar about Proteus. It clearly follows that if Liber has control over seeds then he is also in Varro's naturalizing way identical with seed: he is the immanent power of seed, as it were. Here we are close to my provisional interpretation of the scattering of Orpheus' limbs: that the action resembled the broadcasting of seed.[18]

If we *can* assume an agricultural dimension to the death of Orpheus, we might even consider backdating the opinions which Servius records about Virgil's *mystica uannus Iacchi* (*G.* 1.166) to the time of its composition. Servius writes,

ET MYSTICA VANNUS IACCHI id est cribrum areale.... 'mystica' autem 'Iacchi' ideo ait, quod Liberi patris sacra ad purgationem animae pertinebant, et sic homines eius mysteriis purgabantur, sicut uannis frumenta purgantur. hinc est quod dicitur Osiridis membra a Typhone dilaniati Isis cribro superposuisse: nam idem est Liber pater – in cuius mysteriis uannus est, quia, ut diximus, animas purgat, unde et Liber ab eo, quod liberet, dictus est – quem Orpheus a gigantibus dicit esse discerptum.

AND IACCHUS' MYSTIC FAN that is a sieve used on the threshing floors.... He calls it 'mystica uannus Iacchi' because the rites of Liber pater pertain to the purification of the soul. Men are purified in his mysteries just as corn in purified in winnowing-fans. This is why it is said Isis placed on a sieve the limbs of Osiris after he had been torn to pieces by Typhon. For he is the same as Liber pater – in whose mysteries the winnowing-fan is used, because, as we said, it purifies the soul, which is why Liber is so named, because he liberates – and Orpheus says that he was torn to pieces by the Giants.

---

[15] Ross (1987) 32–54.

[16] 4.10, p. 157, *mare Neptuno tribuitur*; 7.16, p. 294, *Neptunum [esse] aquas mundi.*

[17] Feeney (1991) 135–6. Cf. Hardie (1986) *passim*.

[18] Compare with *G.* 4.522 Ov. *Met.* 5.655, describing the archetypal sowing of seed by Triptolemus: *dona fero Cereris, latos quae sparsa per agros | frugiferas messes alimentaque mitia reddant.*

There is (at least) four-way syncretism here. Dionysiac cult – which is assumed to be identical to the cult of Liber pater – is identified with Isiac cult; and also assumed is an assimilation of Eleusinian and Dionysiac cult. Orpheus is in the frame as well. On the basis of this notice we could say that the expression *mystica uannus Iacchi* at 1.166, with its associations with the dismemberments of Dionysus and Osiris, foreshadows the death of Orpheus in Book 4, lending it a further indubitable connection with the practices of agriculture.

BIBLIOGRAPHY

Ahl, F. (1976) *Lucan: An Introduction* (Cornell Studies in Classical Philology 39). Ithaca, NY
  (1984) 'The art of safe criticism in Greece and Rome', *AJPh* 105: 174–208
  (1985) *Metaformations: Soundplay and Wordplay in Ovid and other Classical Poets*. Ithaca, NY
Allen, A. W. (1950) 'Elegy and the classical attitude toward love: Propertius 1.1', *YCS* 11: 255–77
Allen, W., Jr. (1940) 'The Epyllion: a chapter in the history of literary criticism', *TAPhA* 71: 1–26
Allen, W. S. (1965) *Vox Latina: a Guide to the Pronunciation of Classical Latin*. Cambridge
Ampolo, C. (1980) 'Le condizioni materiali della produzione', *DArch* N.S. 2: 15–46
Anderson, R. D., Parsons, P. J. and Nisbet, R. G. M. (1979) 'Elegiacs by Gallus from Qaṣr Ibrîm', *JRS* 69: 125–55
Anderson, W. S. (1982) 'The Orpheus of Virgil and Ovid: *flebile nescio quid*', in Warden (1982): 25–50
Angus, S. (1925) *The Mystery Religions and Christianity*. London
Apthorp, M. J. (1980) *The Manuscript Evidence for Interpolation in Homer*. Heidelberg
Aucher, J.-B. (1822) *Philonis Judaei sermones tres hactenus inediti*. Venice
Aurigemma, S. (1984) *Villa Adriana*. Rome
Austin, R. G. (1964) *P. Vergili Maronis Aeneidos liber secundus*. Oxford
Babbitt, F. C. (1928) *Plutarch's 'Moralia' II*. London and Cambridge, Mass., Loeb Classical Library
  (1936) *Plutarch's 'Moralia' V*. London and Cambridge, Mass., Loeb Classical Library
Barchiesi, A. (1989) 'Voci e instanze narrative nelle *Metamorfosi* di Ovidio', *MD* 23: 55–97
Bardon, H. and Verdière, R. (1971), edd. *Vergiliana: Recherches sur Virgile*. Leiden
Bassi, D. (1909) 'La sticometria nei Papiri Ercolanesi', *RFIC* 37: 321–63, 481–515
Bather, A. G. (1894) 'The problem of the *Bacchae*', *JHS* 14: 244–63
Beard, M. and Crawford, M. (1985) *Rome in the Late Republic: Problems and Interpretations*. London

Beard, M. and North, J. (1990), edd. *Pagan priests: Religion and Power in the Ancient World*. London

Bell, H. I. and Roberts, C. H. (1948) *A Descriptive Catalogue of the Greek Papyri in the Collection of Wilfred Merton F.S.A., Vol. I*. London

Bernhardt, R. (1975) 'Athen, Augustus und die eleusinischen Mysterien', *MDAI(A)* 90: 233–7

Bettini, M. (1991) *Anthropology and Roman Culture: Kinship, Time, Images of the Soul* (trans. J. Van Sickle). Baltimore and London

Bianchi, U. (1976) *Iconography of Religions 17.3: The Greek Mysteries*. Leiden, EJ Brill

Binns, J. W. (1973), ed. *Ovid*. London and Boston

Blass, F. (1904). *Über einige Leipziger literarische Fragmente auf Papyrus oder Pergament* (Berichte über die Verhandlungen der königlich sächsischen Gesellschaft der Wissenschaften zu Leipzig, philologisch-historische Klasse 56): 205–12

Bömer, F. (1957–8) *P. Ovidius Naso. die Fasten* (2 vols.). Heidelberg

Bolling, G. M. (1925) *The External Evidence for Interpolation in Homer*. Oxford

Bonnet, H. (1952) *Reallexicon der ägyptischen Religionsgeschichte*. Berlin

Bowra, C. M. (1952) 'Orpheus and Eurydice', *CQ* N. S. 2: 113–26

Boyancé, P. (1960–1) 'L'antre dans les mystères de Dionysos', *RPAA* 33: 107–27

Boyle, A. J. (1972) 'The meaning of the *Aeneid*', *Ramus* 1: 63–90, 113–51

(1979a) '*In medio Caesar*: paradox and politics in Virgil's *Georgics*', *Ramus* 8: 65–86

(1979b), ed. *Virgil's Ascraean Song: Ramus Essays on the Georgics*. Melbourne

(1988), ed. *The Imperial Muse. Ramus essays on Roman Literature of the Empire, Vol. I: To Juvenal through Ovid*. Berwick, Victoria

(1993), ed. *Roman Epic*. London

Bramble, J. C. (1970) 'Structure and ambiguity in Catullus LXIV', *PCPhS* 16: 22 41

Braund, S. M. (1996) *Juvenal, 'Satires' Book 1*. Cambridge

Brink, C. O. (1972) 'Ennius and the Hellenistic worship of Homer', *AJPh* 93: 547–67

(1982) *Horace on Poetry, 'Epistles' Book II: The Letters to Augustus and Florus*. Cambridge

Brown, E. L. (1963) *Numeri Vergiliani: Studies in 'Eclogues' and 'Georgics'* (Coll. Latomus 63). Brussels

Brown, J. (1986) *Velázquez: Painter and Courtier*. New Haven

Brown, J. and Elliott, J. H. (1980) *A Palace for a King: the Buen Retiro and the Court of Philip IV*. New Haven

Brown, R. D. (1990) 'The Homeric background to a Vergilian repetition', *AJPh* 111: 182–6

Bruhl, A. (1953) *Liber Pater: Origine et expansion du culte dionysiaque à Rome et dans le monde romain*. Paris

Buchheit, V. (1972) *Der Anspruch des Dichters in Vergils Georgika: Dichtertum und Heilsweg*. Darmstadt

Buchner, E. (1976) 'Solarium Augusti und Ara Pacis', *MDAI(R)* 83: 319–65

Buffière, F. (1956) *Les mythes d'Homère et la pensée grêcque*. Paris, Les Belles Lettres

(1962) *Héraclite: Allégories d'Homère*. Paris, Les Belles Lettres

Burck, E. (1952) *Römische Wesenszüge der augusteischen Liebeselegie*, *Hermes* 80: 163–200

Burkert, W. (1962) *Weisheit und Wissenschaft: Studien zu Pythagoras, Philolaos und Platon*. Nuremberg

(1972) *Homo Necans: Interpretationen altgriechischer Opferriten und Mythen*. Berlin

(1977) *Griechische Religion der archaischen und klassischen Epoche*. Stuttgart

(1987) *Ancient Mystery Cults*. Cambridge, Mass.

Bywater, I. (1877) 'Aristotle's dialogue "On Philosophy"', *JPh* 7: 64–87

Cairns, F. (1979) *Tibullus: A Hellenistic Poet at Rome*. Cambridge

(1984) 'Propertius and the Battle of Actium (4.6)', in Woodman and West (1984), 129–68

(1989) *Virgil's Augustan Epic*. Cambridge

(1992) 'Theocritus, *Idyll* 26', *PCPhS* 38: 1–38

Cardauns, B. (1976) *M. Terentius Varro: Antiquitates rerum divinarum*. Wiesbaden

Carter, J. M. (1970) *The Battle of Actium: the Rise and Triumph of Augustus Caesar*. London

(1982) *Suetonius, 'Divus Augustus'*. Bristol

Cavallo, G. (1983) *Libri scritture scribi a Ercolano* (BCPE 13 Supp. 1). Naples

Chandler, A. R. (1934–5) 'The nightingale in Greek and Latin poetry', *CJ* 30: 78–84

Chomarat, J. (1974) 'L'initiation d'Aristée', *REL* 52: 185–207

Chuvin, P. (1992) *Nonnos de Panopolis: les Dionysiaques III (chants VI–VIII)*. Paris, Les Belles Lettres

Clausen, W. V. (1964) 'Callimachus and Latin poetry', *GRBS* 5: 181–96

(1994) *A Commentary on Virgil, 'Eclogues'*. Oxford

Coleman, K. M. (1988) *Statius, 'Silvae' IV*. Oxford

Coleman, R. (1977) *Vergil, 'Eclogues'*. Cambridge

Coleman, W. S. (1860) *Woodlands, Heaths and Hedges: a Popular Description of Trees, Shrubs, Wild Fruits, etc. with Notices of their Insect Inhabitants*. London

Collart, P. (1933) 'Les papyrus de l'Iliade', *RPh* SER. 3 7: 33–61

(1939) 'Les papyrus de l'Iliade et de l'Odyssée', *RPh* SER. 3 13: 289–307

Conington, J. and Nettleship, H. (1898) *The Works of Virgil, Vol. 1* (5th edn, revised by F. Haverfield). London

Conte, G. B. (1986) 'Aristaeus, Orpheus and the *Georgics*', in *The Rhetoric of Imitation: Genre and Poetic Memory in Virgil and other Latin Poets* (C. Segal, ed.), 130–40. Ithaca

(1992) 'Proems in the middle', *YClS* 29: 147–59

Conticello, B. et al. (1990) *Rediscovering Pompeii: Exhibition by IBM-Italia, New York City.* Rome

Cook, A. B. (1895) 'The bee in Greek mythology', *JHS* 15: 1–24

Corbaud, E. (1899) *Le bas-relief romain à représentations historiques* (Bibl. des Ecoles franç. d'Athènes et de Rome 81). Paris

Courtney, E. (1990) 'Vergil's sixth *Eclogue*', *QUCC* 63: 99–112

(1993) *The Fragmentary Latin Poets.* Oxford

Crabbe, A. M. (1977) '*Ignoscenda quidem*...: Catullus 64 and the Fourth Georgic', *CQ* N.S. 27: 342–51

Cribiore, R. (1995) 'A hymn to the Nile', *ZPE* 106: 97–106

Cristofani, M. (1990) *La grande Roma dei Tarquini: Catalogo della mostra.* Rome

Crowther, N. B. (1970) 'Οἱ νεώτεροι, *poetae novi* and *cantores Euphorionis*', *CQ* N.S. 20: 322–7

(1976) 'Parthenius and Roman poetry', *Mnemosyne* SER. 4 29: 65–71

(1979) 'Wine and water as symbols of inspiration', *Mnemosyne* 32: 1–11

(1980) 'Parthenius, Laevius and Cicero: Hexameter poetry and Euphorionic myth', *LCM* 5: 181–3

Crump, M. M. (1931) *The Epyllion from Theocritus to Ovid.* Oxford

Dahlmann, H. (1977) *Über Helvius Cinna.* Mainz

Davison, J. A. (1956) 'The study of Homer in Graeco-Roman Egypt', in *Akten des VIII internationalischen Kongresses für Papyrologie in Wien, 1955* (Vienna), 51–8

Diels, H. (1929) *Doxographi Graeci.* Berlin and Leipzig

Dodds, E. R. (1944) *Euripides, 'Bacchae'.* Oxford

Dominik, W. J. (1993) 'From Greece to Rome: Ennius' *Annales*', in Boyle (1993), 37–58

DuQuesnay, I. M. Le M. (1984) 'Horace and Maecenas: the propaganda value of *Sermones* 1', in Woodman and West (1984), 19–58

Dwyer, E. J. (1992) 'The temporal allegory of the Tazza Farnese', *AJA* SER. 2 96: 255–82

Eder, W. (1990) 'The Augustan principate as binding link', in Raaflaub and Toher (1990), 71–122

Elia, O. (1961) 'Bacco fanciullo e Dioniso chtonio à Pompei', *BA* 46: 1–6

Elliott, J. H. (1989) *Spain and its World, 1500–1700: Selected Essays.* New Haven

Elsner, J. (1991) 'Cult and sculpture: sacrifice in the Ara Pacis Augustae', *JRS* 81: 50–61

England, E. B. (1921) *Plato, 'The Laws'* (2 vols.). Manchester

Erbse, H. (1977) *Scholia Graeca in Homeri Iliadem (scholia vetera), Vol. 5.* Berlin

Fagles, R. (1976) *Aeschylus, 'The Oresteia'.* Harmondsworth, Penguin

Farnell, L. R. (1896–1909) *The Cults of the Greek States* (3 vols. in 5). Oxford

Farrell, J. (1991) *Vergil's 'Georgics' and the Traditions of Ancient Epic: The Art of Allusion in Literary History.* Oxford

Feeney, D. (1991) *The Gods in Epic: Poets and Critics of the Classical Tradition.* Oxford

Ferguson, J. (1970) *The Religions of the Roman Empire.* London

Festugière, A. J. (1949) *La révélation d'Hermès Trismégiste, Vol. II.* Paris

Fisher, J. M. (1971) 'Catullus 35', *CPh* 66: 1–5

Fiske, G. C. (1920) *Lucilius and Horace.* Madison

Fordyce, C. J. (1961) *Catullus.* Oxford

(1977) *P. Vergili Maronis Aeneidos libri VII–VIII.* Oxford

Forsythe, G. (1994) *The Historian L. Calpurnius Piso and the Roman Annalistic Tradition.* New York and London

Foti, G. and Pugliese Carratelli, G. (1974) 'Un sepolcro di Hipponion e un nuovo testo orfico', *PP* 29: 91–126

Foulkes, A. P. (1983) *Literature and Propaganda.* London

Fowler, D. P. (1983) 'An acrostic in Vergil (*Aeneid* 7. 601–4)?', *CQ* N.S. 33: 298

(1989) 'First thoughts on closure: problems and prospects', *MD* 22: 75–122

(1990) 'Deviant focalisation in Virgil's *Aeneid*', *PCPhS* 36: 42–63

Fowler, W. W. (1911) *The Religious Experience of the Roman People.* London

Fraser, P. M. (1972) *Ptolemaic Alexandria* (3 vols.). Oxford

Frazer, J. G. (1906) *Adonis, Attis, Osiris: Studies in the History of Oriental Religion.* London

Frede, M. (1989) 'Chaeremon der Stoiker', *ANRW* II. 36.3: 2067–103

Friedländer, P. (1941) 'Pattern of sound and atomistic theory in Lucretius', *AJPh* 62: 16–34

Gale, M. (1991) 'Man and beast in Lucretius and the *Georgics*', *CQ* N.S. 41: 414–26

Galinsky, G. K. (1972) *The Heracles Theme: the Adaptations of the Hero in Literature from Homer to the Twentieth Century.* Oxford

(1992) 'Venus, polysemy, and the Ara Pacis Augustae', *AJA* SER. 2 96: 457–75

(1996) *Augustan Culture: an Interpretative Introduction.* Princeton

Gallo, I. (1986) *Greek and Roman Papyrology* (trans. M. R. Falivene and J. R. March). London

Giangrande, G. (1966) 'Parthenius and Erycius', *CR* N.S. 16: 147–8

(1983) 'Parthenius, Erucius and Homer's poetry', *Maia* 35: 15–18

Girard, R. (1972) *La violence et le sacré*. Paris

Gordon, R. (1990) 'Religion in the Roman Empire: the civic compromise and its limits', in Beard and North (1990), 233–55

Gow, A. S. F. and Page, D. L. (1965) *The Greek Anthology: Hellenistic Epigrams* (2 vols.). Cambridge

(1968) *The Greek Anthology: the Garland of Philip* (2 vols.). Cambridge

Gowers, E. (1993) *The Loaded Table: Representations of Food in Roman Literature*. Oxford

Gransden, K. W. (1976) *Virgil, 'Aeneid' Book VIII*. Cambridge

(1988) '*Cosmos* and *imperium*', *CR* N.S. 38: 24–6. Review of Hardie (1986)

Grenfell, B. P. and Hunt, A. S. (1899) *The Oxyrhynchus Papyri II*. London

(1906) *The Hibeh Papyri I*. London

(1915) *The Oxyrhynchus Papyri XI*. London

Griffin, J. (1979) 'The Fourth *Georgic*, Virgil, and Rome', *G&R* N.S. 26: 61–80

(1985) *Latin Poets and Roman Life*. London

(1986) *Virgil*. Oxford

Griffith, M. and Mastronarde, D. J. (1990), edd. *Cabinet of the Muses: Essays on Classical and Comparative Literature in Honor of Thomas G. Rosenmeyer*. Atlanta

Griffiths, J. G. (1970) *Plutarch's 'De Iside et Osiride'*. University of Wales Press

(1975) *Apuleius of Madauros, The Isis Book ('Metamorphoses' Bk. XI)* (EPRO 39). Leiden, EJ Brill

Gruen, E. S. (1990) 'The imperial policy of Augustus', in Raaflaub and Toher (1990), 395–416

Gubernatis, A. de (1872) *Zoological Mythology, or, The Legends of Animals* (2 vols.). London

Guépin, J.-P. (1968) *The Tragic Paradox: Myth and Ritual in Greek Tragedy*. Amsterdam

Gummere, R. M. (1970) *Seneca, 'Ad Lucilium Epistulae Morales', Vol. II*. London and Cambridge, Mass., Loeb Classical Library

Guthrie, W. K. C. (1935) *Orpheus and Greek Religion: a Study of the Orphic Movement*. London

Gutzwiller, K. J. (1981) *Studies in the Hellenistic Epyllion* (Beitr. zur Klass. Philol. 114). Königstein

Haan, E. A. M. (1992), ed. *From Erudition to Inspiration: Essays in Honour of Michael McGann*. Belfast

Habinek, T. N. (1990) 'Sacrifice, society and Vergil's ox-born bees', in Griffith and Mastronarde (1990), 209–23

Hagendahl, H. (1967) *Augustine and the Latin Classics* (2 vols.) (Studia Graeca et Latina Gothoburgensia 20). Gothenburg and Uppsala

Hamerton-Kelly, R. G. (1987), ed. *Violent Origins: Walter Burkert, René Girard, and Jonathan Z. Smith on Ritual Killing and Cultural Formation.* Stanford

Hannestad, N. (1986) *Roman Art and Imperial Policy* (Jutland Archaeological Society Publications 19). Aarhus

Hardie, C. (1971) *The Georgics: A transitional poem* (Third Jackson Knight Memorial Lecture). Abingdon-on-Thames

Hardie, P. R. (1985) 'Cosmological patterns in the *Aeneid*', *PLLS* 5: 85–97

(1986) *Virgil's 'Aeneid': Cosmos and Imperium.* Oxford

(1988) 'Virgil's elements',*CR* N.S. 38: 241–2. Review of Ross (1987)

(1992) 'Augustan poets and the mutability of Rome', in Powell (1992), 59–82

(1993) *The Epic Successors of Virgil: a Study in the Dynamics of a Tradition.* Cambridge

Harmon, A. N. (1923) 'The poet κατ᾽ ἐξοχήν', *CPh* 18: 35–47

Harrison, J. E. (1903a) '*Mystica vannus Iacchi*', *JHS* 23: 292–324

(1903b) *Prolegomena to the Study of Greek Religion.* Cambridge

(1912) *Themis: a Study of the Social Origins of Greek Religion.* Cambridge

Harrison, S. J. (1990) *Oxford Readings in Vergil's Aeneid.* Oxford

(1991) *Vergil, 'Aeneid' 10.* Oxford

(1992) 'The Portland Vase revisited', *JHS* 112: 150–3

Haslam, M. (1997) 'Homeric papyri and the transmission of the text', in I. Morris and B. Powell (edd.), *A New Companion to Homer* (Leiden), 55–100

Heath, J. (1994) 'The failure of Orpheus', *TAPhA* 124: 163–96

Herbert-Brown, G. (1994) *Ovid and the 'Fasti': a Historical Study.* Oxford

Heurgon, J. (1932) 'Orphée et Eurydice avant Virgile', *MEFR* 49: 6–60

Hinds, S. (1987) *The Metamorphosis of Persephone: Ovid and the Self-conscious Muse.* Cambridge

(1988) 'Generalising about Ovid', in Boyle (1988), 4–31

Hollis, A. S. (1970) *Ovid, 'Metamorphoses' Book VIII.* Oxford

(1973) 'The *Ars Amatoria* and *Remedia Amoris*', in Binns (1973), 84–115

(1976) 'Some allusions to earlier Hellenistic poetry in Nonnus', *CQ* N.S. 26: 142–50

(1994) 'Nonnus and Hellenistic poetry', in Hopkinson (1994b), 43–62

Hopkinson, N. (1988) *A Hellenistic Anthology.* Cambridge

(1994a) *Greek Poetry of the Imperial Period: an Anthology.* Cambridge

(1994b) *Studies in the 'Dionysiaca' of Nonnus* (Camb. Philol. Soc. Supp. 17). Cambridge

(1994c) 'Nonnus and Homer', in Hopkinson (1994b), 9–42

Horst, P. W. van der (1984) *Chaeremon, Egyptian Priest and Stoic Philosopher* (EPRO 101). Leiden, EJ Brill

How, W. W. and Wells, J. (1912) *A Commentary on Herodotus* (2 vols.). Oxford

Hubbard, M. (1974) *Propertius*. London

Hunt, A. S. (1911) *Catalogue of the Greek Papyri in the John Rylands Library, Manchester, Vol. I: Literary texts (nos. 1–61)*. Manchester

(1912) *The Oxyrhynchus Papyri IX*. London

Innes, D. C. (1979) 'Gigantomachy and natural philosophy', *CQ* N.S. 29: 165–71

Jahn, P. (1973) *Vergils Gedichte, vol. I* (repr.). Dublin and Zürich

Jebb, R. C. (1886) *Sophocles, the Plays and Fragments, Part II: the Oedipus Coloneus*. Cambridge

Jenkyns, R. (1993) 'Virgil and the Euphrates', *AJPh* 114: 115–21

Johnston, P. A. (1977) 'Eurydice and Proserpina in the *Georgics*', *TAPhA* 107: 161–72

Jones, R. M. (1980) *The Platonism of Plutarch and Selected Papers*. New York and London

Kähler, H. (1948) *Der grosse Fries von Pergamum*. Berlin

Kennedy, D. F. (1984) Review of Woodman and West (1984), *LCM* 9: 157–60

Kenney, E. J. (1971) *Lucretius, 'De Rerum Natura' Book III*. Cambridge

Kerényi, C. (1967) *Eleusis: Archetypal Image of Mother and Daughter* (trans. R. Manheim). New York

(1976) *Dionysos: Archetypal Image of Indestructible Life* (trans. R. Manheim). Princeton

Kern, O. (1922) *Orphicorum fragmenta*. Berlin

Kinsey, T. E. (1965) 'Irony and structure in Catullus 64', *Latomus* 24: 911–31

Kirk, G. S., Raven, J. E. and Schofield, M. (1983) *The Presocratic Philosophers* (2nd edn). Cambridge

Klingner, F. (1956) *Catulls Peleus-Epos* (SBAW 6). Munich (= *Studien zur griechischen und römischen Literatur* (Zurich, 1964), 156–224)

Knauer, G. N. (1964) *Die Aeneis und Homer. Studien zur poetischen Technik Vergils mit Listen der Homerzitate in der Aeneis* (Hypomnemata 7). Göttingen

Knox, P. E. (1985a) 'The epilogue to the *Aetia*', *GRBS* 26: 59–65

(1985b) 'Wine, water and Callimachean poetics', *HSPh* 89: 107–119

(1986) *Ovid's 'Metamorphoses' and the Traditions of Augustan Poetry* (Camb. Philol. Soc. Supp. 11). Cambridge

Koenen, L. (1976) 'Egyptian influence in Tibullus', *ICS* 1: 127–59

Kromer, G. (1979) 'The didactic tradition in Vergil's *Georgics*', in Boyle (1979b), 7–21

Krumme, M. (1990) 'Isis in Praeneste: zur Rekonstruktion des unteren Heiligtums', *JDAI* 105 : 155–65

Lada, I. (1993) 'Initiating Dionysus: Ritual and Theatre in Aristophanes' *Frogs*'. Cambridge Ph.D. Thesis

Lamberton, R. (1986) *Homer the Theologian: Neoplatonist Allegorical Reading and the Growth of the Epic Tradition.* Berkeley

Lamberton, R. and Keaney, J. J. (1992), edd. *Homer's Ancient Readers: the Hermeneutics of Greek Epic's Earliest Exegetes.* Princeton

Lapidge, M. (1978) 'Stoic cosmology', in Rist (1978), 161–85

(1979) 'Lucan's imagery of cosmic dissolution', *Hermes* 107: 344–60

(1980) 'A Stoic metaphor in late Latin poetry: the binding of the cosmos', *Latomus* 39: 817–37

(1989) 'Stoic cosmology and Roman literature, first to third centuries AD', *ANRW* II. 36.3: 1379–429

Lauffer, S. (1971) *Diokletians Preisedikt.* Berlin

Le Bonniec, H. (1958) *Le culte de Cérès à Rome.* Paris

Lee, G. (1981) 'Imitation and the poetry of Virgil', *G&R* N.S. 28: 10–22

Leigh, M. (1993) 'Hopelessly devoted to you: traces of the Decii in Virgil's *Aeneid*', *PVS* 21: 89–110

Levi, M. A. (1938) '*Auspicio imperio ductu felicitate*', *RIL* 71 (SER. 3 NO. 2): 101–18

Lieberg, G. (1982) *Poeta creator: Studien zu einer Figur der antiken Dichtung.* Amsterdam

Liebeschuetz, J. H. W. G. (1979) *Continuity and Change in Roman Religion.* Oxford

Lilja, S. (1978) *The Roman Elegists' Attitude to Women.* New York

Linforth, I. M. (1941) *The Arts of Orpheus.* Berkeley

Ling, R. (1991) *Roman Painting.* Cambridge

Lobeck, C. A. (1829) *Aglaophamus, sive de theologicae mysticae Graecorum causis libri tres.* Königsberg

Long, A. A. (1992) 'Stoic readings of Homer', in Lamberton and Keaney (1992), 41–66

Long, A. A. and Sedley, D. N. (1987) *The Hellenistic Philosophers* (2 vols.). Cambridge

Luck, G. (1973) 'Virgil and the mystery religions', *AJPh* 94: 147–66

Lyne, R. O. A. M. (1974) '*Scilicet et tempus ueniet...*: Virgil, *Georgics* I. 463–514', in Woodman and West (1974), 47–66

(1978a) *Ciris: a Poem Attributed to Vergil.* Cambridge

(1978b) 'The Neoteric poets', *CQ* N.S. 28: 167–87

(1979) '*Servitium amoris*', *CQ* N.S. 29: 117–30

(1980) *The Latin Love Poets, from Catullus to Horace.* Oxford

(1987) *Further Voices in Vergil's 'Aeneid'.* Oxford

Maass, E. (1898) *Commentariorum in Aratum reliquiae*. Berlin

McCormick, M. (1985) 'The birth of the codex and the apostolic life-style', *Scriptorium* 39: 150-8. Review of Roberts and Skeat (1983)

Macleod, C. W. (1977) 'The poet, the critic and the moralist: Horace, *Epistles* 1.19', *CQ* N.S. 27: 359-76 (= *Collected essays* (Oxford, 1983), 262-79)

Maehler, H. (1989) *Pindari carmina cum fragmentis, pars II: fragmenta, indices*. Leipzig

Malaise, M. (1972). *Les conditions de pénétration et de diffusion des cultes égyptiens en Italie* (EPRO 22). Leiden, EJ Brill

Maltby, R. (1991) *A Lexicon of Ancient Latin Etymologies*. Leeds

Mansfeld, J. (1979) 'Providence and the destruction of the universe in early Stoic thought. With some remarks on the "mysteries of philosophy"', in M. J. Vermaseren (ed.), *Studies in Hellenistic religions* (EPRO 78) (Leiden, EJ Brill), 129-88.

Martin, L. H. (1987) *Hellenistic Religions: an Introduction*. Oxford

Martindale, C. (1984), ed. *Virgil and his Influence: Bimillennial Studies*. Bristol

(1993) *Redeeming the Text: Latin Poetry and the Hermeneutics of Reception*. Cambridge

Masters, J. (1992) *Poetry and Civil War in Lucan's 'Bellum Civile'*. Cambridge

Mayer, R. (1994) *Horace, 'Epistles' Book 1*. Cambridge

Mette, H. J. (1936) *Sphairopoiia: Untersuchungen zur Kosmologie des Krates von Pergamum*. Munich

Metzger, H. (1944/5) 'Dionysos chthonien d'après les monuments figurés de la période classique', *BCH* 68/9: 296-339

Meuli, K. (1955) 'Altrömischer Maskenbrauch', *MH* 12: 206-35

Miles, G. B. (1980) *Virgil's 'Georgics': A New Interpretation*. Berkeley

Miller, J. F. (1983) 'Ennius and the elegists', *ICS* 8: 277-95

Morel, W. (1927) *Fragmenta poetarum latinorum epicorum et lyricorum praeter Ennium et Lucilium*. Leipzig, Teubner

Morgan, J. D. (1990) 'The death of Cinna the poet', *CQ* N.S. 40: 558-9

Morgan, Ll. (1998) 'Assimilation and civil war: Hercules and Cacus, *Aen.* 8. 185-267', in H.-P. Stahl, ed., *Vergil's Aeneid: Augustan Epic and Political Context* (London), 175-97

Most, G. W. (1989) 'Cornutus and Stoic allegoresis', *ANRW* II. 36.3: 2014-65

Munro, H. A. J. (1878) *Criticisms and Elucidations of Catullus*. Cambridge and London

Myers, K. S. (1994) *Ovid's Causes: Cosmogony and Aetiology in the 'Metamorphoses'*. Ann Arbor

Mylonas, G. E. (1961) *Eleusis and the Eleusinian Mysteries*. Princeton

Mynors, R. A. B. (1990) *Virgil, 'Georgics'*. Oxford

Nadeau, Y. (1984) 'The lover and the statesman: a study in apiculture (Virgil, *Georgics* 4.281–558)', in Woodman and West (1984), 59–82

Nelis, D. (1992a) 'The Aristaeus episode and *Aeneid* 1', in Haan (1992), 3–18

(1992b) 'Demodocus and the song of Orpheus (Ap. Rhod. *Arg.* 1, 496–511)', *MH* 49: 153–70

Newlands, C. E. (1995) *Playing with Time: Ovid and the 'Fasti'*. Ithaca and London

Nilsson, M. P. (1935) 'Early Orphism and kindred religious movements', *Harv. Theol. Rev.* 28: 181–230

(1940) *Greek Popular Religion*. New York

(1957) *The Dionysiac Mysteries of the Hellenistic and Roman Age*. Lund

Nisbet, R. G. M. & Hubbard, M. (1970) *A Commentary on Horace, 'Odes' Book I*. Oxford

(1978) *A Commentary on Horace, 'Odes' Book II*. Oxford

Norden, E. (1916) *P. Vergilius Maro: 'Aeneis' Buch VI* (2nd edn). Berlin

Norwood, G. (1940–1) 'Vergil, *Georgics* IV, 453–527', *CJ* 36: 354–5

Obbink, D. (1996) *Philodemus, 'On Piety', part 1: Critical text with Commentary*. Oxford

Ogilvie, R. M. (1965) *A Commentary on Livy, Books 1–5*. Oxford

O'Hara, J. J. (1996) *True Names: Vergil and the Alexandrian Tradition of Etymological Wordplay*. Ann Arbor

Ohly, K. (1924) 'Die Stichometrie der herkulanischen Rollen', *APF* 7: 190–220

(1928) *Stichometrische Untersuchungen* (ZBB Beiheft 61). Leipzig

Otis, B. (1963) *Virgil: a Study in Civilized Poetry*. Oxford

Otto, W. F. (1965) *Dionysus: Myth and Cult* (trans. R. B. Palmer). Indiana

Overbeck, J. (1875) *Pompeji in seinen Gebäuden, Alterthümern und Kunstwerken* (3rd edn). Leipzig

Page, D. L. (1942) *Select Papyri III: Literary Papyri (poetry)*. London and Cambridge, Mass., Loeb Classical Library

Papanghelis, T. D. (1987) *Propertius: a Hellenistic Poet on Love and Death*. Cambridge

Parry, A. (1963) 'The two voices of Virgil's *Aeneid*', *Arion* 2.4: 66–80

Parsons, P. J. (1977) 'Callimachus: *Victoria Berenices*', *ZPE* 25: 1–50

Pascal, C. B. (1990) 'The dubious devotion of Turnus', *TAPhA* 120: 251–68

Perkell, C. G. (1989) *The Poet's Truth: a Study of the Poet in Virgil's 'Georgics'*. Berkeley

Pfeiffer, R. (1949–53) *Callimachus* (2 vols.). Oxford

(1968) *History of Classical Scholarship, from the Beginnings to the End of the Hellenistic Age*. Oxford

Platner, S. B. and Ashby, T. (1929) *A Topographical Dictionary of Ancient Rome*. Oxford

Pollini, J. (1990) 'Man or god: divine assimilation and imitation in the late Republic and early Principate', in Raaflaub and Toher (1990), 334–63

Pollitt, J. J. (1986) *Art in the Hellenistic Age*. Cambridge

Porter, J. I. (1992) 'Hermeneutic lines and circles: Aristarchus and Crates on the exegesis of Homer', in Lamberton and Keaney (1992), 67–114

Powell, A. (1992), ed. *Roman Poetry and Propaganda in the Age of Augustus*. Bristol

Powell, J. U. (1925) *Collectanea Alexandrina*. Oxford

Putnam, M. C. J. (1970) '*Aeneid* VII and the *Aeneid*', AJPh 91: 408–30 (= *Essays on Latin lyric, elegy and epic* (Princeton, 1982), 288–310)

Quint, D. (1983) *Origin and Originality in Renaissance Literature: Versions of the Source*. New Haven

(1993) *Epic and Empire: Politics and Generic form from Virgil to Milton*. Princeton

Raaflaub, K. A. and Toher, M. (1990), edd. *Between Republic and Empire: Interpretations of Augustus and his Principate*. Berkeley

Raaflaub, K. A. and Samons, L. J. (1990) 'Opposition to Augustus', in Raaflaub and Toher (1990), 417–54

Reinhold, M. (1988) *From Republic to Principate: a Historical Commentary on Cassius Dio's 'Roman History' Books 49–52 (36–29 BC)* (APhA Mon. Ser. 34). Atlanta

Reynolds, L. D. (1983), ed. *Texts and Transmission: a Survey of the Latin Classics*. Oxford

Reynolds, L. D. and Wilson, N. G. (1991) *Scribes and Scholars: a Guide to the Transmission of Greek and Latin Literature* (3rd edn). Oxford

Richter, C. E. (1830) *Philonis Iudaei opera omnia VIII*. Leipzig

Richter, G. M. A. (1971) *Engraved Gems of the Romans*. London

Rist, J. M. (1978), ed. *The Stoics*. Berkeley

Robert, C. (1878) *Eratosthenis Catasterismorum reliquiae*. Berlin

Roberts, C. H. and Skeat, T. C. (1983) *The Birth of the Codex*. London

Rohde, E. (1894) *Psyche: Seelencult und Unsterblichkeitsglaube der Griechen*. Freiburg i. B. and Leipzig

Romm, J. S. (1992) *The Edges of the Earth in Ancient Thought: Geography, Exploration and Fiction*. Princeton

Ross, A. (1984) 'Virgil and the Augustans', in C. Martindale (1984), 141–67

Ross, D. O. (1987) *Virgil's Elements: Physics and Poetry in the 'Georgics'*. Princeton

Ross, W. D. (1910–52) *Aristotle: the Works* (12 vols.). Oxford

Rouse, W. H. D. (1940) *Nonnus, 'Dionysiaca' I (Bks I–XV)*. London and Cambridge, Mass., Loeb Classical Library

Rudd, N. (1989) *Horace, 'Epistles' Book II and 'Epistle to the Pisones'*. Cambridge

Russell, D. A. (1979) 'De imitatione', in West and Woodman (1979), 1–16

(1992) *Dio Chrysostom, 'Orations' VII, XII & XXXVI*. Cambridge

Russo, J., Fernández-Galiano, M. and Heubeck, A. (1992) *A Commentary on Homer's 'Odyssey' Vol. III*. Oxford

Ryberg, I. S. (1955) *Rites of the State Religion in Roman Art* (MAAR 22). Rome

Sandbach, F. H. (1969) *Plutarch's 'Moralia', Vol. XV: The Fragments*. London and Cambridge, Mass., Loeb Classical Library

(1975) *The Stoics*. London

Sattler, P. (1960) *Augustus und der Senat. Untersuchungen zur römischen Innenpolitik zwischen 30 und 17 v. Christus*. Göttingen

Scazzoso, P. (1956) 'Riflessi misterici nelle *Georgiche* di Virgilio', *Paideia* 11: 5–28

Schiesaro, A. (1994) 'The palingenesis of the *De Rerum Natura*', *PCPhS* 40: 81–107

Schlunk, R. R. (1974) *The Homeric Scholia and the 'Aeneid': A Study of the Influence of Ancient Literary Criticism on Vergil*. Ann Arbor

Schmidt, M. G. (1986) *Caesar und Cleopatra: philologischer und historischer Kommentar zu Lucan, 10.1–171*. Frankfurt am Main

Schofield, M. (1991) *The Stoic Idea of the City*. Cambridge

Schrijvers, P. H. (1970) *Horror ac divina voluptas: Etudes sur la poétique et la poésie de Lucrèce*. Amsterdam

Scodel, R. S. and Thomas, R. F. (1984) 'Virgil and the Euphrates', *AJPh* 105: 339

Scott, K. (1925) 'The identification of Augustus with Romulus-Quirinus', *TAPhA* 56: 82–105

Scullard, H. H. (1981) *Festivals and Ceremonies of the Roman Republic*. London

Seaford, R. (1978) *Pompeii*. Florence

(1981) 'Dionysiac drama and the Dionysiac mysteries', *CQ* N.S. 31: 252–75

Segal, C. (1966) 'Orpheus and the fourth *Georgic*: Vergil on nature and civilization', *AJPh* 87: 307–25

Seth-Smith, A. (1981) 'Parthenius and Erucius', *Mnemosyne* SER. 4 34: 63–71

Simon, E. (1975) *Pergamum und Hesiod*. Mainz

Skiadas, A. D. (1965) *Homer im griechischen Epigramm*. Athens

Skutsch, O. (1985) *The 'Annals' of Quintus Ennius*. Oxford

Smith, A. H. (1892–1904) *A Catalogue of the Sculpture in the Department of Greek and Roman Antiquities, British Museum* (3 vols.). London

Smith, R. A. (1990) 'Ov. *Met.* 10.475: An instance of "meta-allusion"', *Gymnasium* 97: 458–60

Smith, R. R. R. (1987) 'The Imperial reliefs from the Sebasteion at Aphrodisias', *JRS* 77: 88–138.

(1988) '*Simulacra gentium*: the *ethne* from the Sebasteion at Aphrodisias', *JRS* 78: 50–77

Solmsen, F. (1972) 'The world of the dead in *Aeneid* Book 6', *CPh* 67: 31–41. (= Harrison (1990), 208–23)

Spoerri, W. (1959) *Späthellenistische Berichte über Welt, Kultur und Götter*. Basle

Stadtmüller, H. (1906) *Anthologia Graeca epigrammatum Palatina cum Planudea, Vol. III.1*. Leipzig

Stahl, H.-P. (1985) *Propertius: 'Love' and 'War'. Individual and State under Augustus*. Berkeley

Stambaugh, J. E. (1972) *Sarapis under the Early Ptolemies* (EPRO 25). Leiden, EJ Brill

Syme, R. (1939) *The Roman Revolution*. Oxford

Syndikus, H. P. (1958) *Lucans Gedicht vom Bürgerkrieg: Untersuchungen zur epischen Technik und zu den Grundlagen des Werkes*. Munich

Thomas, R. F. (1983a) 'Virgil's ecphrastic centerpieces', *HSCP* 87: 175–84

(1983b) 'Callimachus, the *Victoria Berenices* and Roman poetry', *CQ* N.S. 33: 92–113

(1985) 'From *recusatio* to commitment: the evolution of the Vergilian programme', *PLLS* 5: 61–73

(1986) 'Virgil's *Georgics* and the art of reference', *HSCP* 90: 171–98

(1988) *Virgil, 'Georgics'* (2 vols.). Cambridge

(1991) 'The 'sacrifice' at the end of the *Georgics*, Aristaeus, and Vergilian closure', *CPh* 86: 211–18

Thomson, G. (1941) *Aeschylus and Athens: a Study in the Social Origins of Drama*. London

Tillyard, E. M. W. (1923) *The Hope Vases: A Catalogue and Discussion of the Hope Collection of Greek Vases*. Cambridge

Toynbee, J. M. C. (1964) *Art in Britain under the Romans*. Oxford

Tsantsanoglou, K. and Parássoglou, G. M. (1987) 'Two gold lamellae from Thessaly', Ελληνικα 38: 3–16

Tucker, R. A. (1975) 'The banquets of Dido and Cleopatra', *CB* 52: 17–20

Turner, E. G. (1968) *Greek Papyri: An Introduction*. Oxford

(1971) *Greek MSS of the Ancient World*. Oxford

Versnel, H. S. (1970) *Triumphus: an Inquiry into the Origin, Development and Meaning of the Roman Triumph*. Leiden, EJ Brill

Veyne, P. (1988) *Roman Erotic Elegy: Love, Poetry and the West*. Chicago and London

Villefosse, A. H. de (1899) *Le trésor de Boscoreale* (MMAI 5). Paris

Wallace-Hadrill, A. (1987) 'Time for Augustus: Ovid, Augustus and the *Fasti*', in Whitby, Hardie and Whitby (1987), 221–30

Warburton, W. (1738–41) *The Divine Legation of Moses Demonstrated on the Principles of a Religious Deist, from the Omission of the Doctrine of a future State of Reward and Punishment in the Jewish Dispensation* (2 vols.). London

Warden, J. (1982), ed. *Orpheus: The Metamorphoses of a Myth*. Toronto

Warmington, E. H. (1935–40) *Remains of old Latin* (4 vols.). London and Cambridge, Mass., Loeb Classical Library

Watson, L. C. (1982) 'Cinna and Euphorion', *SIFC* N.S. 54: 93–110

Webster, T. B. L. (1964) *Hellenistic Poetry and Art*. London

Weinstock, S. (1971) *Divus Julius*. Oxford

Wender, D. S. (1969) 'Resurrection in the Fourth *Georgic*', *AJPh* 90: 424–36

West, D. (1990) *Virgil, the 'Aeneid': A New Prose Translation*. Harmondsworth

West, D. and Woodman, A. J. (1979), edd. *Creative Imitation and Latin Literature*. Cambridge

West, M. L. (1966) *Hesiod, 'Theogony'*. Oxford
(1982) 'The Orphics of Olbia', *ZPE* 45: 17–29
(1983) *The Orphic Poems*. Oxford

West, S. (1967) *The Ptolemaic Papyri of Homer*. Cologne

Whitby, M., Hardie, P. R. and Whitby, M. (1987), edd. *Homo Viator: Classical Essays for John Bramble*. Bristol

White, P. (1993) *Promised Verse: Poets in the Society of Augustan Rome*. Cambridge, Mass.

Wild, R. A. (1981) *Water in the Cultic Worship of Isis and Sarapis* (EPRO 87). Leiden, EJ Brill

Wilkinson, L. P. (1969) *The 'Georgics' of Virgil*. Cambridge

Williams, F. (1978) *Callimachus, 'Hymn to Apollo', a Commentary*. Oxford

Williams, G. D. (1994) *Banished Voices: Readings in Ovid's Exile Poetry*. Cambridge

Williams, R. D. (1979) *Virgil, 'Eclogues' & 'Georgics'*. London

Wills, J. (1996) *Repetition in Latin Poetry: Figures of Allusion*. Oxford

Wimmel, W. (1960) *Kallimachos in Rom: die Nachfolge seines apologetischen Dichtens in der Augusteerzeit*. (Hermes Einzelschriften 16). Wiesbaden

Wiseman, T. P. (1974) *Cinna the Poet and other Roman Essays*. Leicester
(1979) *Clio's Cosmetics: Three Studies in Greco-Roman Literature*. Leicester
(1991) 'Democracy and myth: the life and death of Remus', *LCM* 16: 115–24

Wistrand, E. (1958) *Horace's Ninth 'Epode' and its Historical Background* (Studia Graeca et Latina Gothoburgensia 8). Gothenburg

Witt, R. E. (1971) *Isis in the Graeco-Roman world*. London

Woodman, A. J. (1983) *Velleius Paterculus: the Caesarian and Augustan narrative (2.41–93)*. Cambridge

Woodman, A. J. and West, D. (1974), edd. *Quality and Pleasure in Latin Poetry*. Cambridge

(1984), edd. *Poetry and Politics in the Age of Augustus*. Cambridge

Wormell, D. E. W. (1971) '*Apibus quanta experientia parcis*. Virgil, *Georgics* 4. 1–227', in Bardon and Verdière (1971), 429–35

Wyke, M. (1989) 'In pursuit of love, the poetic self and a process of reading: Augustan elegy in the 1980s', *JRS* 79: 165–73

Zanker, P. (1987) *Augustus und die Macht der Bilder*. Munich

Zeller, E. (1892) *The Stoics, Epicureans and Sceptics* (trans. O. J. Reichel). London

Zetzel, J. E. G. (1995) *Cicero, 'De Re Publica': Selections*. Cambridge

Zuntz, G. (1971) *Persephone: Three Essays on Religion and Thought in Magna Graecia*. Oxford

Zwierlein, O. (1974) 'Cäsar und Kleopatra bei Lucan und in späterer Dichtung', *A & A* 20: 54–73

INDEX

DATE DUE

NOV 1 2 1999	

UPI 261-2505 G

PRINTED IN U.S.A.